Advance praise f--

Our New World of A

"*Our New World of Adult Bullies* is tir
Bill Eddy explains not only the damagi
lying but the psychological understanding of how to stop it. Poignant
examples from history and everyday life bring it home. This book
empowers and offers solutions instead of reactions. Much needed in
a time of great divide and polarization."

—**Karyl Mcbride, Ph.D.,** author of *Will the Drama Ever End? Untangling and
Healing from the Harmful Effects of Parental Narcissism*

"As always, Bill delivered a book that is easy to digest and full of practical insights and advice. Make the decision to take back your power.
Start by reading this book."

—**Catherine Mattice,** CEO, Civility Partners and workplace bullying expert

"Bill Eddy has had a long and distinguished career as a mediator,
trainer, and author. He brings this experience and wisdom to his
latest book. Having read the book, I feel more confident with not
just identifying bullies but more importantly how to pull the plug on
bullies. Given the heightened levels of divisiveness and polarization
in society, this book couldn't have come soon enough."

—**Steven P. Dinkin,** president, National Conflict Resolution Center

"Crystal clear, eye-opening take on the bullies in our lives, whether
at work, at home, or in our culture. Eddy's easy-going conversational
tone belies the solid science that drives his ideas and spot-on practical advice. Learn how to recognize bullies, understand how they
get into our heads, and how to evict them."

—**Dr. Richard A. Warshak,** author of *Divorce Poison: How To Protect Your
Family from Bad-mouthing and Brainwashing.*

"Great book—I really enjoyed reading it. I learned several things that I will be able to use! In a world where bullying and aggressive behavior are increasingly prevalent, Bill Eddy's latest book is a must-read. His approaches in managing high-conflict behaviors are a cornerstone of my practice. Offering practical solutions and deep insights, backed by real-world examples, this book is an invaluable resource for anyone looking to navigate and mitigate such conflicts effectively."

—**Susan Guthrie,** attorney, mediator, chair of American Bar Association Section of Dispute Resolution

"Drawing from over a decade of dedicated service in childhood anti-bullying education, I recognize the great importance and urgency of this book. Bill Eddy, through his multifaceted career, has laid bare the intricate dynamics of adult bullying, whether in the workplace or home, but also equips readers with the crucial strategies to identify, confront, and effectively tackle such behavior. We must no longer be silenced when it comes to bullying and feeling alone, enough is enough!"

—**Sunnie McFadden-Curtis,** filmmaker, award winning director, advocate for women and children, and director of *Bullying: A Culture of Silence*

"Bill Eddy gives elaborate explanations, with myriad examples at every level of society, of why and how adults with persistent aggressive and domineering behaviors get their power and how to most effectively respond without getting caught in their sticky webs of influence. This book will serve as an instructional manual for readers in understanding and responding to dominating behaviors by individuals within various contexts, including their families, their workplaces, online, and even in elections."

—**Don Saposnek, Ph.D.,** author of *Mediating Child Custody Disputes* and co-author of *Splitting America*

"Bill Eddy sheds light on the why and the how of bullying and gives the other 90% of the world tools to help stop this epidemic from ruining our families, communities, and nations. He offers a highly focused and effective application of compassionate accountability you can use to manage bullies in your life and keep yourself from getting sucked into the toxic win-lose vortex."

—**Nate Regier, Ph.D.,** CEO, Next Element Consulting, author of *Compassionate Accountability: How Leaders Build Connection and Get Results*

"What a fantastic book. Yet again Bill Eddy has distilled decades of wisdom into down-to-earth concepts that resonate deeply and strategies that are attainable for practitioners at all levels. A must-read for family violence survivors seeking tips on how to safely and effectively instruct counsel, work with a mediator, or self-represent in court."

—**Hilary Linton, J.D., LLM,** president, Riverdale Mediation Ltd. and mediate393 inc.

"While educators are normally quite adept at resolving problems on a daily basis, the increasing visibility of adult bullies in the educational arena has been perplexing. This practical guide will empower educators to set realistic limits on adult bullies—with consequences that will effectively stop their polarizing behavior. Administrators and school board members, in particular, will benefit from the steps outlined in this timely publication."

—**Dennis Doyle, Ph.D.,** retired superintendent

"Witnessing the scars of bullying within families, I know the pain it inflicts. *Our New World of Adult Bullies* offers a lifeline. It exposes the often-hidden reality of adult bullies and equips readers with the tools to not only protect themselves, but also children from these damaging dynamics when attacked by an adult, including a family member. This book is a powerful resource for anyone caught in the crosshairs of adult bullying."

—**Ginger Gentile,** director of *Erasing Family* and coach for High Conflict Divorce

"Bill Eddy has done it again! After reading his brilliant book on adult bullies, I am going to redesign my training courses for mediators and lawyers and rewrite client materials for my own private practice to include Bill's wisdom from this book. By profiling the behaviour of adult bullies in business, sex abusers, and tyrants in political life whose bullying I know about, Bill has even helped me better deal with adult bullies in my own life."

—**Forrest (Woody) Mosten,** cofounder of Mosten Guthrie
Online Mediation Training Academy; mediator and
family collaborative lawyer at La Jolla, California;
author and adjunct professor of law at UCLA

"*Our New World of Adult Bullies* is a timely book, full of practical advice on how to 'spot' and 'stop' them. Bill Eddy uses multiple case examples, mostly from high profile media cases, to illustrate the many faces of adult bullying. Like an anatomist, he dissects their strategies and offers victims valuable insights as well as a highly practical toolbox. Like a Zen master, his writing is full of empathy, optimism, and hope."

—**Corine de Ruiter, Ph.D.,** professor of forensic psychology,
Maastricht University, the Netherlands

"This outstanding, easy to read book includes some great summaries and real life (and at times very sad) examples of bullying as well as tips about how bullies can be managed or stopped. Importantly, the way that technology is creating more opportunities for bullying without consequences is explored. Eddy analyses how bullying works and then, importantly, follows this up with some great practical steps that we can take as individuals, groups, and as a society."

—**Tania Sourdin,** University of Newcastle, School of Law and Justice;
president Academic Senate, University of Newcastle;
fellow, Australian Academy of Law

Our New World of
ADULT BULLIES

HOW TO SPOT THEM · HOW TO STOP THEM

BILL EDDY

Health Communications, Inc.
Boca Raton, Florida
www.hcibooks.com

Library of Congress Cataloging-in-Publication Data
is available through the Library of Congress

© 2024 Bill Eddy

ISBN 13: 978-0-7573-2510-6 (Paperback)
ISBN 10: 0757325106 (Paperback)
ISBN 13: 978-0-7573-2511-3 (ePub)
ISBN 10: 0757325114 (ePub)

Publisher: Health Communications, Inc.
       301 Crawford Boulevard, Suite 200
       Boca Raton, FL 33432-3762

Cover, interior design, and formatting by Larissa Hise Henoch.

To the
TARGETS
of bullies around the world,

you're not alone.

CONTENTS

INTRODUCTION

I DON'T LIKE BULLIES. I never have. I could say I'm not sure why, but I think I know where this started. I have a very clear memory about this. When I was eight years old in the third grade, I had my own personal bully: Glen M. He would trap me at the foot of the stairs in the stairwell outside the exit from our classroom. He would try to beat me up, hitting me on the head, shoulders, and chest, and kicking me in the legs. I'm not sure why he picked on me in particular, but I think it had something to do with my parents teaching me and my three siblings that we weren't allowed to fight. We were not allowed to hit anybody.

"It takes two to make a fight," they said. "But what if I can't avoid the other person?" I replied. They just repeated: "It takes two to make a fight. Just get away. Find a way to do that." So, all I was allowed to do was to try to block Glen with my arms from hitting and kicking me. I tried to figure out where he was at the end of class so that I could leave with the other students. But occasionally he would catch me off guard. He knew that out of all the kids in my class, I wasn't allowed to fight back.

Glen showed up at my school sometime during third grade. He was actually slightly smaller than I was, but he was a fierce fighter, as if his goal was to destroy me. Why me? I hadn't done anything to him. I generally ignored him in class, but he often got into trouble with the teacher.

One day on the weekend, my mother was reading the newspaper and said, "Isn't the M. boy in your class at school?" "Yes," I said. "Well, it says here in the paper that his father hung himself in the garage yesterday and died. He must have been a very troubled man."

I was shocked and confused. I remember I suddenly felt sorry for Glen. It occurred to me that his father may have been treating him the way that he treated me. After all, when I was five, my mother had taught me that "we don't judge people; we try to understand them." I had been trying to understand Glen's intensity in attacking me and generally getting into trouble at school. Now I thought I might understand his behavior because of his father's behavior, whatever it was.

I decided to tell Glen the next day at school that I was sorry to hear about what happened to his father. I think I had the beginnings of what I later learned was empathy for my bully. But of course, Glen never came back to school after that. His mother instantly moved their family out of the area, and I never heard about them again.

While this experience probably doesn't sound very dramatic compared to children who are abused by their parents or assaulted by other adults, it left a huge impression on me coming from a fairly peaceful and loving (but strict) family. I think it made me into a more cautious kid, but it also made me into a keen observer. I didn't want this to happen to me again, so I developed a bit of bully radar to help me keep an eye on who to avoid as I grew up and I mostly succeeded at that.

But I wonder, even today, if this experience played a big part in my career choices to become a social worker, lawyer, and mediator, often protecting clients from bullies. While I have always been more concerned about their targets/victims, I also wanted to understand bullies, and from time to time I find myself having empathy for them like I did for Glen.

As you read this book, you may notice how I try to balance strongly setting limits on bullies with understanding them and having some compassion for them. There is no excuse for their behavior—and some of it is very evil—but at the same time I think I have figured out why there are bullies, where their behavior comes from, and how to influence it.

I understand that many bullies were bullied as children (although many were not but were simply born this way) and that there are many other aspects to who they are besides their bully personalities. Many have good contributions to make to society, but they still need to be restrained. I hope that you too will have some compassion for them as you learn the many strategies contained in this book for spotting them and stopping them.

In short, we don't judge bullies, but we shouldn't let them be in charge of anyone else's life. As you read this book, try not to be judgmental. Be strategic.

CHAPTER 1

Preparing Yourself

BULLIES USED TO BE KEPT ON THE FRINGES OF SOCIETY. As a result, they only bothered a small percentage of unlucky people. But in recent years, because of many changes in technology, media, politics, and culture, bullies have been launched to the forefront of our society. Today they are far more prevalent, more powerful, more persuasive, and more dangerous than they were even a decade ago. Now, everyone is likely to have a bully in their life sooner or later—including you. Are you prepared to spot them and stop them?

Over the past forty years I have studied bullying as a therapist, lawyer, mediator, and cofounder of the High Conflict Institute. Since 2008 my institute colleagues and I have taught skills for managing high-conflict people (bullies and other difficult folks) to over 250,000 professionals, including lawyers, judges, therapists, mediators, human resource managers, law enforcement professionals, teachers, administrators, and many other people. I've seen the mistakes that all of us make, and I've learned that bully behavior is surprisingly predictable, as you will see.

Most people are terrible at spotting bullies and fail to act in ways to protect themselves. Will you make the same mistakes that most people make? Will you underreact or overreact? Will you wish that you had known the simple tips and tools contained in this book much earlier? That's what most of our consultation and training clients at the High Conflict Institute tell us when they desperately seek help in getting a bully out of their lives or in learning how to manage one.

As we teach our clients—and as you will learn in this book— much of what works with bullies is counterintuitive. Most of what we naturally think will work only makes our situations worse. And some of what we need to do with bullies is precisely the opposite of what we naturally do with reasonable, caring adults.

A fundamental theme of this book is that with bullies *the issue is not the issue—the personality is the issue* driving the intensity of the conflict. This book explains ten hidden *primitive emotional powers (PEP)* of bullies that poison our minds, bodies, and communities— without us even realizing it. (New terms that I will use, such as PEP, will appear in italics the first time for ease of remembering.) In many ways, the primitive emotional power of bullies is the flip side of emotional intelligence, which is the ability to understand and manage emotions in relatively equal and respectful relationships. That's why a bully's PEP has such power over us—we haven't expected it and haven't understood it, until now. Instead, we expect everyone to make an effort to get along. But bullies don't, which gives them an advantage over us. By breaking down these powers, we can reduce bullies' impact, predict them, remove them from our psyches, and energize our will to overcome them. For each of the ten bully powers discussed, I offer six strategies for how you can stop that power of the bully.

Foundational to a bully's aggressive character is the **power of unrestrained personality** and lack of self-restraint, which gives bullies more power to overwhelm everyone around them. They use the **power of primitive emotions** to persuade, intimidate, intrude, dominate, and sometimes destroy people. PEP allows bullies to blatantly use deception and the **power of surprise attacks** in plain sight. In the pages that follow, we will look at several examples of how anyone can succumb to these primitive powers until they understand how they work and how to spot them.

We also look at the **power of the bully's story**—their "BS." This is the story that every bully uses to create fear of a *fantasy crisis*, anger at a *fantasy villain*, and *love/loyalty* for the bully as a *fantasy hero*. Their BS helps their **power to makes things very personal,** as their attacks are on the *whole person*, not just a criticism of your behavior, and may include devastating effects to you, your reputation, your life, or all three. This BS is amplified through intense repetition—the **power of emotional repetition** in isolation—as bullies cut off their victims from all other points of view and drill their bully's story into their heads. This story can immobilize you or mobilize you against another one of their targets. This is further enhanced by the **power of negative advocates** who support them and their ability to employ the **power to project and play the victim**. If you've ever dealt with a bully, you may know how alone all of this can make you feel. Meanwhile, everyone around you usually won't understand what is really happening to you and may minimize it.

Finally, we look at most bullies' drive to use the **power of bullies as leaders** and how they use the **power of polarization** to seize unlimited power over their family, their work group, their commu-nity, and possibly even their nation while they get everyone else to fight with one another. The power of today's *high-emotion media* is explained in training more and more bullies. Lastly, we look at successful methods of turning bullying into positive behavior and changing our world culture to encourage win-win relationships.

Surprisingly, by analyzing a wide range of examples—family, workplace, community, national, and international—you will see that bullying behaviors are the same at every level. Since most bul-lying goes on in private, I use many public examples and current events, as well as made-up examples based on real cases, to show the subtle details of how the *adult bully* really works and will continue to work in the future in new situations. In a few cases, I analyze public events as far back as fifty years ago, because we know a lot about them. But I also explain why the same patterns of bully dynamics are going to persist for another fifty years, until a sufficient number of people understand them and set limits on them.

When enough of us recognize these ten powers and learn to use the six strategies, we can stop bullies in their tracks over and over and create a much healthier world—with safer families, workplaces, and communities for us all. In other words, it's time to prepare yourself.

CHAPTER 2

Why Adult Bullies Now?

*58 percent of respondents agreed that "the display of
bullying, disrespect and intolerance of the opinions
of others by politicians and public figures affected
workplaces," because they "encouraged aggression"
and "granted permission to ignore rules."*

—U.S. Workplace Bullying Survey

Are Adult Bullies Really a Problem?

MOST PEOPLE ARE UNAWARE of how many adult bullies there are in
the world these days, for two big reasons. First, most people who
have been targeted by adult bullies suffer alone, in private. Many
are embarrassed or afraid. Some feel that their situation is somehow
their own fault. (It's not, as I explain in this book. No one deserves

to be bullied.) They are ashamed to tell anyone, or they may have been threatened with severe consequences (even death) if they expose what is happening to them. Second, most people think that each bullying situation is unique and unpredictable. They don't realize that all adult bullies have the same basic personalities and the same predictable patterns of behavior, whether they're a family bully, a workplace bully, an online bully, or a bully leader.

Who Are Adult Bullies?

Adult bullies have *high-conflict personalities*. People with high-conflict personalities have four key patterns of behavior: (1) They are preoccupied with blaming other people without taking responsibility for themselves; (2) they think in all-or-nothing terms (winners and losers, friends and enemies, and heroes and villains); (3) they regularly express extreme emotions; and (4) they often engage in extremely harmful behaviors that most people would never do.

Yet bullies are the *most* high-conflict people. In addition to the listed behavior patterns, they have a deep-seated drive to dominate or destroy other people. They don't just want to win; they want other people to lose, to suffer. They compulsively turn win-win situations into win-lose relationships. In the process, they deliberately target innocent people, blaming them for anything and everything for no good reason. I call these their *targets of blame*. They all use the same set of hidden powers to accomplish this domination or destruction— powers that can be easily recognized once you know what to look for.

Bullies exist in all levels of society: in families, workplaces, communities, business, government, and organizations of all types and sizes. Yet all bullies act in similar ways, regardless of their demographics and context. In families, bullies are common perpetrators of domestic violence, child abuse, parental alienation, and false allegations in family courts. In the workplace, they are bully bosses, bully employees, sexual harassers, and sometimes CEOs or even company owners. In communities, they often wreak havoc on school boards, in homeowners' associations, and in religious congregations. Too often they are becoming the heads of states and nations, bullying their own citizens and sometimes neighboring countries.

Bullies have narrow patterns of behavior, which make them more predictable than the average person. Most people are unaware of these common patterns. Recognizing them is the first step to stopping bullies in their tracks.

Not Talking About Children as Bullies

In this book, I'm not discussing playground bully boys or high school mean girls, because the vast majority of them outgrow their bullying behaviors by adulthood. Most children are bullies and also victims of bullies as they navigate all kinds of relationships growing up and suffer the consequences of their actions until they learn how to engage successfully with their peers and others. It's normal for children to test their powers and learn their limits from experience. We're born with the ability to engage in aggressive behaviors, but childhood and adolescence are when we learn what succeeds and what fails based on our family, friends, and community cultures. Many books have been written on childhood bullies.

I'm talking about *adults* who are compulsive bullies—alleged grown-ups who regularly act like angry, domineering children. I estimate that they make up 5 to 10 percent of adults, for reasons I explain in Chapter 3. Most of them were also bullies as children, but for one reason or another they entered adulthood with their bullying behavior intact and refined.

Changing Cultures and an Increase in Bullying

COVID-19 accelerated a variety of cultural changes that favored bullies. During the early days of the pandemic, from 2020 to 2021, domestic violence increased 25 percent to 33 percent around the globe with the isolation of victims at home with their perpetrators.[1] The percentage of employees directly experiencing bullying rose to 30 percent, with 43 percent for those doing remote work, which removes the normal restraints of in-person contacts.[2] A 2021 survey by the Workplace Bullying Institute reported that 58 percent of respondents agreed that "the display of bullying, disrespect, and intolerance of the opinions of others by politicians and public figures affected workplaces," because they "encouraged aggression" and "granted permission to ignore rules."[3]

On the international stage, a 2021 *Atlantic* article by Anne Applebaum titled "The Bad Guys Are Winning: How a New League of Autocrats Is Outsmarting the West," noted that bully leaders around the world have taken over democracies and are expected to become ever more aggressive toward their neighbors. Since Applebaum's article was published, this is precisely what has happened with Putin in Russia and Xi in China. Then, in 2023, a *New York Times* article titled "America's Foes Are Joining Forces" pointed out that Cuba and Iran are helping Russia and China in a new "axis of authoritarians."[4]

By identifying that the same personality patterns of behavior are operating in personal life and public culture, you will be more aware of how to spot and protect yourself from adult bullies who hope to create a widespread *culture of fear and blame*, which covers up their own drive for dominance and destruction at every level of society.

In many ways adult bullying has been building for years. It isn't one person's fault or one group's fault. It's the collision of humanity and our own technological progress. We need to understand the big picture in order to understand what is happening, what to do, and what not to do. The following chart compares what most of us value in our relationships—and what we want children to learn growing up—with the way that bullies of all ages are learning to think and act in today's world.

Relationship Skills Versus Bullying Skills

DESIRED SOCIAL SKILLS	TYPICAL BULLYING SKILLS
Provide empathy for one another.	Be tough; show empathy for no one.
Treat other people as equals.	Show off as a superior person; repeatedly show disdain for others.
Take turns being the center of attention.	Always try to be the center of attention.
Find common ground for mutually respectful conversations.	Dominate others; tell people what to think and how to behave.
Learn to listen well.	Don't listen. Tell others what to do. Insult others in order to look strong and tough.
Impress people with sensitivity, intelligence, and problem-solving skills.	Impress people with strong fighter skills. Dominate others.
Be cooperative in dealing with others.	Demonstrate power through domineering and vindictive behavior.
Show vulnerability from time to time.	Never show vulnerability, only strength.
Learn whom to trust and whom not to trust.	Prize self-reliance.

Relationship Skills Versus Bully Skills (continued)

DESIRED SOCIAL SKILLS	TYPICAL BULLYING SKILLS
Use respectful and realistic language; avoid using dramatic and exaggerated terms.	Speak in dramatic, exaggerated, superior terms.
Do what is possible to calm crises, conflicts, chaos, and fear in order to maintain relationships.	Stir up crises, conflicts, chaos, and fear. Then present themselves as a hero, to protect others from what they created.
Speak modestly; appreciate others' accomplishments as well as your own.	Speak arrogantly and exaggerate (or make up) accomplishments.
Be a team player. Work to accomplish many tasks with teammates.	Show off as an individual. Accomplish many tasks single-handedly—or claim to do so.

© 2024 Bill Eddy

How Technology Promotes Bullies

In recent decades, our world has steadily changed in ways that value these bullying skills and give bullies an ever-increasing advantage. Technology has weakened our social relationships without us even noticing. Instantaneous communication and easy travel have made mobility and individualism a way of life. Family and community connectedness, as well as responsibility and restraint, have diminished, creating a vacuum that bullies have been happy to fill.

Throughout human existence, communities have formed around shared tasks, beliefs, and enemies. With most shared tasks taken over by technology (and more to come with artificial intelligence), shared beliefs and shared enemies become more important. And bullies are skilled at exploiting opportunities to build communities around their enemies—their targets of blame. The emotional intensity that this can create is almost irresistible. Meanwhile, the Internet and social media have made it possible for anyone to bully anybody anywhere in the world—long-distance, anonymously, without a conscience, and usually without consequences.

The Impact of Technology on Our World Culture

TECHNOLOGY AT HOME AND AT WORK	HIGH-EMOTION, HIGH-TECH MEDIA
Weakens family and community ties.	Strengthens bullies and their powers.
Weakens restraints on bullying behavior.	Strengthens images of bullying behavior.
Weakens respect for others.	Strengthens disrespect and disdain.
Weakens our shared sense of responsibility.	Strengthens selfishness.
Weakens compassion for people we know—and for other people like us.	Strengthens arrogance.
Weakens compassion for strangers and people not like us.	Strengthens judgmentalism.
Weakens consequences for bad behavior.	Strengthens bad behavior by giving it more and more attention.
Weakens unity of purpose.	Strengthens division.
Weakens tolerance for benign differences.	Strengthens fear, anger, and the exaggeration of differences, even small ones.
Weakens understanding of real problems.	Strengthens belief in fantasy crises.
Weakens our reliance on real people.	Strengthens belief in fantasy heroes.
Weakens our use of skilled leaders.	Strengthens opportunities for bully leaders.

If we take a close look at our shifting cultural trends and technology, we can see how our tech-driven lives are creating this new world of adult bullies—why they are gaining and the rest of us are losing. That is the bad news.

Turning the Tables on Bullies

Now for the good news: Although this may be our current predicament, it is not our destiny. And being bullied does not have to be your destiny. We have the knowledge and the tools to turn this around. The following chapters provide you with information, inspiration, and practical guidance.

Many people scratch their heads about why adult bullies succeed repeatedly, but they are looking in the wrong places for answers. Most people who become adult bullies' targets of blame wonder what they did to cause bullies to attack them. They often feel isolated and ashamed. They look for issues and causes and root problems. They don't understand that all these are completely beside the point. They don't recognize that adult bullies have distinctly different personalities from most people. They think, feel, and act differently. They are driven to dominate others, regardless of the situation or the people involved. With bullies, there often is no issue or cause or problem other than that the bully feels driven to overpower everyone else at all times.

Because of this, when many people find themselves dealing with a bully, they often overreact or underreact. Thus, they make things worse for themselves and others without even realizing it. Meanwhile, other people around bullies tend to minimize the bullies' behavior. They urge bullies' targets of blame not to get so upset or worry so much. But if you've ever been bullied, you know that this advice only makes things worse. It empowers the bully.

Most people don't expect bullies to enter their lives. This catches them off guard. That's why there is surprise domestic violence by a newlywed, surprise sexual assault by an employer such as Harvey Weinstein, a surprise invasion of Ukraine by Vladimir Putin's Russia in 2022, and new surprises personally and publicly in the news every year.

The truth is that all adult bullies—from the abusive spouse to the toxic boss to the online troll to the murderous dictator—share some very predictable personality patterns of behavior and use the same ten hidden powers—over and over.

SIX STRATEGIES TO OVERCOME BULLIES' POWERS

Each chapter in this book explains a primitive emotional power, and at the end of each chapter, I provide six strategies for overcoming that power. These are generally the same for all bullying situations although I have given examples to show the differences in some contexts. Most of the examples of these strategies include success stories in which individuals or groups strengthened themselves and stopped or slowed a bully. Combined, these methods help individuals gain confidence and allies in spotting and stopping bullying behavior.

Here are the six strategies:

1. Open your eyes to the patterns of bullies.
2. Pull the plug on bullies.
3. Set limits on bullies with credible threats.
4. Impose serious consequences on bullies.
5. Communicate effectively about bullies to others.
6. Stand strong against bullies with other people.

Since we are all part of this new world culture, we can all play a role in decreasing bullying, in ways small and large. Overall, the more awareness there is for everyone, the more effective our whole culture will be in discouraging adult bullying behavior. As you'll see, it's not that complicated. We have the knowledge. This book will give you hope and skills.

CHAPTER 3

The Power of Unrestrained Personalities

I'm smart. I'm loving. My love will cure.
This is going to work out.

—**Victim of domestic violence**

BULLYING IS MORE THAN ONE ISOLATED ACTION. It's a predictable pattern of behavior. The American Psychological Association defines it this way: "Bullying is a form of aggressive behavior in which someone intentionally and repeatedly causes another person injury or discomfort. Bullying can take the form of physical contact, words, or more subtle actions."[1] It usually takes place where there is a power imbalance or perceived power imbalance. It can lead to health problems for the victims or targets of bullying. (I use the terms *victims* and *targets* interchangeably throughout this book.) Most people think that bullies have the ability to come to their senses, realize how much harm they're doing, and stop themselves. Years ago I used to think this also.

But that's a fantasy. Adult bullies don't—and can't—come to their senses and catch themselves. After four decades of working with bullies and their victims, this is one of the most important lessons I have learned: Many adult bullies are born that way. Others learn to be bullies in early childhood through abuse or indulgence (or both). Bullying is not just something they do; it defines who they are. Bullying by adults doesn't stop on its own because it is part of a bully's personality. Fundamental to this personality is deliberately targeting others for abuse and domination. Adult bullies have a personality-based pattern of *unrestrained, aggressive behavior.*

Remember this. It may save your life.

Yet most people don't believe that people like this actually exist in large numbers. In a civilized society, we count on everyone to stop themselves, to be reasonable and self-restrained, and to stay in their lanes. Bullies do none of these things.

We are hardwired to trust people, especially strangers in need. This gives bullies incredible powers to manipulate us. You might be thinking, *Of course bullies can stop themselves. They just don't want to.* Or *They know they're acting badly. I just have to point it out to them.* Or *I can get them to stop. They'll listen to me.* Or *They'll calm down and stop bothering me soon enough. I just have to wait it out.* Or *I think he's learned his lesson now.* Or *I believe there's good in everyone. She'll come to her senses. You'll see.* Sadly, they don't suddenly change into reasonable people—although we may keep waiting for that to happen. Bullies can pretend for a while, but they are fundamentally different in how they act in relationships. Their personalities lack empathy, remorse, and self-control.

Win-Lose, Dominant Relationships

Bullies desire—and create—win-lose relationships. They don't *just* want to be on top, *just* to be superior, *just* to be in charge. They also want *you to lose*. Bullies want to get into your head and manipulate you, to make you doubt yourself and believe in them. Some may enjoy hurting you. They mostly want to have power and control over you. Their goal is to overpower—and if they can't, then they may try to ruin or destroy.

Most people—maybe 80 to 90 percent of us—assume that we live in a world where conflicts are problems to solve in a civilized manner, in a win-win way. Sports and business have rules and incentives so that, in the end, people don't kill one another or overrun others' lives. They just win or lose an event and move on.

But winning is *never* enough for bullies. For an adult bully, somebody else *has* to lose, and lose big, in order for the bully to feel okay. Sometimes this even includes violence. Bullies keep going until they get what they want, or until they are stopped by someone or something else. It's programmed into them by the time they are adults. When most people debate or argue, they think they are trying to solve a problem or come to a resolution. That is not the case for bullies. The surface issue is irrelevant to them. While the goal for most people is to resolve conflicts and get along, for bullies' the goal is to achieve power and control.

If you don't realize this, you will be continually caught off guard by bullies' behavior. It won't make sense. *Why does he do that? Doesn't he realize . . . ?* Nope! He doesn't. It's not who he is. Bullies repeatedly get away with their unrestrained aggressive behavior because people don't believe anyone they know could be that extreme.

Let's look at what happens if you don't realize that bullies have this aggressive drive and will stop at nothing to get what they want—even if it's just to have power over someone else.

The Handsome Surgeon

When Gail Katz met Robert Bierenbaum in the early 1980s in New York City, he seemed like an ideal husband-to-be. Soon he became a successful doctor. But over time some red flags appeared. Once, at dinner with Gail's sister, Alayne, after Gail and Robert married, Robert forcibly shoved food into Gail's mouth, and then into Alayne's as well. Another time, Robert tried to drown Gail's cat in the toilet of their Upper East Side apartment. Things soon got worse. One day, when Robert, who disliked smoking, caught Gail enjoying a smoke on the balcony of their apartment, he choked her to unconsciousness, a clear sign that his pattern of power and control was escalating. She reported this to the local police station, but nothing was done. (It was 1983.)

You and I can see a pattern of unrestrained aggressive behavior emerging. But Katz couldn't. Victims of domestic violence often can't see the warning signs because they have become acclimated to this coercive control. Instead, she naively told her sister, "I'm smart. I'm loving. My love will cure. This is going to work out."[2]

In 1985 Katz disappeared. She was never seen or heard from again. Bierenbaum went on to marry again and lived a pleasant new life with his new wife. But she too eventually became concerned about him—and separated from him.

It wasn't until fifteen years later that Bierenbaum was convicted of Gail Katz's murder. And it wasn't until 2020, at a parole board hearing, while serving a twenty-year-to-life sentence, that Bierenbaum finally admitted that he had killed her, and how. He explained to the board that he strangled her and threw her body out of a small plane he was piloting over the ocean. When asked why, he stated, "I wanted her to stop yelling at me, and I attacked her." He further admitted that he killed her because he was "immature" and "didn't understand how to deal with his anger."[3]

In short, Bierenbaum couldn't stop himself.

This is important to remember. Bullies are often driven to act in ways that even they don't understand. This is why it is so essential for all of us to stop bullies: because they often cannot stop themselves.

When the truth finally came out, Katz's sister, Alayne, said he was exactly the same man she had known thirty-five years earlier. "He is incapable of a shred of remorse."[4]

Was this man a bully? It sure sounds like it.

Why Do Bullies Lack Self-Restraint?

Every day, there are people born or raised with high-conflict personalities. As I mentioned in the first chapter, they have a behavior pattern of blaming others, all-or-nothing thinking, unmanaged emotions, and extreme behavior. Bullies, as the most high-conflict people, are driven to dominate others and potentially ruin their families and their businesses. We need to understand their personalities and how to restrain them, since they don't—and can't—restrain themselves.

Many of them also have what are called *personality disorders,* as defined in the *Diagnostic and Statistical Manual of Mental Disorders,* Fifth Edition, Text Revision (commonly referred to as the

DSM-5-TR). This is the manual that mental health professionals use to diagnose mental disorders. A personality disorder means that the person is stuck in "an enduring pattern of behavior" that can lead to "social impairment."[5] In short, they can't stop themselves. Personality disorders have been closely studied and have been detailed in the manual for over forty years.

Of course, most people with personality disorders are not killers like Robert Bierenbaum. Mostly, they lead frustrated lives, not understanding how they are stuck in whatever pattern of behavior they have. They lack self-awareness and, therefore, most also lack the ability to change, although a few do find ways to get unstuck and improve their lives. It is very important to understand that not all people with personality disorders are high-conflict people and most are not bullies.

But one category of personality disorders may help explain bullies. Of the ten identified personality disorders, those known as Cluster B personality disorders include narcissistic, borderline, antisocial, and histrionic personalities. These are interpersonal disorders, and research looking at 127 studies has shown that these Cluster B personalities have "significant associations with domineeringness, vindictiveness, and intrusiveness."[6]

Sound familiar? Essentially, bullying behavior.

Of course, bullying and personality disorders can both vary widely in terms of degree. But this connection helps us understand many things about bullies—in particular, why they lack self-restraint and rarely change. Remember, personality disorders have an enduring pattern of behavior. The *DSM-5-TR* lists several factors that go with each Cluster B personality disorder. Three of these disorders stand out as having a significant factor that is associated with bullying and a lack of self-restraint:

- **Narcissistic personalities (NPD):** "Lacks empathy: is unwilling to recognize or identify with the feelings and needs of others."
- **Antisocial personalities (ASPD):** "Lack of remorse, as indicated by being indifferent to or rationalizing having hurt, mistreated, or stolen from another."
- **Borderline personalities (BPD):** "Inappropriate, intense anger or difficulty controlling anger (e.g., frequent displays of temper, constant anger, recurrent physical fights)."[7]

In other words, these personalities lack the internal brakes that 90 percent or more of people have that help them get along with others. A subgroup of these Cluster B personalities would appear to be our bullies, who will go all the way to dominate or destroy their targets. This can at times include violence although most people with personality disorders are not violent.[8]

How Do These Personalities Develop?

About 4.5 percent of adults around the world may have a Cluster B personality disorder, according to the *DSM-5-TR*. But it's important to note that not everyone with one or more of these personality disorders or traits is a bully. For example, some narcissists are self-absorbed and feel entitled—but they don't have targets of blame the way that bullies do. Some people with borderline personality disorder are primarily hard on themselves and focus much of their anger inward. Some antisocials (also known as sociopaths) may steal or otherwise break financial laws, but they don't target any human beings for domination or abuse. Indeed, many people with Cluster B personalities are also the targets and victims of bullies and may benefit from reading this book as well.

But a significant number of people with one or more of these three disorders are bullies. When they have a personality disorder, that means that they are very unlikely to change (it's an enduring pattern per the *DSM-5-TR*), they lack self-awareness, and they have an "inability to care about the needs of others."[9] This surprises many people who believe that everyone wants to change and improve their own lives. However, this repetitive pattern of interpersonal dysfunctional behavior is at the core of a personality disorder. The reason that bullies have no interest in changing the way they are is that they can't see their own part in their problems and truly believe that others are to blame for everything that goes wrong in their lives. It's an unfortunate blind spot, and you can't get them to see it because it's part of their personality.

Perhaps these personalities evolved over time to cope with a much more dangerous interpersonal world. One leading team of cognitive therapists puts it like this from today's perspective:

> Strategies of predation, competition, and sociability that were useful in the more primitive surroundings do not always fit into the present niche of a highly individualized and technological society, with its own specialized cultural and social organization. A bad fit may be a factor in the development of behavior that we diagnose as a "personality disorder."[10]

With this in mind, being domineering in primitive times makes sense. It's better than being dominated. But in today's world, being domineering and vindictive can get you into big trouble in families, at work, and in communities. While our culture and technology have changed dramatically, we still have the same human personalities and genetic tendencies we have had for thousands of years.

Don't Label Anyone

What I'm about to say is vitally important: Don't tell a bully you think they are a bully, have a high-conflict personality, or have a personality disorder. They can quickly become very defensive and perhaps even dangerous—possibly for months or years. You can easily become their next target. It's easy to judge people with these disorders as jerks, as hateful, or as evil people. Please don't. Instead, think of them more like you'd think of alcoholics and addicts who don't have control over their substance use, and who may require outside intervention.

Therefore, as you read this book, please avoid judging or labeling people. Instead, try to understand their personalities. Think of how to restrain them or stop them—and to protect yourself and others from their bullying behavior. Labels aren't helpful. Don't think of how to change them. Think of how to change what *you* do in relation to them or how to steer clear of their primitive emotional powers in the first place. People constantly argue over whether a person is all good or all bad while missing the hidden patterns of behavior that are really the issue. As I said in the Introduction: Don't be judgmental; be strategic. For example, don't tell someone they are being a bully in a hostile conversation. Instead, tell them that if they continue talking that way, you are going to leave the conversation.

Lance Armstrong

Let's look at another bully who caught everyone by surprise—except for the people close to him. This sort of example can happen in any social or recreational group. From 1999 to 2005, Lance Armstrong was the most world-famous, highly regarded athlete; he had won seven Tour de France cycling races—the world's most respected and difficult cycling event. All this success came *after* he recovered from near-fatal testicular cancer. Put together, these accomplishments made him into a wildly popular American hero.

Except that Armstrong repeatedly took illegal performance-enhancing drugs to give him an advantage in races. For years he denied having done so, but eventually those around him could no longer keep it a secret. He would eventually admit to this use in a television interview with Oprah Winfrey in 2013.

As news began to surface that Armstrong may have been doping, he sharply attacked his critics. In one widely covered press conference in 2009 when he was pressed on this question, he said to Irish sports journalist and former pro cyclist Paul Kimmage, "You're not worth the chair you're sitting on, with a statement like that."[11] And later, in a 2019 interview regarding his book, *Positively False*, Armstrong's teammate Floyd Landis said:

> A lot of times he would push people out of the way. He was a bully. . . . It's his way of doing it. It worked for him, but he didn't have a lot of friends. . . . For Lance it was basically a war, and sometimes it wasn't even a war to win, it was a war to inflict suffering. . . . He got satisfaction out of making people lose. He likes to see people lose.[12]

To be fair, Lance Armstrong has also done some good work for people with cancer. Not every bully is 100 percent bad, 100 percent of the time—though a few may be (Hitler comes to mind). But Armstrong followed the standard adult bully pattern of bullying others until he got himself into trouble and others had to restrain him. He eventually destroyed his own stellar reputation as a prize-winning cyclist by being stripped of his seven Tour de France titles, thereby losing millions of dollars in bonuses and lucrative advertising contracts.[13]

HOW YOU CAN STOP THIS POWER

1. Open Your Eyes to the Pattern

Watch out for patterns of behavior that can pull you into a win-lose relationship with a bully. Most people want relatively equal win-win relationships, so this behavior usually stands out once you look for it. But you don't need to be paranoid and constantly on guard—you just need to be observant. Practice looking for these patterns by thinking about who has these patterns in the news and in entertainment. Get used to noticing that a lot of people demonstrate the typical signs of bullying. (For a full list of 40 Predictable Behaviors of High-Conflict Personalities, see the Appendix 1 on page 246) Be careful about getting too close to such people. Remember that they have unrestrained aggressive behavior.

Once you see one or more warning signs of a bully or high-conflict personality (preoccupation with blaming others, all-or-nothing thinking, unmanaged emotions, and extreme behavior), you can predict some of the following:

1. They won't reflect on their own behavior.
2. They won't understand why they behave the way they do.
3. They won't change their behavior.
4. They will claim their behavior is normal and necessary, given the circumstances.
5. They lack empathy for others although they may say the right words.
6. They may have a public persona that's very good, but that covers (and hides) a private negative personality.
7. They are preoccupied with blaming others, even for very small or nonexistent events.
8. They will turn on family and good friends in an instant.
9. They have targets of blame who are intimate others or people

in positions of authority.

10. They may assault their target(s) of blame financially, reputationally, legally, emotionally, or physically.[14]

Several years ago, I recognized what I call the 90 Percent Rule. Ninety percent of people will *never* do some of the things that bullies or high-conflict people do repeatedly. So, when you hear about someone acting this way, there is usually a pattern of similar behavior that has existed for a long time that you can spot.

2. Pull the Plug on the Bully

Bullies count on your cooperation with their terrible treatment of others—or of you.

For example, by 2021 there were concerns that Governor Andrew Cuomo of New York was sexually harassing women on his staff. Unknown to anyone else at first, he had several encounters with his Executive Assistant #1, which included unusually close hugs, unwanted kisses on the cheeks and (once) the lips, grabbing her butt while taking a selfie with her, and ultimately reaching under her blouse and touching her breast.

At first, the assistant kept this to herself, planning to take it "to the grave." But when he stated at a press conference that he never "touched anyone inappropriately," she couldn't contain herself and told certain colleagues, who told senior staff.[15] It was clear that he wasn't going to stop himself.

After more women came forward about Cuomo's treatment of them, he resigned in August 2021. They pulled the plug on his bullying behavior. If it wasn't for Executive Assistant #1 refusing to keep Cuomo's behavior a secret any longer, he might have continued for years. This is a good example of how people—individually and collectively— can pull the plug on a bully. It's also a good example of the struggle individuals go through with themselves over whether to stop protecting a bully by keeping secrets. It helps to know that other people have chosen to pull the plug on bullies' power. If you're in a situation like this, you're not alone. You too can pull the plug, especially if you get some help.

3. Set Limits with Credible Threats

Credible threats are threats that the bully *knows* will definitely be implemented if they violate the limit that has been set. While many bullies simply can't stop themselves no matter what, many others may at least try to stop to avoid undesirable consequences. Letting a bully know in advance that there will be consequences, and that their power will be taken away, will sometimes slow them down.

One way of letting bullies—and everyone else—know in advance that there will be consequences for certain bullying behaviors is to post or announce a policy of expected behavior, especially in public. An example of this is the Respectful Meeting Policy, a method I designed for a tech company. In the firm, older consultants, all of them male, attended company meetings that needed their technical input. The meetings were often led by younger female managers—and the older men regularly bullied them. The men had specialized information that was needed for decision-making, but they did not take the young managers seriously. They interrupted, had side conversations, and made occasional sexist insults. I recommended the following procedure, which the company has used successfully ever since. Some homeowners' association boards and other groups with open meetings have employed it also.

Respectful Meeting Policy:

At our Company, much of our work is accomplished at meetings. In order to ensure the smooth, respectful, and efficient management of meetings, the meeting chair shall manage the Agenda and the right of members to speak. On rare occasion, a meeting member may become disrespectful in communicating their information and opinions. In such a case, the meeting chair shall ask the meeting member to revise their manner of speech to be respectful. In the event that the meeting member does not thereafter speak respectfully, the chair may announce a short break or end the meeting, at the meeting chair's discretion. Other meeting members shall support the chair in making such decisions.[16]

The benefit of this approach is that it gives the meeting chair the ability to end the meeting, if necessary, without feeling ashamed that they cannot restrain unrestrained (and perhaps unrestrainable) people. The older male consultants soon learned to respect this. In addition, the young women managers gained confidence that they could stop a meeting, if necessary, so that they would not be bullied. They no longer feared they would look bad or weak if they took this action. This Respectful Meeting Policy is designed to set limits rather than to cancel a meeting outright. Many bullies will adhere to this type of limit if they realize—but *only* if they realize—that the meeting chair will actually enforce it if they don't behave. Many people don't realize how effective a credible threat can be because they are used to seeing empty threats that are not enforced. That failure to enforce actually encourages *more* bullying behavior, not less. Some bullies can't restrain themselves even a little bit, so imposing consequences on them, perhaps over and over, may become necessary in some situations.

A similar approach has become necessary for school board meetings, as acknowledged by the California School Board Association in developing procedures to handle increasing disruptions: "In 2021, we have seen a marked increase in political division at school board meetings, open hostility toward board members, mass protests, disruptions that forced the board to pause or abandon meetings, and physical abuse and death threats against trustees and their families."[17]

By informing participants at public meetings that disruptions may cause the termination of the meeting, they are on notice to follow the rules, or they will not be heard. Some school boards have had to stop meetings because of these disruptions, and the abruptly ended meetings have been reported in the media, so setting such limits has a lot of credibility.

Is this an infringement of free speech? No. According to legal standards, it is not a violation of the First Amendment right to free speech for government officials to shut down certain public meetings, if necessary, because they are known as limited public forums; they can be subject to time, place, and manner restrictions to avoid disruptions, citing, "If speech is irrelevant, repetitious, lengthy, speaking out of turn, refusing to leave the podium, hateful obscene gestures, thoughts of harm, those are all considered disruption."[18] As one court of appeals decision, *White v. City of Norwalk*, explains about First Amendment rights at city council meetings:

> A speaker may disrupt a Council meeting by speaking too long, by being unduly repetitious, or by extended discussion of irrelevancies. The meeting is disrupted because the Council is prevented from accomplishing its business in a reasonably efficient manner. Indeed, such conduct may interfere with the rights of other speakers.[19]

4. Impose Serious Consequences

Speaking of boards, many large businesses have boards of directors that have the potential to impose serious consequences on a bully—even a bully CEO. Whether and when they will impose serious consequences is the big question. It's common for a start-up to have a high-powered innovator who is also a bully. Their bullying behavior may help them promote their ideas, product, or service, but it also may eventually destroy their efforts—and even their company. Will they crash their own business? Some innovator bullies do.

This almost happened to Uber, the ride-sharing company founded in 2009, primarily by Travis Kalanick, who became its CEO. Uber very quickly revolutionized the taxi business—but trouble was brewing with a series of privacy scandals, gross manipulations of Apple products with its Uber app,[20] and complaints of discrimination and sexual harassment at the company. Kalanick was considered to be at the center of the bullying culture that permeated Uber. It all came to a head in 2017. He was caught by surprise when two representatives from one of Uber's biggest shareholders showed up in the middle of a business trip. They gave him a letter signed by five of Uber's biggest investors demanding that he resign "by the end of the day." Kalanick called Arianna Huffington, a friendly board member, and she told him to take this letter seriously. Kalanick resigned from his job as CEO that same day.[21]

It was another two years before he resigned his own seat on the board of directors in 2019. By then, the company had received 6,000 complaints and multiple lawsuits by riders regarding sexual assault—but Uber had taken a bullying approach to the victims, challenging their credibility, and stonewalling disclosure.[22] In 2020 a judge found that Uber had refused to comply with court disclosure requirements "without any legitimate legal or factual grounds" and recommended that their permits to operate be suspended if they didn't pay a fine within thirty days. Uber ultimately paid a $9 million penalty for that.[23] While this further forced the company to change its culture, in some ways it highlights the need for more serious and swift consequences for bullies *before* they do too much damage rather than afterward as punishment.

We all need to realize from the start that even a bully as successful as Kalanick often cannot stop their own bullying behavior. What is stunning about his case is that brilliant business leaders are overlooked as being truly bullying. How could he be a bully and be so successful? Remember, bullies can show up anywhere at any time. Unless you have a healthy skepticism and recognize these bully dynamics, you too may excuse their unrestrained bullying behavior rather than impose consequences and instead rely on wishful thinking that they will stop themselves. Hopefully, you are starting to get the idea that, even at the highest levels of the business world, it's not the position. It's the personality.

5. Communicate Effectively About Bullies to Others

Most people don't know about these unrestrained personalities. Therefore, those who do understand can help communicate to others how a significant number of people indeed lack empathy, remorse, and self-control. This communication can be done in individual conversations, educational seminars, and books and other writings.

Throughout this book I mention people who are engaged in such communications and making a positive impact in many settings. For example, child abuse is an obvious and all-too-common form of bullying. This can take many forms: physical abuse, sexual abuse, emotional abuse, and neglect. However, because this topic is already widely discussed and too vast to cover effectively here, I want to address one of the most hidden and misunderstood types of bullying behavior in families that is often experienced in families going through a separation or divorce. This is called *parental alienation*, also known as *child alienation* or simply *alienation*. This occurs when a child resists or refuses to see one of their parents after separation or divorce, even though they previously had a good relationship and there was no abuse.

To be clear, it's not alienation if a parent has engaged in some form of abuse that is causing the child's resistance. This is called *estrangement* instead because it's that parent's own abusive behavior that caused the resistance. Telling the difference between alienation and estrangement takes understanding primitive emotional power and its unconscious influence on children's behavior that causes them to resist or refuse seeing a parent.

In cases of alienation, the child may reject one parent's whole side of their family, including grandparents, aunts, uncles, and even pets. The cause is typically one of the parents intensely and emotionally telling the child terrible (and often false) things about the other parent. You can see how a bully parent can easily weaponize and optimize this power when alone with a vulnerable child after a separation or divorce, yet much of this is done unconsciously. Resisting or refusing contact has grown into a significant problem around the world for about 11 to 15 percent of all separated and divorced families. The number is almost twice as high for families that end up in court with custody disputes, as about 20 to 27 percent of those families have resistance or refusal issues.[24]

One of the people who is effectively educating parents and professionals about parental alienation is psychologist Richard Warshak. In 2001 (and updated in 2010), he published a book explaining this problem: *Divorce Poison: How to Protect Your Family from Bad-Mouthing and Brainwashing.* He recognized this poisonous power, which occurs mostly out of sight as does most bullying. The effect is to create a win-lose relationship between the child and the other parent (the "rejected parent") that no one else can see. It goes on primarily in private and is absorbed mostly *emotionally* and not logically or even consciously by the child from the bullying parent's behavior (the "favored parent"). These unrestrained alienating behaviors can be so poisonous that they will sever some parent-child relationships for years—or even a lifetime. Yet some parents really can't stop themselves from engaging in alienating behaviors.

We will revisit this often-hidden pattern of unrestrained bullying behavior in families in later chapters, starting in Chapter 6. With education about the hidden dynamics of this problem, parents, professionals, and courts can learn to stop it early before parental alienation takes hold. Once again, it's an issue of restraining bullying behavior that may be mostly unconscious for the parent engaging in it.

6. Stand Strong with Others Against Bullies

Given a bully's unrestrained behavior, it often takes more than one person to stop them. The case of Elizabeth Smart is a perfect example.

Smart was fourteen years old when she was kidnapped from her home in Utah at knifepoint by Brian Mitchell. He took her to a remote location in the mountains, where he lived with his wife. Smart became his "second wife." His plan was to kidnap several more fourteen-year-old "virgin brides" to create his own polygamous religious family. Apparently, he figured that girls of this age would be the easiest to manipulate and to train to accept his domination.[25]

Fortunately, Smart's parents were very assertive about getting public attention. The day she was kidnapped, more than one hundred officers joined the search for her, including many from nearby counties. As the day progressed, the hunt expanded to Wyoming and Idaho. Soon her father was on nationwide television promoting a massive nationwide search. Police and citizens were on the lookout everywhere.[26]

They didn't give up. From time to time, Mitchell and his two "wives" would go shopping in the nearby city, dressed as pious religious people in white robes. Smart wore a veil and a wig as he instructed her to. She did not try to escape at times when she might have, because he had told her that if she did, he would kill her family. Finally, after nine months, a stranger saw the three of them on a sidewalk in town and thought one of them might be Smart. Police were contacted and stopped them. Mitchell insisted they were pious people who should be left alone, as he had done before. This time the police asked if the young woman behind the veil was Smart. She was afraid to answer. But the police insisted and separated her from them. After some conversation Smart finally admitted who she was. Police took her into protective custody and arrested Mitchell and his wife.[27]

Smart was saved from a possible lifetime of dominance and mind control by this unrestrained bully. She could not have done that without the help of her parents spreading the word far and wide, an alert stranger, and the police. This is a perfect example of the large school of fish chasing the bully on the cover of this book because so many people helped stop this man who couldn't stop himself. Instead of being bitter and immobilized, Elizabeth Smart came out of this ordeal dedicating her life to teaching others about child safety, self-defense, and recovery from sexual assault. Her own words should give all of us encouragement, whatever we're facing: "Now, whenever there is a challenge in front of me, I say to myself, 'Elizabeth, you can do this. You survived nine months with those creeps. If you could survive that, you can do anything.'"[28]

CONCLUSION

It's a hard concept to accept, as we want to see everyone as fundamentally well-intentioned and interested in self-improvement, but 5 to 10 percent of adults appear to have unrestrained personalities, which means they have an enduring pattern of lack of empathy for others, lack of remorse for their harm to others, lack of self-control of their emotions and behavior, or all three. This gives them, as bullies, the ability and drive to dominate and possibly destroy the people around them. This perhaps primitive behavior may have helped humans thousands of years ago but has undermined our relationships in the modern world. In other words, bullies aren't evil, they're ancient.

At the same time, we have an equal or greater ability to stop their unrestrained behavior using six strategies. With a healthy skepticism, we can recognize when these bullying patterns are present and unlikely to change. Rather than enabling bullies' unrestrained behavior by thinking that the "issue" justifies it, we need to pull the plug on our own cooperation with their bullying. With practice we can gain confidence in threatening consequences and imposing them. We can educate others about these patterns of bullying behavior, and we can stand with others to put on the brakes—especially when others can't do it alone. Lack of self-restraint is the underlying problem of bullies, so those around them need to stop them.

COMMON MISTAKE:

Bullies can stop themselves but choose not to do so.

REALITY:

Bullies are unable to stop themselves.
Others must do so.

CHAPTER 4

The Power of Three Primitive Emotions

*The plaintiff alleges that Mr. Cowell
created an intimidating atmosphere that he knew she
found oppressive. Mr. Cowell knew that the plaintiff
felt intimidated and uncomfortable in his presence,
but he didn't care. . . . Mr. Cowell had a particular
attitude, flowing from his personality.*

—Supreme Court of Victoria in
Swan v. Monash Law Book Co-operative

WHY DON'T PEOPLE JUST WALK AWAY from or ignore bullies? Some-times people can't because the bully is their boss, coworker, parent, sibling, or elected official. But sometimes the psychological powers of bullies trigger in others some very deep and ancient parts of the human psyche. Bullies gain control over these parts of our brains by using *primitive emotional powers (PEP)*. This is how they get into your head.

The powers described in this book are all forms of PEP—all put together, think of them as the *PEP formula*. This is what you want to spot. Since these powers are based on primitive emotions, they are not logical, and most people absorb them without even realizing it.

Our Ancient Brains

Bear with me as I try to be brief with this explanation. It's the foundation of understanding bullies' primitive emotional power and why it is so problematic. I'm not a brain scientist, but I have developed this theory of bully dynamics based on forty years of observing and dealing with bully behavior combined with readings and seminars in brain science and early human history.

Our primitive emotions mostly operate outside our conscious minds, yet they can drive our most basic behavior. This is what therapists often help their clients gain access to in order to understand their own behavior. Three primitive emotions in particular that operate deep within us appear to be activated by bullies without us even being aware of it on a conscious level:

FEAR

ANGER

LOVE/LOYALTY

In understanding our own brains, *The Archaeology of Mind* by Jaak Panksepp and Lucy Biven is particularly helpful in describing our "higher" brains and our "lower" or "ancient" brains. The upper parts of our brain—the cortex—represent our uniquely developed human thinking cap, generally the conscious part of our minds. The lower parts of our brain—the subcortical brain networks—are common to all mammals. While not identical, we mammals have the same seven emotional systems.[1]

Two of these emotional systems are fear and anger, which bullies constantly manipulate. Two of the other ancient emotional systems are care and panic/grief. When combined, care and panic/grief explain the empathy or love/loyalty that bullies elicit in their targets in order to dominate them or get them to help in their domination of others. As Panksepp and Biven explain, "The roots of human empathy reach deep into the ancient circuits that engender caring feelings in all mammals, where we identify our own well-being with the well-being of others. Feelings of panic/grief in others may be one of the most powerful emotional resonances to promote empathic devotions."[2]

This may explain the devotion that bullies activate in their targets and others, which I call love/loyalty—because the bullies pretend to express love but what they really expect is your loyalty—your devotion—and they don't reciprocate it. When this love/loyalty is activated at the primitive level, people don't understand their own actions in relation to their bullies. *Why did I do that? Why did I fall in love with him! Why didn't I fight back? Why did I follow her in attacking this other person whom I don't even know?* Bullies often inspire this love/loyalty by constantly telling you they love you (often called "love-bombing") or by playing the victim, so that you feel sorry for them and very protective of them against others. (Playing the victim is explained in depth in Chapter 9.)

Immobilized and Mobilized

All put together, these three primitive emotions (fear, anger, love/loyalty) are easily manipulated and triggered by bullies and their primitive emotional power (PEP). Because these feelings are primitive, we are not used to them and surprised when we have them. They activate our unconscious and automatic fears for our survival as individuals and as a group. People don't recognize these powers, don't understand them, may overreact and make things worse because of them, or may be consumed with self-criticism because of them. Yet these unconscious responses may have saved our lives in many circumstances in primitive times and remain hardwired within us.

For example, many women who have been raped describe being frozen and unable to scream or fight back. Singer/songwriter Lady Gaga said this happened to her when she was raped at nineteen: "'I just froze.' Years later, she said, her body still remembered the feeling, and she experienced a 'total psychotic break.'"[3]

When criticized by friends or in court, rape victim/survivors often can't explain their responses. Yet some researchers have said that this may be because of "tonic immobility," suggesting that it is a way of defending against predators and surviving. Yet in court, victims are often unable to get convictions because they didn't resist. "It seems ironic," the researchers wrote, "that victims should be legally penalized for exhibiting a reaction that has such adaptive value and may be firmly embedded in the biology of our species."[4]

Being emotionally *immobilized* by bully behavior is one common outcome of PEP as applied to individual targets in any setting. Another common use of a bully's PEP is to emotionally *mobilize* people to attack the bully's other targets. This can help explain mob action. Rage may be activated in addition to or without fear. All or most of this appears to occur at a primitive emotional level outside our consciousness.

Another researcher explains how our brains process these emotions without thinking. In his book *Right Brain Psychotherapy*, Allan Schore explains that the left brain is the "thinking brain" and the right brain "processes all of our intense emotions," including fear, anger, and love. When these emotions are intense enough, our left brain "goes offline and the right hemisphere dominates." Our right brain reads "subtle facial (visual and auditory) expressions and other nonverbal communication" so fast that "our body and mental state is altered before we become conscious of what we are feeling."[5]

In other words, by invoking these intense primitive emotions with their faces and voices, others can bypass our rational thinking and get us to respond instinctively. I call this becoming *emotionally hooked*. Then, according to another brain scientist and surgeon, Antonio Damasio, the left brain guesses at reasons to justify the intensity of the right brain emotions: "The left cerebral hemisphere of humans is prone to fabricating verbal narratives that do not necessarily accord with the truth."[6] The result of this brain processing is that a person who is emotionally hooked may be ready to believe the bully's explanation for why they are upset. This explanation may then immobilize them ("It's all your own fault!") or mobilize them against others ("It's those people who are causing all our problems").

In the workplace when several people gang up on one person like this, they call it *mobbing*, which can refer to various types of harassment, spreading rumors, and sabotaging the person's projects. The PsychCentral mental health website explains that this term originated in describing mammals' predatory behavior in the wild. It can occur at all levels of an organization, from the boardroom to the janitor's closet.[7] Keep in mind that mobbing is usually started by one bully who mobilizes others who become emotionally hooked into this group behavior.

PEP 101: Bully Dynamics

In the hands of bullies, the combination of these three primitive emotional powers can be highly aggressive, highly adversarial, and highly contagious. The goal of PEP is always to dominate others—to gain power and control over them. PEP grows stronger as others reinforce and repeat it, similar to how a pep talk or pep rally builds a group's energy to win sporting events, new customers, or greater market share. Driven by this combination of intense "subcortical" emotions, bullies attempt to dominate individuals, groups, and even nations. If they don't get what they want, rather than calming down their PEP energy, they often escalate into violence—because, remember, their goal is always to dominate, no matter what it takes.

In ancient times, violence and power often went together. In modern times, however, we have tried to separate power from violence, so that we don't destroy ourselves, either individually or collectively. Unfortunately, in our new world culture of adult bullies, primitive emotional powers are making a comeback. The violence that comes with PEP has started to make a comeback as well.

How PEP Is Communicated

Bullies communicate their power through primitive images, sounds, and words of strength rather than providing useful information or problem-solving. They hook our primitive responses this way without us even realizing it.

Images of Strength. Bullies communicate dominance through primitive facial expressions of hostility, various forms of chest thumping ("I'm in charge here!"), and images of widespread support that they supposedly have behind them ("Everyone agrees with me"). Such images have nothing to do with the quality of bullies' information, knowledge, or skills. It's all about looking big and strong to get us emotionally hooked. In primitive days, that's often all that everyone had to go on. Our human existence as Homo sapiens goes back about 200,000 years, but we didn't have speech until about 60,000 to 70,000 years ago.[8] We mostly communicated nonverbally, through facial expressions, hand gestures, and other body language, for the first two-thirds of our existence. It's not surprising that so much of human communication is nonverbal even today—perhaps 80 to 90 percent. Yet we're so used to focusing on words that we miss the power of images on our primitive, lower brains, even when the images are right in front of us.

Today, bullies may show you their muscles, their stock portfolio, their big car, their big weapons, their fancy suits, or the number of followers they have on Facebook. They may sit surrounded by other people to make them look even bigger. They may stand on a podium to look taller or sit at a huge table in their office to show how powerful they are. Take notice when you see such displays. Consider how they make you feel.

Sounds of Strength. Bullies also use primitive vocal sounds—domineering tones of voice, sounds of great confidence, and threatening exclamations that are meant to strike fear in their targets. They may yell unnecessarily. Some bullies may speak almost in a whisper, to make you strain to hear them, and also to make you feel like you are their best buddy, whom they are telling something in the strictest confidence. Some people alter their voices to make them deeper to seem more authoritative and powerful. Most perpetrators of domestic violence don't hit their victims every day, but their voices, faces, and body language make it clear they are in charge. These are forms of what is called *coercive control.* You feel it, but you don't quite understand why. Bullies may not understand why what they do works so well at intimidating others, but they learn how powerful these images and sounds can be over time.

Words of Strength. Bullies also regularly use *hyperbole* (extremely exaggerated words and phrases, or "hype") in order to activate the more primitive, defensive parts of people's brains rather than the parts used for thinking and analyzing. Bullies say things like "You always" and "You never," or "She's the worst person to ever live on this planet," or "I know more about _____ than anyone in history," or "You will seriously regret what you're doing."

This language is designed to inspire in others a powerful mix of extreme fear, extreme anger, and extreme love/loyalty for the hero. This mix of extreme emotions can activate violence against others—especially any identified villains. Meanwhile, the bully who uses hyperbole can deny any responsibility for what it inspires. ("It's just words." "I wasn't being literal." "I was just joking." "I meant 'get murdered' as in 'lose at the ballot box and reach the end of their political career.'")

These words can hook people's brains in ways that no one can see—not even the people who are being hooked. When you hear a bully's rant, you may not remember a single word they said or a single point they made. You just know that you feel deeply upset and in personal danger or enraged at their targets—but you can't quite put your finger on why.

Target Dynamics

We've just looked at what bullies do. Now let's look at the primitive emotional responses that they often trigger in their targets. (And keep in mind that *anyone* can be the target of a bully.)

First, a bully picks a target and uses PEP energy to dominate them—*as a whole person*. Typically, the target absorbs the PEP energy and then does one of several things:

- Flees the bully in a panic for personal survival. The bully then chases after the target, either literally or metaphorically (e.g., on social media or in the press), and keeps inflicting damage or threats of extreme harm.

- Fights for their life against the bully—verbally or physically—who fights back, almost always raising the stakes—sometimes quite dangerously.
- Freezes in shock and confusion, and then the bully rolls over them.
- Turns the PEP energy inward, against themselves, often blaming themselves or doubting their own judgment.
- Submits to the bully and turns the PEP energy outward, toward the bully's other targets—that is, becoming one of the bully's negative advocates.

Both ends of this dynamic—the bully's aggressive behavior and their target's range of potential responses—appear to be (at least partly) hardwired in all of us. How does this primitive emotional power operate? Why is it so powerful? Where does it come from? How can it occur right under people's noses, yet most people don't see it?

If we look at primate history, we may find some answers. Humans are primates. So are chimpanzees (our closest primate cousins), bonobos (also close cousins), gorillas, monkeys, baboons, and orangutans. Primates constantly fight for power within each group, and sometimes between groups. They establish a *dominance hierarchy* so that everyone knows their place—either above or below someone else. But everyone wants to get higher on the hierarchy, so there may be frequent fights over who has higher status than whom.

Such dominance hierarchies were very effective among early humans. They helped to establish order and to give leadership to the strongest individuals—the *alphas* (usually alpha males, but sometimes alpha females). Physical strength mattered, especially when competing with other large animals (for example, lions long ago found humans tasty, until they learned how to fight back together), when coping with dramatic weather conditions (such as floods and fires), and when fighting one another.

For a long time, these hierarchies may actually have contributed to human progress. In more recent centuries, however, more flexible, rule-driven, and collaborative social structures have proved more intelligent, creative, strong, and effective. Nowadays, when you and your two coworkers compete for a promotion, or when you and three other candidates run for a position on your local school board, you are vying for power—temporary power—fighting like all other primates but in a respectful, civilized, controlled way. We humans have figured out that temporary hierarchies based on elections make for a much more stable and less violent and dangerous society. Bullies are part of the old-school approach that most of humanity has outgrown.

Many bullies appear to be oblivious to how their behavior affects others. Many lack empathy, remorse, and emotional self-control. While this is not an excuse, it helps us understand that we must stop them because they are incapable of stopping themselves. Over time their behavior usually gets steadily worse, and the harm they do only spreads.

A Bully at Work

Let's look at an example of primitive emotional power in the workplace. Workplace bullies are especially good at getting into coworkers' heads by using PEP because they may have to encounter or work with the same bully day after day. Catherine Mattice, a workplace bullying expert, emphasizes that workplace bullying goes far beyond minor disruptions or small annoyances. As Mattice explains,

"It creates a psychological power imbalance between the person doing the bullying and their target or targets, to a point where the person at the receiving end develops a feeling of helplessness."[9]

This can become very emotional, triggering primitive emotional responses the target may not understand. Some people develop headaches and stomachaches and may stay home and miss work. Some become depressed. Others are motivated to simply quit. Many wish their employer would do something, and occasionally someone sues their employer.

While the United States is just starting to have antibullying laws in some states for workers, Australia has had such laws since 2014. Let's look at an example of one such case that went to court there. It may be an example of a bully who had watched too much dominance behavior on television and applied it to real life.

Wendy Swan alleged that her supervisor at a law book cooperative, Kriston Cowell, had caused her psychiatric injury, over a period of years, by "exposing her to an unsafe workplace in which she was subject to bullying, harassing, and intimidating conduct." Examples of that conduct included, as stated in the opinion of the Supreme Court of Victoria (her state in Australia), repeatedly subjecting Ms. Swan to sarcasm, hostility, and rudeness; throwing a book at Ms. Swan's head; using foul and offensive language; threatening to dismiss Ms. Swan (when he had no authority to do so); rudely interrupting Ms. Swan and belittling her in front of third parties; issuing unreasonable instructions such as directing her regarding how she answered the phone; excessively scrutinizing Ms. Swan's work and whereabouts; and so on.[10]

Events reached a peak in July 2007 when, after the two disagreed about where to place some books, Mr. Cowell told Ms. Swan to "get out . . . and go and find another job, and just go away." In terms of the overall atmosphere between the two, the justice writing the opinion noted that "Mr. Cowell knew that the plaintiff felt intimidated and uncomfortable in his presence, but he didn't care. . . . Mr. Cowell had a particular attitude, flowing from his personality."[11]

The court couldn't have described bullying more clearly. It became clear from this list that Mr. Cowell used a variety of tactics to intimidate and induce fear in Ms. Swan. Even the court understood that it was about his personality and not about disagreement over any real issues. Remember that bullies often have Cluster B personality disorders frequently associated with domineeringness, vindictiveness, and intrusiveness. His scrutiny of her work and whereabouts demonstrates all three of these. This fits into our High Conflict Institute saying: "The issue's not the issue; the personality is the issue" that's driving the high-conflict situation.

HOW YOU CAN STOP THIS POWER

1. Open Your Eyes to the Pattern

This pattern is emotional rather than logical. Look for the exaggerated primitive images: trying to impress you with signs of overwhelming physical strength, facial expressions that regularly show dominance, powerful hand gestures, a dominating tone of voice, implications that the entire organization or profession or community supports the bully and will overwhelm you, and regular use of hyperbole—the extremely exaggerated emotional words they use but deny mean anything. These are all easy to spot if you're looking for them. Sometimes it helps to memorize a phrase to tell yourself to avoid absorbing these unconscious influences, such as *It's just a bully's primitive emotions, and I'm not going to get hooked.*

2. Pull the Plug on the Bully

Bullies require the inaction of their targets and the tolerance (or ignorance or complicity) of lots of other people in order to continue their bullying. Some of the best examples of this problem are the victim/survivors of sexual harassment and assault by movie mogul Harvey Weinstein, who got into his victims' heads. He showed his strength by making lots of threats to end their acting careers by telling others not to hire them. He made them feel isolated and unable to talk to others about what happened to them. He overwhelmed them with his aggressive legal team, others in his company, and various collaborators, who helped plant negative stories in the press.

Over the years, Weinstein is alleged to have sexually harassed or assaulted more than eighty women. One example was Asia Argento, an Italian film actress and director, who didn't speak out for twenty years, until 2017, because she was sure he would crush her. "The thing with being a victim is I felt responsible," she said. "Because, if I were a strong woman, I would have kicked him in the balls and run away. But I didn't. And so I felt responsible."[12]

This is a good example of how she felt immobilized by her bully yet blamed herself. In her mind it became her fault, not his. This is how primitive emotional power can activate a primitive emotional response of targeting oneself. Taking this a step further, actress Lucia Evans turned against herself in several ways after being abused by Weinstein. "I had an eating problem for years. I was disgusted with myself. It's funny, all these unrelated things I did to hurt myself because of this one thing."[13] These primitive emotional responses felt wrong but were based on self-protection at the primitive emotional level.

For most of human history, people didn't have the choices they have today, and it may not have been safe to "kick him in the balls and run away." When there's only one community, where do you go?

People couldn't easily survive on their own. Unconsciously and automatically, your very primitive responses can take over—and may save your life. People need to understand where these primitive emotional responses come from, so they don't judge themselves negatively and instead praise themselves for surviving. Then, it's possible to overcome any sense of isolation and take positive action in the modern world.

That is exactly what these and other women did by eventually telling their stories. They unplugged the power that Weinstein used to get into their heads. With strength in numbers, they went public despite the many nondisclosure agreements that Weinstein required them to sign. Weinstein was convicted and sentenced to twenty-three years in prison in New York in 2020 and then sentenced to another sixteen years in Los Angeles in 2023.[14]

3. Set Limits with Credible Threats

In domestic violence cases (also known as *intimate partner violence* or *IPV*), the presence of "coercive control" has been recognized in some state laws as the underlying ability to control victim/survivors without actually using violence. I believe that coercive control is a form of primitive emotional power, which is why people haven't seen it or recognized its power up until now. Based on this recognition, California enacted a new law in 2021 allowing courts to issue restraining orders in cases of present or past couple relationships (intimate partners), even if there has not been physical violence.

The law emphasized that coercive control includes "disturbing the peace of the other party," defined as "a pattern of behavior that . . . unreasonably interferes with a person's free will and personal liberty." Other examples of coercive control include "Isolating the other party from friends, relatives, or other sources of support. Depriving the other party of basic necessities. Controlling, regulating, or monitoring the other party's movements, communications, daily behavior, finances, economic resources, or access to services."[15]

Since violations of restraining orders can get a person arrested, the specifics of this law make it clear what behaviors are not allowed. Once a restraining order has been issued, jail time becomes a very credible threat if the restraining order is violated. This law appears to recognize the concept of PEP and is one of the first to set limits on it. Several other states and countries have now added coercive control to their laws restraining relationship behavior that involves dominating or bullying the other party.

4. Impose Serious Consequences

Consequences are usually the biggest factor in changing any behavior. Bullies who think they are strong enough try to avoid consequences. While consequences don't change personalities, they can stop people from their bullying behavior at least for a while. This can include putting people in prison, firing them, severe financial penalties, ending relationships with them, or other options that fit the situation. In the earlier case regarding workplace bullying by Mr. Cowell, the court agreed that Ms. Swan had suffered significant psychiatric injury and required the book co-op to pay about $600,000 (in Australian dollars, or about US $425,000) for her pain, suffering, and loss of enjoyment in life.[16]

The case served, not only to hold Cowell to account, but to warn all employers that they needed to protect employees from bullying—and, if they failed to do so, serious consequences *could* result. It also provided the bookstore's management and managers at other establishments with a very specific list of things that constituted bullying behavior. This is an example of imposing consequences and also setting limits for the future with what is now a credible threat. Imagine the improvement in employee and manager behavior if the United States were to support such strong consequences for bullying in the workplace.

5. Communicate Effectively to Others About Bullies

Many people are already communicating about the dangers and dynamics of adult bullies in many settings. Jaron Lanier is one such person who is deep inside our high-tech world as a computer scientist, an inventor in the field of virtual reality, a pioneer in several other high-tech areas, and a major critic of today's social media (which he no longer uses). He is one of the technology experts interviewed in the movie *The Social Dilemma*. His concern isn't the networking aspects of social media (such as sharing pictures with family and friends) but its algorithms that manipulate people's minds and their online behavior. Lanier lays out the dangers in detail in his book *Ten Arguments for Deleting Your Social Media Accounts Right Now*. While he doesn't use the term PEP, he explains that the very design of social media activates our lower brains in dangerous ways.

> Social media is biased, not to the Left or the Right, but downward. The relative ease of using negative emotions for the purposes of addiction and manipulation makes it relatively easier to achieve undignified results. An unfortunate combination of biology and math favors degradation of the human world. . . . The unplanned nature of the transformation from advertising to direct behavior modification caused an explosive amplification of negativity in human affairs.[17]

I'm glad he points out that our biology sets us up for this manipulation. Social media targets our negative emotions in the same manner that bullies do. This helps us understand why people often have escalated fear, anger, love/loyalty responses (or all three) to the most popular social media posts. "This country is so messed up, we have to move!" "I hate those people in that post!" "I'm totally in love with so-and-so!"

But if you recognize this primitive emotional power to manipulate, you may be able to resist it. Of course, this may require you to limit your social media use one way or another or practice some bully resistance mantras, such as "You won't emotionally hook me!" "I make no assumptions." "I need a second opinion before I believe anything!" "It's all an exaggeration, so I don't have to buy it!"

6. Stand Strong with Others Against Bullies

One of the strongest themes of this book is that we need to help one another in dealing with bullies. Our individual bully resistance mantras will only get us so far.

Brandon Farbstein is an example of someone who was bullied and now turns bullies around. Farbstein, a young man in his early twenties who has dwarfism, was bullied mercilessly by his classmates when he was in high school. But now he testifies at government hearings and gives presentations about his experiences of being bullied. This work has resulted in new antibullying legislation in the state of Virginia, empathy training for youths who bully their peers, and social and emotional intelligence curriculum in Virgina public schools.[18]

Farbstein has written books about self-love and given hundreds of speeches around North America. The feedback he has received has been incredible, including an apology from one of the bullies from Farbstein's high school years who explained he was a victim of abuse in his own home at the time and didn't know how to manage his anger other than to bully others.[19] Examples like these give this work so much hope for the future.

CONCLUSION

As we've seen, bullies often get their way by exercising three primitive emotional powers (PEP) that activate three primitive emotional responses in their targets: extreme fear, extreme anger, and extreme love/loyalty. These emotions engage the unconscious, lower parts of people's brains and are processed unconsciously in the right brain. PEP causes bullies to create a win-lose relationship with each of their victims, often driving them into submission. This submission frequently includes self-doubt and shame about themselves.

Bullies generally isolate their victims so that they keep the bullying a secret and suffer in silence. In some cases, this win-lose relationship may be hardwired from both ends, so that the targets of bullies (e.g., sexual abusers, spousal abusers, workplace bullies) often automatically shut down in order to survive. However, every single day, people stand up to bullies. In fact, in the absence of secrecy and isolation, *most* people and groups naturally do not tolerate bullies and will set limits on them. That is one of the goals of this book: to give you and other people confidence, strength, and awareness by hearing the stories of so many others who have been successful at stopping bullies.

COMMON MISTAKE:

We are always in rational control of our feelings and behavior.

REALITY:

Much of our feelings and behavior is socially influenced,
so that bullies can activate our primitive emotional responses
without our conscious awareness.

CHAPTER 5

The Power of Making It Personal

Everybody . . . knows who you are.
You are a bad person and everybody hates you.
Have a shitty rest of your life. The world would
be a better place without you.

—"Josh," an online adult bullying a thirteen-year-old girl

BULLIES DO NOT JUST CRITICIZE YOU or attack some decision you made or some action you took. They try to dominate or destroy you as a *whole person*. This is the line that bullies cross all the time. Instead of disagreeing with your values, beliefs, or behavior, they attack your being. They'll tell others—or the world—that you are a terrible, sinful, shameful human being. Perhaps this is the biggest change in recent times: More and more people (bullies) won't just disagree with you anymore; they'll want to control, dominate, crush, or eliminate you (or your group). We respond to these powerful emotional messages with our own primitive emotional responses—usually by automatically fighting, fleeing, freezing, or submitting.

Humans have been using primitive emotional power (PEP) on one another throughout human history. PEP appears to be baked into our DNA, and it causes us to respond in very automatic and predictable ways. Bullies often manipulate people into feeling that they are isolated and that everyone else is on the bully's side. When you're not part of the group but on the fringe, your very existence may feel at risk. And in primitive times, it often was. You couldn't survive alone. This can create a visceral sense of desperation. Bullies know this and use it to get what they want—or just to feel powerful.

Your Reputation

Your reputation and your job are two of the most important things in your life—your *personal place* in the world. Bullies may make their attacks personal by threatening to ruin your reputation or your career and to isolate you from others in your occupation. When this happens to someone, they may feel like their personal survival is at risk. This can be especially painful for a teenager, young adult, or anyone just getting started in a career. Bullies may tell you, "No one will believe you," or "Your professional colleagues will look down on you or expel you." These are all cruel things to say—and most people would never think them, let alone say them out loud. But remember, bullies lack self-restraint—and they often relish the idea of dominating others in this way.

Threatening your reputation can be especially cruel if you are involved in a helping profession, such as health care, education, social work, police work, ministry, and specialized businesses, where people are expected to be honest, caring, and helpful. This type of work is often more than just a job—it can be a person's life's work. They may be dedicated to making the world a better place, usually by helping one person at a time. Unfortunately, this offers a great opportunity for bullies, who are skilled at manipulating helping professionals by threatening their reputations. "I'll tell the world that you're uncaring or unethical." "I'll tell your boss and your professional association and the police that you violated my confidentiality, my trust, my privacy, and your own professional standards."

Your Life

It's one thing to threaten your reputation or career, but another to threaten your very life—your physical existence. Bullies are doing that more and more now. The Internet provides numerous opportunities for people to threaten one another's lives. This is often brushed off as "just words" allowed by free speech, but it can also lead to actual murder or suicide.

For example, in 2006, a mother and her eighteen-year-old employee repeatedly went online and pretended to be a teenage boy named Josh who claimed to like thirteen-year-old Megan Meier. The two adult women wanted to humiliate Megan for allegedly gossiping about the mother's daughter, who was in Megan's class. "Josh's" fake messages started out friendly, then turned hostile. "Josh" said, "I don't know if I want to be friends with you anymore because I've heard that you are not very nice to your friends." "Josh's" final message was "Everybody knows who you are. You are a bad person, and everybody hates you. Have a shitty rest of your life. The world would be a better place without you."[1]

Megan had been bullied before and had a history of depression and occasional suicidal thoughts. After reading that message, she killed herself. She had absorbed all the PEP energy and turned it against herself. This personal attack did, in fact, destroy her.

Words matter, especially when adults direct them toward children and adolescents. The human brain—and the ability to manage one's emotional reactions for most people—isn't fully developed until around age twenty-five. People younger than this age are particularly susceptible to the manipulation of their primitive emotional responses, which aren't yet under full control of the brain's control center of functioning—the prefrontal cortex, which is the last part to develop. Managing fear responses and managing anger are all related to this twenty-five-year task of developing impulse control and self-reflection. As the authors of *The Archaeology of Mind* explain, "We can bite our tongues when we are angry and not say things that make matters worse. But many 'choose' not to. We used quotes in the previous sentence because for many people their emotions are not under the control of their higher mind."[2]

Sadly, this appears to have been true for the two adult women who told Meier her life was worthless, as well as for the girl herself. The Internet and bullies have helped change our world back into one in which minor conflicts are addressed as matters of life and death.

This is also a lesson for all of us about using hyperbole (exaggerated words) on the Internet and in ordinary conversations. If we say someone should just up and die, we may be activating other people's primitive emotional responses (such as fear and anger) without even realizing it. We need to try not to make it personal, so that we focus our criticisms of others on their specific behavior rather than their very existence.

Bully Dynamics

Let's break down the ways in which bullies typically make things personal. They seem to apply several methods instinctively and automatically:

Gross exaggeration: *A bully takes a tiny or inadvertent error, magnifies it, and relentlessly smears their target with it to make their target look like evil incarnate. "You know, she's always on the phone doing personal business while she's supposed to be working." (The reality is that once she had to reschedule a doctor's appointment for her daughter during worktime and otherwise is a very committed worker.)*

For example, in a high-conflict divorce, a bully parent may accuse the other of being an unfit parent because they lost their young child for a minute at the beach or brought the four-year-old into the opposite-sex public bathroom or was thirty minutes late in returning the child to the other parent. Then the bully parent may loudly broadcast a stack of these minor incidents to neighbors, friends, and even judges as if the other parent were the most horrible caregiver in the world. By sharing these minor events with a lot of emotional intensity and repetition, they can come to feel extremely major and inspire people to intensely dislike the target of these statements.

Outright lies: *A bully may widely and loudly spread absurd and outrageous lies to family, friends, coworkers, and sometimes the world. These lies often include very deliberate—and entirely bogus—personal attacks. "You know, he's a child abuser. You should watch out for him, especially if your kids are around."*

For fifteen years, I represented divorcing parents in family court. Some of these cases included allegations of child sexual abuse. Sometimes these accusations were true, and people were appropriately sent to prison. But sometimes the allegations were fabricated by bully parents. In one case involving divorced parents, the mother of an eight-year-old girl accused the father of sexually abusing their child. (He had been the primary custodial parent because of an incident of domestic violence against him five years earlier by the mother, which she didn't contest.)

Understandably, hearing this allegation of child sexual abuse, a judge immediately granted the mom full-time custody of her daughter with supervised visitation for the father pending the outcome of an investigation. Finally, an investigation by a psychologist and a lawyer for the child concluded that the mother's accusations were unfounded. I took depositions of the mother and the people she enlisted to support her claims. Their stories quickly fell apart, revealing a plot by the mom to obtain sole custody of the child—and child support (which she didn't get while he was the primary custodial parent).

It soon became clear that the mother and her new husband were both bullies. They had taken the eight-year-old girl on a camping trip, and throughout the trip they bullied her into making false allegations against her dad. In the end, the judge ordered financial sanctions against the mother—and took away custody of her daughter but allowed supervised contact. The girl returned to living peacefully with her father and brother.

Making an example: *A bully may instantly and widely smear someone they want to dominate, then crow about what they did to teach others what is in store for them if they speak up. "Look at what I did to Jack and to Jill. Is that what you want?"*

For example, Joanna was one of several new employees in her business unit. She was asked by her supervisor, Clarisse, to change a report to cover up a serious ethical violation that Clarisse herself had committed. When Joanna refused, Clarisse threatened to blame the violation on Joanna. When Joanna still refused, Clarissa altered the report herself, then spread the rumor that Joanna had engaged in unethical conduct and needed coaching on ethical behavior. Since Joanna was new, many established employees believed this story and treated her more cautiously. Meanwhile, all the other new hires got the message that Clarisse could get away with anything.

Accusing their target of overreacting: *As a bully relent-lessly attacks their target, other people—and possibly even the bully themselves—may say to the target, "Why are you so upset? Why are you overreacting?"*

All this can make that person feel crazy. This is often called *gas-lighting*: telling someone that their accurate perceptions are wrong, and the bully's exaggerated or made-up story is the one that is right. That's precisely the bully's plan—to get into their target's head and stay there.

For example, in a hospital, a doctor missed an important family meeting about a patient who was about to be discharged, even though the social worker for the hospital had reminded the doctor. At a subsequent hospital team meeting where difficult cases were discussed with about twenty doctors and staff, the complaints from the family were raised. This doctor explained that he had not been notified of the family meeting by the social worker and would have certainly been present if he had—thereby blaming the social worker for his own error.

While the social worker had good relations with almost all the doctors and other hospital staff, this doctor had been rumored to be a bully. In the hallway, just after that meeting, the social worker confronted the doctor with the fact that he had been informed of the family meeting by the social worker and that what he said in the meeting was not true. "Oh, don't take it so personally," the doctor said. "It was nothing. You've got to loosen up." The social worker was devastated and wondered: Is there something wrong with me? Am I taking things too personally? Is this the kind of criticism I should expect in the future?

If you've ever been bullied, you will recognize this. You spend much of your time and emotional energy preoccupied with where the bully is and what he or she is going to do next. You feel as if at any moment you could be in danger, caught in the bully's crosshairs —and you might be right. And yet you may blame yourself for "allowing" this to happen to you. Remember, you can understand why your self-doubts—your primitive emotional responses—are triggered and that you don't have to accept them.

HOW YOU CAN STOP THIS POWER

1. Open Your Eyes to the Pattern

Recognize PEP energy when you see it, and don't let it get into your head. Is the person attacking you as a whole person or giving you helpful feedback on a specific behavior? Do you feel like your status, reputation, body, or even your existence is being threatened? Do you worry a lot about where the person is or what they are doing now? These are warning signs that you are dealing with a bully. Remember that you always have choices.

For example, the social worker in the prior scenario could say, *I know about primitive emotional power and bullies immobilizing their targets. I know I'm feeling defensive right now, like I have to prove to him that I'm worthy of respect and better treatment. But I realize that this is my own primitive emotional response, and he's not going to get into my head.*

2. Pull the Plug on the Bully

When you realize someone is personally attacking you, find someone to talk to about it—almost anyone!—to help you figure out how to get away from the bully or get the bully to stop. Many people don't know the right person to talk to, such as in your workplace. Just talk to somebody, in or out of work, to get you started so that you don't let the bully shut down your own thinking and sense of yourself. Just get started. Then you can find out more about who to talk to in your organization or community. Don't assist the bully in their treatment of you by suffering alone silently.

In the prior scenario, the social worker could say, *I know what he did was wrong and that my feelings and actions make sense. Yes, what the doctor said was personal—it could threaten my whole reputation with everyone else. But I'm not going to let him immobilize me into becoming self-critical. I know I have choices. I can choose to report this to the administration, or talk about it with my friends, or just forget about it. But I'm not going to turn his negative energy against myself. I'm going to unplug his power over me.*

3. Set Limits with Credible Threats

Bullies *do* stop bullying sometimes—but *rarely* because they suddenly feel empathy and remorse for their victims. They stop *only* because of potentially painful consequences or the credible threat of such consequences. Below is an example of the failure to set limits with credible threats.

Jeffrey Epstein was a wealthy financier who mixed with high-society people and powerful government officials. He also had a fixation on having sexual encounters with girls as young as fourteen. By 2006 he had reportedly abused dozens of teenage girls. He was arrested in 2006 and pled guilty to one felony count in a sweetheart deal that gave him only eighteen months in prison, but with work release from prison every day to go to his office. This was not a remotely appropriate prison sentence, given his crimes. But he had many friends in high places.[3]

People involved with the case thought that he had learned his lesson and from then on would avoid having sex with teenage girls. But remember this: Bullies can't stop themselves. For Epstein, the light prison sentence was not enough of a credible threat for the future. He quickly returned to his old ways. Over the next dozen years, Epstein continued to have sex with many more teenage girls, often procured for him by his companion Ghislaine Maxwell. In 2019 Epstein was arrested once again. This time, he likely faced living the rest of his life in prison. The threat had now become credible. A month later he died in prison, reportedly a suicide.[4]

While most of my examples demonstrate people succeeding in stopping bullies in a positive way, this is a good one for showing how opportunities were missed. If the people handling Epstein's case in 2006 were aware that bullies cannot stop themselves and are comfortable ruining people's entire lives—in this case teenage girls with their whole lives ahead of them who had to deal with Epstein's actions—they would have hopefully set much firmer limits.

4. Impose Serious Consequences

In this example, if Epstein had been given an appropriate sentence in 2006, he would have been restrained from gaining access to teenage girls while in prison. Then, when he got out, the credible threat of returning to prison might have stopped him from risking his prior behavior. Depending on the severity of his personality, he might have been one of those who really worked hard at staying out of prison or he might have simply relapsed into an enduring pattern of behavior.

This is the type of situation in which it can help to have a mental health professional testify at court about whether Epstein had a personality disorder or not, such as the antisocial personality disorder of many bullies. Regardless of his pattern of behavior, if he had a personality disorder he would have been unlikely to change; that's what the enduring pattern means. If he didn't have a personality disorder, then he might have been able to change his ways after a strong enough consequence motivated him, such as a more appropriate prison sentence in 2006.

5. Communicate Effectively About Bullies to Others

Much of the potential to communicate about various bullies around the world comes from journalists. They have the training and experience to get deep into the facts of a case as well as explaining those facts to the world in easy-to-understand terms. The next example comes from a Canadian journalist, Sarah Berman, who wrote the book *Don't Call It a Cult: The Shocking Story of Keith Raniere and the Women of NXIVM.*

NXIVM was a self-improvement business. In her book, Berman explains the tactics that the leader, Keith Raniere, used to captivate his followers, most of them smart and successful women. These included claiming—falsely—that he had one of the world's highest IQs, making it look like many important people endorsed him—and routinely inflicting large doses of deeply personal and intrusive shame on people. He had the women in his inner circle painfully branded with a cryptic symbol, which turned out to be his initials, on their flesh. He also kept one woman, whom he had brainwashed, psychologically confined to her room for two years even though she could physically leave.[5]

When complaints from some of his followers started surfacing, Raniere created smear campaigns against anyone who crossed him. He abused "his position as leader in order to sexually manipulate women in the company." This included four women who were on the executive board: Raniere secretly maintained sexual relationships with each of them. He "successfully ruined the lives of several people who tried to expose him, usually through lawsuits, private investigators, and criminal complaints in several states." When Raniere's abusive behavior and many unethical business practices were finally exposed, he received a 120-year prison sentence. Four of the women leaders received prison sentences as well for bullying members and for their roles in manipulating the business's finances.[6]

Berman's book explains in detail how this bully of many smart and wealthy people was able to succeed for twenty straight years. Telling others about these kinds of stories may help them avoid falling into such traps and help prevent another bully from getting away with similar behavior in the future.

6. Stand Strong with Others Against Bullies

Once again, learning about how other people have come together to stop bullies can be inspiring and instructive. One of the best examples of this is the women of Fox News, who in 2016 collectively exposed regular sexual harassment by Roger Ailes, the network's founder and chairman.

At first, Gretchen Carlson, one of the cable channel's star anchors, brought a lawsuit against Ailes personally. She had substantial evidence, including recorded conversations with Ailes, but Ailes's bullying looked like an isolated incident. Even when three other, lower-level women came forward, the parent company, 21st Century Fox, said that

Ailes had their "full confidence." But it agreed to conduct a limited internal review of these cases.

At that time, the highest-ranking female star at Fox was Megyn Kelly. Ailes asked her to defend him, since he had strongly promoted her within the organization. But he had also sexually harassed her ten years earlier, when she first started out with the company.

For a while, Kelly was silent. Her own words describe her internal struggle:

> I knew of my story and that of my friend, but these were events from a decade earlier. Was I really prepared to get him in trouble for something we had long since gotten past? To undermine this man who had done so much for my career, and who had my back in some ugly situations? I didn't want to hurt him. But could I stay silent? What if there were other victims? What if—God forbid—he was *still* doing it to someone? The choice became clear: honor my ethical code or abide by my loyalty to Roger.[7]

Kelly chose to stand with the other women and disclose Ailes's prior harassment. While he may have gotten into her head with secrecy and shame ten years earlier, he didn't get into her head this time around. Kelly's disclosure led to a full-scale investigation by an outside law firm—and, ultimately, to Fox's firing of Ailes.

Remember, bullying is a *pattern of behavior*, so if you are being bullied by someone, there are almost always others who are experiencing the same thing from that person. If the bully also has a personality disorder, then they have an enduring pattern of behavior that is unlikely to stop on its own. And remember that this pattern is likely to be very personal, which in these last three cases is about harassment and assault against the physical person of these women.

CONCLUSION

Understanding the dynamics of bullies' primitive emotional powers and how they attack the whole person, you will become less vulnerable to them, better able to set limits on them, and better positioned to live life with confidence. Keep your eyes wide open and pay attention to your own emotions and when you may feel attacked or in danger as a whole person. Your own responses are often a helpful sign that you may be dealing with a bully. Don't ignore what you are experiencing or become self-critical. You may be truly facing a bully and totally justified in being concerned and seeking help. Don't let others say, "Oh, don't take it personally." It may really be personal after all.

COMMON MISTAKE:

Don't take bullies personally; they are just being ridiculous.

REALITY:

It is personal—a threat to your life, your body,
or your reputation, which can be just as devastating.
Bullies really do want to dominate or destroy you.

CHAPTER 6

The Power of the Bully's Story (BS)

I don't know why Mom hates Dad so much. . . .
But she's not gonna get me to say he's a bad daddy.
I know better.

—Nine-year-old girl talking to her therapist

THE *BULLY'S STORY (BS)* is an exaggeration or totally untrue. It's often a *con*, which is bigger than a lie because it has a hidden purpose. A con is designed to gain power over you and others. It's how they get you to do something you wouldn't do if you knew the truth. It's how they win, and you lose—and get you to *help them* take advantage of you or others by using their primitive emotional power (PEP) on you.

Most of this is unconscious. Bullies really believe they should be in charge. They don't connect the dots from their story to other people's behavior. In fact, not connecting the dots is one of the biggest problems for bullies and all high-conflict people. They honestly don't

73

see how they affect other people. This disconnect can make their lives miserable because they are frequently being caught by surprise by other people's frequently negative behavior toward them. They don't see that their own behavior provoked it. When confronted with what they have said or done as being inappropriate, they usually deny any bad intent—and often believe it. "I never told her to say that!" "So many people are out to get me!" "I don't know why people turn on me. They must be jealous."

As mentioned before, when most people are talking to a bully, they think an issue is being discussed or a problem is being solved. They don't realize that the goal of the conversation from the bully's perspective is to dominate their target—possibly you—rather than to solve a problem. They are driven to control others so that they can feel okay. To do this they often tell a bully's story, to get you to accept their explanation for events rather than your own, and to get you to take the action that they want on their behalf.

Gaslighting

When someone is trying hard to persuade you to adopt their point of view of reality and to doubt yourself, it is often called *gaslighting*. This term originates from a play and then a movie called *Gaslight*, in which an 1800s villain in London secretly turns the lights (lit by gas in those days) up and down in the apartment he shares with his wife. Since there is a serial killer on the loose, she becomes very fearful. But he denies that the lights are flickering in order to make her think she's going crazy.

Bullies behave in the same manner. The bully says, "What you see and hear isn't true. What I'm telling you is true." In other words, "You're crazy to believe what you believe. Everyone knows that what I'm telling you is what's really going on. And if you challenge me to others, I will tell them you're crazy." You start to doubt yourself. Maybe you didn't really hear it right.

But there's more to the bully's story. There are three predictable parts, which you can easily recognize once you know what to look for.

The Three-Part Story

The three parts are based on a bully's imagination—a partial or complete fantasy with made-up facts designed to give them power. All three parts trigger primitive emotions, the same primitive emotions we discussed in Chapter 4. The combination can lead to action, sometimes including violence. The three essential parts are a *fantasy crisis*, a *fantasy villain*, and a *fantasy hero*. This combination triggers our primitive fear, primitive anger or rage, and love/loyalty for the bully—a mixture of emotions that is powerfully seductive and almost irresistible. It immobilizes their victims, energizes other people to attack their victims, and inspires decision-makers to take their side in a conflict.

Keep in mind, all three parts are a fantasy—made up by the bully—so that the message of the BS is emotional rather than logical. It gets into your head without you even knowing it because it activates your primitive emotions. Of course, sometimes what bullies call a crisis *is* a problem that does need solving, usually with teamwork and planning, not just blindly following an alleged leader. But bullies exaggerate problems into fantasy crises to shut down your ordinary thinking and get you to simply follow whatever they say.

The fundamental point for bullies is that in order to gain power, they have to convince people that there is a crisis. This is because people don't like to be told what to do or to follow anybody else. This has been a trait from primitive days when people lived "in groups of up to 150 that were relatively egalitarian and wary of alpha males." However, there were exceptions: "We also evolved the ability to rally around leaders when our group is under threat or is competing with other groups." Likewise, "Strangers will spontaneously organize themselves into leaders and followers when natural disasters strike."[1]

In other words, without a crisis no one is going to turn to a bully for leadership. So, that's where their stories always begin.

1. **Fantasy Crisis:** *There's a terrible, urgent crisis! This instills extreme fear.*

In cases of domestic violence, a bully might say, "You're nothing without me! No one else would ever want you!" In the workplace, they might insist, "You're sabotaging the entire project we've all worked so hard on!" In today's current events, they might proclaim, "Today's music is ruining our youth! We've got to shut it down!"

Effect: The urgency and intensity of the crisis gets into your head. And when we're anxious, research shows that we are more likely to absorb other people's emotions. In addition, in crises that instill extreme fear, we become willing to follow anyone who will save us from danger—or gives the impression with carefully crafted images, sounds, and words of strength that they will save us.

2. **Fantasy Villain:** *The crisis is caused by an evil villain or crazy person! This instills extreme anger or hatred.*

The villain is actually the bully's *target of blame,* who the bully wants to dominate or destroy. In cases of domestic violence, a bully may insist to their victim, "You're stupid! You're crazy! I have to control you!," which instills self-hatred. In the workplace, they may broadcast this message: "Anita has sabotaged all of our efforts. She's out to destroy our team. We have to stop her! She should be fired!" In politics, they might insist, "It's ALL the fault of [boomers, millennials, Jews, Muslims, Blacks, gays, Democrats, Republicans]!"

Effect: A villain is pure negative, so the emotions that are triggered are pure and extreme. It isn't just dislike. It's hatred because they are portrayed as the cause of the crisis that everyone extremely fears. This allows bullies to make it personal. The villain is deserving of being dominated or destroyed. This instills anger and often rage against the villain.

3. **Fantasy Hero:** *I can save you! I will be your hero. I love you! This instills extreme love/loyalty.*

Consider some cases of domestic violence: "I can save you from yourself! I'll protect you! You don't need your family or friends anymore—I'm all you need!" For someone who feels that this relationship is providing true, intense love, they won't be willing to even acknowledge the abuse or give up the abusive relationship. The decision is made by their primitive emotions, not their logical analysis of the situation. In the workplace: "I can save the project from this disaster. Put me in charge now, before it's too late! I know what everyone needs to do!" Since everyone is stressed and no one knows what to do, it can be easy to just accept the leadership of the person who appears confident that they know what to do. In politics: "Elect me! I will save you from the subhumans who want to destroy us and our great nation! Only I can solve this crisis and protect our nation! My plan is guaranteed to work!"

Effect: By now, if you are anxious enough because you believe in the crisis and angry enough at the alleged villain, you may fall in love/loyalty with this person as a savior because you are now emotionally desperate. This seals your loyalty to the "hero" (who is actually the bully).

The Best Storytellers

Bullies are highly talented storytellers, and by telling this emotional story they can often win over an individual or a group of people. The BS is simplistic and primitive, so that it hooks our primitive emotional responses and overrides our logical thinking. We end up accepting the bully's behavior and often do what they say.

Lack of Ambivalence

The emotions triggered by the bully's story are not ambivalent. They are pure fear, anger, and love/loyalty. There is no ambivalence like people have when they are upset with real people whom they actually know. Sure, a real person may be a jerk, but you know they have some useful qualities, and you may rely on those even though they're a jerk. However, contagious emotions are based on what others say rather than based on real experience, so the emotions are usually pure this way (you only hear the most negative story). This helps explain situations when someone who hasn't met you hates you and doesn't know anything meaningful about you.

Stuck in the Past

One thing that surprises most people is how often bullies are stuck in the past, always complaining about a crisis of being treated badly and how terrible certain people are—their villains. In these stories, the bully is a *fantasy victim* rather than the fantasy hero. This is designed to get your sympathy *and* anger at the fantasy villain.

The reason they may be stuck in the past is that they don't appear to go through the natural grieving and healing process that is associated with recovering from any major loss and moving forward in one's life. This process usually includes five stages: denial, anger, bargaining, depression, and acceptance. Unfortunately, bullies (and many of those with Cluster B personality disorders) appear to get stuck in the second stage: anger. For this reason, they haven't gotten over the past in the way that most people do who have reached acceptance. Perhaps this is why they are always trying to rewrite history, so that they are not to blame and do not experience an irresolvable sense of loss.

Not being aware of this, many legal professionals and others constantly tell their clients to "just get over it," especially if they don't have a case or only a small case. Yet many legal clients—notably bullies—just keep telling their bully's story and eventually get others to believe it and join in helping them against their "villains." They may file lawsuits and appeal them if they don't win, in a belief that someday, somewhere they can persuade a judge or jury that they were treated badly by someone else and have done nothing wrong themselves.

If you notice this constant repetition of the bully's story, don't be surprised. You can't talk them out of it because it is so essential to their shaky sense of themselves. This is especially true of narcissistic bullies because they can't stand that they have experienced a *narcissistic injury*, which is something that exposes their flaws rather than their superiority. They have to rewrite the past in order to cope with it. They can't allow their superior image to be tarnished. Since real life tarnishes all of us, they are constantly having narcissistic injuries. Just get over it? No way! They endlessly try to rewrite history instead.

A Bully's Story: A Case of Domestic Violence

Many cases of domestic violence are based on a bully's story. This binds the victim/survivor of abuse to the bully because of the use of primitive emotional power, as the following example demonstrates.

FKA twigs is a famous British singer, producer, and actress—born Tahliah Debrett Barnett—who ended up in an abusive relationship with the actor Shia LaBeouf for a year. Her explanation fits so many domestic violence situations, but most of these cases are kept hidden by both the bully and the target. In 2020 Barnett publicly filed a lawsuit against LaBoeuf and said she came forward to show how someone like her "with money, a home and a strong network of supporters" could end up in such a situation. She spoke out to "raise awareness on the tactics that abusers use to control you and take away your agency."[2]

At first LaBeouf showed "over-the-top displays of affection." This is common. Remember, the power of PEP includes intense love or obsession (love bombing), but its true goal is to seal the target's loyalty. This is one of the earliest warning signs of a win-lose personality. It can be very compelling. Then the full personality comes out. Even though he squeezed and grabbed her to the point of bruises, she didn't go to the police because of a "misguided concern" that it would harm his career. She also thought that her description would be discounted. She felt helpless. In addition, he didn't want her to speak to or look at other men, including male waiters. Instead, she would have to "keep her eyes down when men spoke to her." In addition, he had rules about how often she had to kiss him and touch him. He constantly harangued her and criticized her.[3]

Even though Barnett's professional life was in England, LaBeouf got her to stay with him in Los Angeles. This way he was able to isolate her and claim that her creative team "used her." He got her to doubt her own friends and colleagues.

By saying that Barnett's creative team was working against her, LaBeouf used the bully's story of a fantasy crisis (no one cares about you except to use you) and a fantasy villain (her creative team). LaBeouf was her fantasy hero, taking her side against the villains, he apparently told her. This way her isolation grew progressively worse and worse, which is why so many domestic violence victims have such a hard time leaving—or never leave. This is how she explained it in an interview: "The whole time I was with him, I could have bought myself a business-flight plane ticket back to my four-story townhouse in Hackney," in London, she said. And yet she didn't. "He brought me so low, below myself, that the idea of leaving him and having to work myself back up just seemed impossible," she said.[4]

Remember, PEP is progressive in its impact on its victims. It brings the bully's target increasingly lower self-esteem and higher self-doubt, which makes it harder and harder to change the situation. In this case, twig's manager, Michael Stirton, could see something was happening, but he didn't know what. Twig was becoming more isolated and withdrawn from everyone but LaBeouf. "This was an extreme change in her personality and character. . . . I could speak to her," he said. "But I couldn't reach her."[5]

This dramatic change took hold of her within less than a year. What is amazing is that she got out so quickly, as many domestic violence victims become more and more stuck. Even as a successful entertainer, she had more resources than most. She finally extricated herself from him, with the help of a therapist, after several attempts to leave.

Overall, twig's experience reinforces our understanding that the center of a bully's hidden power is a story that weakens their victim's self-esteem and makes them more and more dependent on the bully. There are "crises" and "villains" out there, so the message is that you *need* a hero, and so you become more and more dependent on the bully to be that "hero." Look for the three parts of such a story. If you start seeing them, watch out!

What was LaBeouf's justification for his own behavior? He just said he had no excuse for his drinking and aggressive behavior. In an e-mail to the *New York Times,* he wrote, "I have been abusive to myself and everyone around me for years. I have a history of hurting the people closest to me. I'm ashamed of that history and am sorry to those I hurt. There is nothing else I can really say." But he also added that he is "a sober member of a 12-step program" and in therapy.[6]

Once again, as with some of the other bullies in this book, he seems surprised at his own behavior and acknowledges it (which is a good thing). Whether significant change will occur is unknown. If this is part of his personality—his *enduring* pattern of behavior—it will take strong efforts to change it.

A Bully's Story in a Case of Parental Alienation

Cloaked under the broader topic of child abuse is another type of emotional abuse that is related to primitive emotional power: parental alienation. It's much harder to see and its complexities make it difficult to understand because it often occurs after parents separate or divorce and is based primarily on one parent's intense bully's story about the other parent, such as the one in the chapter opening quote:

> My mom is so mad at Dad. She's always telling me how bad he is and that she's sorry I have him for a father. I know she wants me to be mad at him too. . . . I don't know why Mom hates Dad so much. . . . But she's not gonna get me to say he's a bad daddy. I know better.[7]

This nine-year-old girl shows a lot of insight as she talks to her therapist about not adopting her mother's bully's story. But if her mother keeps repeating this story enough, the daughter is very likely to develop a similar extreme view over time. By thirteen or fourteen she may refuse to even see her father. I have seen this happen several times to fathers. I have also seen it happen to mothers in some cases when the father is telling the child a bully's story.

This is how it works: A parent with a bully personality and a lack of normal parent-child emotional boundaries (they don't know how to "hold their tongue," as the *Archaeology* authors put it)[8] repeatedly tells the child an emotional story about the other parent, such as that the separation or divorce is all the other parent's fault. Therefore their happy childhood is destroyed, there isn't enough money to do things now, and they will have to move across town—all because of that other parent. It's *all* his or her fault.

In other words, using the example of the nine-year-old girl, there is a crisis (triggering fear), the father is the cause of the crisis (triggering anger), and her mother is the only one she can count on (triggering love/loyalty). If the girl has limited contact with the father and the mother tells her this bully's story often enough, this story will replace her positive real experience with her father and she will grow to fear or hate him for no good reason.

I want to make clear that alienation is different from occasional expressions of anger by a parent at the time of a divorce who regularly supports the child's relationship with the other parent. It's also not alienation if the other parent has actually engaged in behavior that is abusive or very negative for the child, so that the child resists contact for understandable reasons. As mentioned above in Chapter 2, this is known as estrangement or realistic estrangement.

Alienation appears to be driven significantly by this repeated pattern of negativity and blurred boundaries so that the child is exposed to the parent's primitive emotional power, which activates the daughter's primitive emotional responses of fear, anger, and love/loyalty. Yet this is generally unconscious for both the parent and the child, and not obvious to others.

The problem for legal professionals and family courts is figuring out the cause of this resistance or refusal, which occurs in up to 27 percent of child custody disputes with endless confusion, anger, and repeated court hearings.[9] While children's resistance to contact with a parent in separation and divorce has been an issue in family courts for several decades, it appears to have increased since the mid-2000s and then more so after COVID-19 isolated families and created new power struggles between the separate parent households.[10]

Usually, though, the child's resistance is often a mystery to everyone involved and the source of endless court battles that sometimes go on for years without a clear resolution. The "favored" parent believes that the "rejected" parent must have done something to cause the child to resist contact, such as abusing the child, domestic violence, or being an incompetent parent. The rejected parent believes that the favored parent has embarked on a purposeful campaign to turn the child against them. Typically, grandparents, aunts and uncles, friends, and many professionals join in the battle on opposite sides, trading accusations of engaging in knowingly bad behavior. In the 1980s divorce researcher Janet Johnston and associates described such large-scale family conflicts as reaching the level of "tribal warfare."[11]

The outcomes of these cases are usually extreme. From my experience with many such cases, the rejected parent or the courts just give up, and the child may have no further contact with the rejected parent throughout the rest of their childhood and, in many cases, throughout their adulthood as well. Over and over again, when individual child counseling is ordered to solve this, I have seen it fail 99 percent of the time—because the child isn't the cause of the problem. In other cases, reunification counseling is ordered between the child and the rejected parent, but that approach also fails 99 percent of the time—because the rejected parent isn't the source of the problem. When family counseling is ordered for *everyone involved,* then some cases have been successful but other cases have been treatment failures because they need something stronger.

In these extreme cases, courts have ordered a change of custody to the rejected parent and a no-contact period of sixty to ninety days for the favored parent, so that the rejected parent and child can experience each other full-time without interference—and many of these cases actually show rapid success.

I believe that PEP explains what is happening in these cases—and what works and what doesn't work. Rather than being the result of intentionally bad behavior, children are primarily picking up their parents' primitive emotions—and one parent's bully's story.

Alienation is further addressed in parts of the next two chapters.

Bullies' Stories Taking Over Politics

Most politicians are sincere and are not bullies. I truly believe that. But in this new world of bullies, many of the reasonable ones are getting out of politics and many bullies are pouring in. While politicians often talk about policies and accomplishments, these new bully politicians seem to be focused mostly on telling a bully's story.

One example of a politician like this might be Boris Johnson, former prime minister of England who was forced out of office by his own party. He is well known as a storyteller. *The Atlantic*, in 2021, said of Johnson, "To him, the point of politics—and life—is not to squabble over facts; it's to offer people a story they can believe in."[12]

Yet Johnson's stories may have been bully's stories and at the center of his downfall. He was a key proponent of Brexit, which pulled England out of the European Union in 2016. He had said that withdrawing from the European Union would bring political freedom and great fortune to Great Britain. In studying him, Princeton professor Harry Frankfurt suggests that most of his stories were

BS. "To Johnson's critics, of course, he is the bullshitter *par excellence*. Some insist that he was never really a euroskeptic journalist, or that he never really believed in Brexit but was happy playing the part because it brought him fame, notoriety, and power."[13]

Once again, the goal of the bully isn't truth or solutions to real problems, it's power. His bully's story was that belonging to the European Union was a crisis because it was controlled by the "evil" EU government in Belgium and allowed hordes of immigrants to swamp the nation. But his "crisis" didn't fit the facts. It was mostly a fantasy crisis blamed on a fantasy villain government. Britain needed immigrants for many jobs because its population is aging, and the European Union provided many economic benefits to the United Kingdom. The savings in funds for Britain's healthcare system were grossly exaggerated.

Yet while many analysts were preoccupied with fact-checking in the lead-up to Brexit, they totally missed what was going on with the bully's PEP and how easy it is to gain power this way. It's the *emotional truth* that the listeners feel after they have been fed the fantasy crisis. PEP *feels* real, which is how con artists have worked for millennia. It's PEP all the way.

If immigration and decision-making in the European Union could be interpreted as a "crisis," then the EU government in Brussels could be made out to be the "villains," and Johnson and his fellow Brexiters could become "heroes" and gain power. Facts didn't matter. What really happened was product shortages, a "brewing crisis" in Northern Ireland, and a "disastrous early response to the pandemic." Furthermore, "After winning the referendum and becoming prime minister, Johnson promised there would be no tax raises on his watch. Then, this month [October 2021], he announced

Britain's most significant tax increase in twenty years—to pay for an increase in health spending."[14] As of May 2023, seven years after the Brexit vote, 56 percent of Britons say Brexit was "the wrong choice," and only 31 percent say it was "the right choice." Even more believe it is a failure (62 percent), and only 9 percent believe it is a success.[15]

For a time, it seemed that Johnson's BS—his PEP—was winning. However, his lies about attending parties and allowing sexual abusers in his government eventually caught up with him and he was forced by his own party to resign as prime minister in July 2022 and then as a Member of Parliament in June 2023.

Looking back, one British analyst said he was "narcissistic and slapdash" in regard to most of his administration's challenges:

> Overall, he showed a selfish disregard, verging on corruption, towards many of the most basic rules and ethics of government. A year ago it was clear that he did not understand he was not up to the job. That is still true a year on. In a new interview, asked about the events that led up to his resignation, he leans his head to one side and pretends to snore. He just doesn't get it. But he just doesn't care either.[16]

From this description, he seems to fit our bully analysis: He did not understand he was a bully and "not up to the job." He did not self-reflect or self-correct. He deceived himself as well as a majority of voters four years earlier. He liked his stories, and everyone else did also for a while. Yet, in looking back, many in the United Kingdom wondered how he came to "undermine the dignity of his post" and "take us all for fools."[17] Unfortunately, they were conned by his bully's stories, and they were fantasies. This would have been avoidable if a majority of their voters understood primitive emotional power. The warning signs were there from the start.

HOW YOU CAN STOP THIS POWER

1. Open Your Eyes to the Pattern

Question every story of a terrible crisis. Maintain a healthy skepticism. Regularly ask yourself these three questions:

- Is this problem really a crisis?
- Is this target really a villain?
- Is this "hero" really a hero?

Beware of the emotional power of a seemingly heroic leader. Research the story in a variety of sources, then ask yourself whether there is a genuine crisis—or a made-up one.

Practice on the stories in this chapter. Was there really a crisis for FKA twigs? Were her work colleagues really villains who just wanted to take advantage of her? Was LeBeouf really her hero? Was the relationship of England to the European Union really a crisis requiring Brexit? Were the policymakers in the European Union really villains? Was Boris really a hero?

2. Pull the Plug on the Bully

Check yourself and be wary of a bully's story (ask the three questions above). Avoid repeating any story of a crisis-villain-hero without checking it out. Then stop cooperating with anything that paints the bully as a hero. It took her a year, but eventually FKA twigs pulled the plug on her relationship with Shia LaBeouf. It took England six years for Boris Johnson's party to push him out as prime minister, but then they did. The earlier you see the pattern, the easier it is to pull the plug and get out.

3. Set Limits with Credible Threats

Bullies routinely try to violate boundaries, one after another. Once you recognize that someone is a bully, it's essential to deliberately strengthen existing boundaries and add new, equally strong ones.

For example, I was the lawyer for a woman who needed to work out a divorce settlement with her violent husband. He had a restraining order against him that prohibited him from even speaking to her—so he had to talk with me to negotiate various issues in their divorce. He would call and tell fabricated stories of terrible things his wife had ostensibly done (I had enough proof to believe her, not him). As he and I talked, he would use insults and refer to her with highly offensive names. I realized there was no benefit to my client of me having this conversation. I stopped him and insisted that he could not speak that way to me about my client—and that if he did once more, I would hang up on him. "It's up to you," I said.

In classic bully fashion, he ignored me and returned immediately to the insults and name-calling. I told him, "Okay, you've decided that I need to hang up. When you're ready to speak respectfully about her, call me and we'll talk." Then I hung up.

The next day he called me—and almost immediately started speaking disrespectfully about her again. I told him that after one more insult, I would have to hang up again. He said, "No, no. Don't hang up. I'll try not to say those things." He watched his language after that. He also got a lawyer, which made my job much easier, because I could talk with her, not him.

4. Impose Serious Consequences

When a bully creates a fantasy crisis and a fantasy villain (or set of villains), that bully will usually stick by their story until the bitter end—that is, until they are fired, sanctioned, or sent to prison, and sometimes even after that. Therefore, it's essential that there are serious consequences for bullies' stories to make them occur much less often.

For example, in 2019 actor Jussie Smollett claimed that a crisis had occurred: He had been the victim of a hate crime by two men, at least one white, who shouted, "MAGA country!" He received widespread sympathy—but it turned out that he had paid two people to fake the attack. It turned out to be a bully's story with a fantasy crisis and fantasy villains. He told the police that one of the men poured bleach on him and the other put a noose around his neck. This was a big story in the press, and he received a lot of sympathy. Since he is Black and a gay man, this was considered a hate crime because he was targeted as a member of a minority group.

But then, two Nigerian men came forward and revealed that he had paid them to fake the attack. This news turned his case around, and he was prosecuted for lying to police. He still refuses to recant his story, but he was ultimately sentenced to five months in prison. However, as of this writing, he is not in prison as he is awaiting the outcome of an appeal.[18]

What was his bully's story? The "crisis" was a hate crime, which actually never occurred. The "villains" who attacked him were actually two people he paid. The "hero" was himself as a victim who survived an attack—a total fabrication—a bully's story that deserved consequences.

5. Communicate Effectively About Bullies to Others

When a bully begins to make headway with their bully's story, explain the three fantasies to others, and show them how each one—the bogus crisis, villain, and hero—applies to what the bully is saying and doing. I have found that—once they know what to look for—people like being able to spot the patterns of other people's personalities and predict their likely future behavior.

For example, suppose a candidate for office tells you that the politician who they are running against took bribes in exchange for a vote to grant an exception for a business. That's a crisis and a villain, and the politician telling you this may claim (or imply) that they are a hero. Check it out before you repeat it to others. Be especially cautious when someone could gain power by telling you a story that doesn't seem right. It's easy to *claim* that the "other side" is corrupt and evil, but that doesn't make it true. If you find out it's not true, explain to others what happened. Bullies will often change stories when one doesn't work and then start conning again with a new bully's story. Teach the three parts of the bully's story to others so that they can protect themselves and their loved ones.

6. Stand Strong with Others Against Bullies

Support efforts anywhere to weed out those who spread false bully's stories. Most occupations have a percentage of bullies who are tolerated by those around them. They are usually defended against outside criticism by other members of their occupation, simply because they are "one of us." However, this appears to be changing as there is more public awareness of what was previously hidden bullying behavior and bully's stories by people in various occupations.

For example, after police officer Derek Chauvin caused the death of George Floyd, he and some other police officers tried to blame Floyd for his own death, claiming that he was uncooperative and under the influence of drugs. However, several people took videos of the murder and shared them publicly. Around the world, people marched in protest. At Chauvin's murder trial, multiple police experts stood with the truth and testified against Chauvin, who was convicted of murder. It was brave of them to speak out for the truth against one in their own occupation. More of us need to be willing to weed out the bullies in our own occupations, since they exist in every field, telling their bully's stories until someone else stops them.

CONCLUSION

The bully's story is at the core of bullying. It uses and reinforces the exact same three primitive emotions that we have been discussing: fear, anger, and love/loyalty. Bullies use all their primitive emotional power to tell bully's stories, which trigger primitive emotional responses in their targets without the targets even realizing it. The fantasy crisis triggers fear, the fantasy villain triggers anger, and the fantasy of the bully as hero is designed to trigger love/loyalty for the bully. Such a story is usually absorbed emotionally, not logically (because it often defies logic).

Yet it *feels true* to the target and others because the story makes sense of the feelings of fear, anger, and love—so it is not questioned and is accepted as logical and true. This is also known as gaslighting. The bully causes these emotions by using the primitive emotional power of the bully's story but can innocently deny doing anything while the target feels intense fear, anger at the villain, and love/loyalty for the bully. Just remember, it's a con. The bully's story is BS. Look for the three parts. And don't let the BS emotionally hook you into acting against yourself or others.

COMMON MISTAKE:

Bullies are telling the truth about real crises and evil people.

REALITY:

Bullies make up stories of crises and villains so that others will believe they are heroes and give them power over others.

CHAPTER 7

The Power of Emotional Repetition

Repetition can affect beliefs about truth.
People tend to perceive claims as truer if they have
been exposed to them before. This is known as
the illusory truth effect, and it helps explain why
advertisements and propaganda work, and also
why people believe fake news to be true.

—*Cognitive Research: Principles and Implications*

PEOPLE BELIEVE ALMOST ANYTHING if the message *is emotional enough,*
repeated enough, and *isolated enough* from any other message that
would contradict it. It's just the way humans are built for survival.
Repetition is how we learn languages, songs, sports, culture, and so
much more. As highly social animals, we need to have mostly shared
beliefs to get along, so we constantly repeat these to one another.
Emotional repetition is part of the social glue of human cultures.

Bullies know this intuitively, if not consciously. That's why they are constantly talking, repeating their simple bully's stories so much that people will believe them. This is central to a bully's primitive emotional power. This is equally true for bullies in families, groups, communities, and nations, and on the Internet—especially on the Internet! If you don't realize that you and everyone else are vulnerable to this power of *emotional repetition,* then you will be even more vulnerable to it.

The "Illusion of Truth" Effect

Research shows that each repetition of a statement is perceived as more truthful although it has slightly less impact than the one before it. Researchers report that "Repetition can affect beliefs about truth. People tend to perceive claims as truer if they have been exposed to them before. This is known as the illusory truth effect, and it helps explain why advertisements and propaganda work, and also why people believe fake news to be true."[1]

This occurs "even when participants are explicitly told that the source of the statements is unreliable or when the initial statement had a qualifier that cast doubt on the statement's validity." Moreover, the effect still occurs when statements are "highly implausible or when the repeated statements directly contradict participants' prior knowledge."[2] How can this be? Apparently, the way our brains process information is designed to be as efficient as possible. We can't stop and analyze (or fact-check) every one of the thousands of bits of information that comes our way each day, so the brain takes shortcuts.

Researchers believe that the *illusion of truth effect* that comes from repetition is because of "fluency"—the ease with which the brain receives the information. Each repetition makes it easier to absorb because you have heard it already. Researchers note that "As the number of repetitions of a given stimulus increases, there are exponential decreases in the firing rates of the neurons." In addition, communications are considered more fluent and truthful if they are "presented in easy-to-read font or easy-to-understand speech" and are considered to be "more truthful than information presented in a less perceptually fluent format."[3]

All put together, this supports the idea that simple bully's stories that are repeated a lot are some of the easiest messages for our brains to digest and remember. Add primitive emotions to the message, and the story becomes automatic in our brains—especially the lower parts of our brains: the crisis–villain–hero story activates the fear, anger, and love/loyalty emotions in response.

Bullies routinely use this illusion of truth effect to mislead us, enhanced by their use of extreme words, intense facial expressions, and powerful tones of voice (PEP) to assist in dominating us—including what we believe. Over time, the message becomes harder and harder to challenge. Eventually, it may even become widely accepted as the one and only truth on the subject—even when it's false.

Cognitive scientist Tom Stafford argues, however, that if we use our reasoning abilities, we can double-check whether something is really true. He says, "If something sounds plausible, is it because it really is true, or have we just been told that repeatedly? This is why scholars are so mad about providing references—so we can track the origin on any claim, rather than having to take it on faith." He also emphasizes that we should not repeat things unless we have verified them as true. Our own repetition can add to the problem if we are not careful. "So, please, think before you repeat," he says.[4]

Repetition in Isolation

If the emotional message of a bully's story is repeated endlessly in isolation, without any other competing message, then it can truly *feel* like the truth.

The next two examples show the extreme impact of a bully's story told with emotional repetition in isolation. They were current events that drew a lot of attention during the 1970s, when values were in flux as they are today, and bullies were playing an outsize role in society as they are today. Do the PEP patterns of bullies then and now seem to be the same?

Patty Hearst

The saga of Patty Hearst in the 1970s is a good example of how emotional repetition in isolation can escalate into highly aggressive and dangerous behavior turned toward a bully's other targets. Patty was a nineteen-year-old college student and an heir of the super-wealthy William Randolph Hearst (owner of the nation's largest media company at one point). She was kidnapped in 1974 by a handful of members of the radical leftist group that called itself the Symbionese Liberation Army (SLA). They wanted to use her as a hostage to get a huge ransom, which would help them start a war against the U.S. government and overthrow the "capitalist state." The kidnapping stunned the nation and made front-page news.

While in captivity, she was locked in a closet. They bombarded her with the group's bully's story of a terrible crisis (the capitalist control of the nation), evil villains (like her wealthy family), and the SLA as the heroes. This *emotional repetition in isolation* was so powerful that within two months she changed her name to "Tania," released a video saying she was joining the cause, and then participated with the group in a bank robbery to raise funds for their efforts. She wielded an assault weapon and was "barking orders to bystanders and providing cover to her confederates." Eventually the FBI caught up with her two years and several violent episodes later.[5]

At trial, her lawyers emphasized that she was brainwashed, but the jury found her guilty. She received a seven-year sentence but served only two years. Her sentence was commuted by President Carter, and she was later pardoned.[6]

Was Hearst brainwashed? Did emotional repetition in isolation by bullies play a role in her change of behavior? She said she was brainwashed, and some experts agreed. However, that defense was not an option in her trial. For Hearst to secure an acquittal on the grounds of having been brainwashed would have been completely unprecedented. However, she was certainly isolated, and there were several signs this may have occurred.

> At the time of her arrest, Hearst's weight had dropped to 87 pounds (40 kg), and she was described by psychologist Margaret Singer in October 1975 as "a low-IQ, low-affect zombie." Shortly after her arrest, signs of trauma were recorded: her IQ was measured as 112, whereas it had previously been 130; there were huge gaps in her memory regarding her pre-Tania life; she was smoking heavily and had nightmares.[7]

True, there were also several indications that Hearst's actions may have been voluntary. For two years she apparently had opportunities to escape but did not. She participated in other violent robberies. She was convicted of bank robbery and using a firearm during the commission of a felony. After the trial, one juror stated that they believed she was lying about being coerced. She apparently had sex with two of the SLA members and kept a trinket given to her by one of the men. Since several of the members were women, it was argued that these radical women would not have allowed the men to rape her, so having sex must have been consensual. She was very engaged in making SLA statements and actions for two years, which they found unlikely to have occurred totally under coercion by the group. Yet she totally disavowed the group and their politics forever after she was caught and separated from the group.

While not a legal factor, emotional repetition in isolation appeared to play some part in her extreme behavior, which was so different from who she was before and after those two years. At what point does a kidnapping victim become a voluntary believer and pick up a gun for those beliefs? Or was this PEP in the form of brainwashing that others just couldn't see or believe was possible—and she herself didn't understand?

Jonestown

Another example of the extreme power of emotional repetition in isolation occurred with Jonestown, also in the political turmoil of the 1970s. In this case, it was a whole group who lived together on a farm in a faraway country. Could they be convinced to believe—and do—anything?

Jim Jones was a preacher in San Francisco in the 1970s who founded a church known as the People's Temple. His church was politically active on behalf of poor people of all races and quite popular with many other church leaders, politicians, and celebrities. In 1977 he started moving his flock to a "socialist paradise" in South America that would be a sanctuary from all the problems in the modern city, including an intrusive media, possible spies in his church, and his fear of eventual American martial law and concentration camps.

Jones and his followers built a farming community they called Jonestown in the middle of the jungle of the small nation of Guyana, next to Venezuela, which also identified itself as a socialist country. The Guyanese government welcomed them as a buffer against Venezuela, with whom they had a potential border dispute. Having Americans on their land would prevent the much larger country from invading.

Daily life in Jonestown was rugged, but most of those who moved there found the camaraderie of hard work very enjoyable. However, after Jones himself arrived, things changed. They had to go to nightly meetings to hear his accounts of the evils happening in the United States and around the world, with his own exaggerations. He claimed that the U.S. military was planning to kill Black people, which was particularly unsettling—and effective as a bully's story—because two-thirds of Jonestown members were Black.

The emotional repetition was relentless. Almost every night, he would describe some terrible thing that was happening in the United States that they had escaped only because of him. In the daytime, there was a loudspeaker system throughout the main settlement where most of them worked that played music interrupted regularly by additional lectures from Jones, expanding on a topic from the night before or even playing a recording of a previous evening's lectures.[8]

Over the nearly four years of Jonestown, he had made several enemies in the United States, including some former members of his church in San Francisco, People's Temple, who had children in Jonestown. Congressman Leo Ryan from San Francisco decided to make a visit to Jonestown to see if anyone was being held against their will as several relatives had told him. After the visit, highly supervised by Jonestown staff, Ryan and his entourage headed to the small airport nearby and were shot and killed by Jones's henchmen.

Jones then told his followers that the U.S. government would be coming, and troops would wipe out Jonestown. He ordered everyone to commit suicide by drinking poison mixed with Flavor Aid (mistakenly called Kool-Aid).

Most of his followers did drink the poison after holding their children to have it squirted into their mouths. While there was evidence that some adults had it forcibly injected against their will, at least two-thirds went willingly.

> Some went proudly; they worshipped Jim Jones, believed that they were making a grand revolutionary statement, and looked forward to a new consciousness on some higher plane. Others accepted poison as a preferable alternative to slaughter by the enemy forces they believed must be converging on Jonestown. . . . A few people in the poison line thanked Jones for all that he'd done for them.[9]

Remember: fear, anger, and love/loyalty. Some even left notes saying to the world, "We died because you would not let us live in peace!" and "Why couldn't you leave us alone?" They apparently accepted Jones's rants that the world was out to get them. The daily emotional repetition in isolation of his bully's story (fantasy crisis–villains–hero) drove them to believe *anything* he said and to do anything he told them to. Here's how one journalist summed it up:

> Jim Jones had wanted his grand gesture to make an impression on the entire world, and, to that extent, he succeeded. But the Jonestown deaths quickly became renowned not as a grandly defiant revolutionary gesture, but as the ultimate example of human gullibility.[10]

The Angry Son

When the Smiths (not their real name) separated, their eleven-year-old son, Jack, stayed primarily with his mother, whom we shall call Olivia. But their father, whom we shall call Noah, really didn't want to separate and divorce. He was quite angry with Olivia, but she was determined to divorce him, significantly because of his bully personality. When they separated, Olivia and Jack stayed with friends for a few months.

Unfortunately, while staying with the friends, Jack developed a rash in his groin area, which was apparently from bedbug bites. A doctor examined him and recommended that the mother treat the area with an ointment that cleared it up over a few weeks. This was known to the father, and he grew very upset about it. He claimed she was sexually abusing the boy by applying the ointment, which took all of thirty seconds a day to apply for a couple weeks. He complained to therapists and even Child Protective Services about this seven times, but no one agreed with him, and the case was closed as unfounded.

Over the next few years, Jack told his mother that his father repeatedly told him,

"Dad says you broke up our family because you didn't want to be a part of it anymore."

"Dad's right, you are controlling."

"Dad's right, you push and push until you make me explode."

"You don't spend money on us, you just spend it on yourself."

"You do not want to spend time with us, you only want to spend time with your friends."

Olivia explained that none of this was true and none of it even fit who she was. She told Jack that neither parent should be discussing their divorce with him. She herself was careful not to talk about the divorce with Jack. However, Noah took Olivia to court several times over the next six years to fight for more time with Jack. Because of his aggressive behavior and continued allegations of abuse against Olivia, the court eventually gave her sole legal custody (decision-making) and specifically admonished Noah to stop talking about their divorce with Jack during his parenting time.

Unfortunately, over the next few years, Noah kept saying Jack was sexually abused to his pediatricians and therapists and fired them when they wouldn't go along with his demands to evaluate Jack as a victim of child sexual abuse. He kept talking to Jack about the divorce and blaming everything on his mother.

When Jack was seventeen, with a year and a half left to go in high school, and after six years of repeated allegations and emotional statements by his father against the mother, he had a conflict with his mother over his cell phone use. She had rules, whereas Noah was very permissive. She put Jack on restriction and around midnight he called his father and asked him to pick Jack up and take him to his father's house. Noah quickly picked him up and took him to his house. In order to say that he had done nothing wrong, because this violated their court-ordered parenting schedule, Noah called the police and informed them that he picked up Jack "because of an incident that occurred" six years earlier.

The police came out the next day to the father's house and took a statement from Jack and quickly concluded that there was no abuse they needed to address. Jack readily admitted that the ointment application took thirty seconds a day for two weeks and that neither he nor his mother were aroused by this. But Noah rushed to family court before the police report came out and won big. He told the new judge that the boy had called him to protect him from his mother, who had abused him six years earlier. "He finally felt safe to say what happened to him."

At court, the judge readily accepted Noah's statements without the mother being present (allowed because it was a special emergency ex parte hearing for a protective order) and awarded Noah the sole custody of Jack on the spot, allowing no contact with his mother until a full hearing.

Before the full court hearing, the court counselor interviewed Jack. He sounded even more negative about his mother, not less, after being isolated with his father for the past month. The counselor wrote, "He stated that he ran away from the mother's home that night, stating that he had had enough of her behavior and insanity. Jack reported that the mother has historically been mentally abusive toward him, with them fighting all the time, never giving him any freedom, and with her attempting to fully control him."

Was this a crisis? Or a bully's story that Jack had absorbed? The mistake the court counselor made is that he did not ask any follow-up questions, which really should be done in a contested case like this: Can you give me an example of the "insanity"? Of being "mentally abusive"? Of the "control"? Of "never giving you any freedom"? And: What do "sanity" and "freedom" look like in your father's home? Often children under the emotional influence of a parent with alienating behaviors cannot describe anything extreme that would fit their dramatic and emotional statements. They have absorbed the emotional repetition but don't seem to know why they feel that way. This fits with how our brains directly absorb intense emotions from other people without wasting time on logical processing, which is why primitive emotional power is so strong.

The reality was that Olivia had a good relationship with Jack until the last few months, when his father's negativity seemed to be grabbing hold of Jack. The reality was that she operated as a fairly average parent who had put his cell phone in "time out" the night he decided to run away. This is a normal adolescent consequence for misbehavior.

Yet Noah, on the other hand, prided himself on having few rules and consequences. He allowed Jack to have unlimited screen time, which meant that he often fell asleep during his classes, didn't do his homework, and was experiencing increasing anxiety. Since he did have frequent issues with anxiety, allowing him to avoid responsibility and avoid his mother was likely to increase his anxiety rather than reduce it.

However, at the full hearing the judge was clearly emotionally hooked by Noah's allegations of child sexual abuse and was very negative toward Olivia. When Olivia's lawyer pointed out that the law says that properly applying doctor-prescribed medicine is not child sexual abuse, the judge reluctantly agreed that this was not a case of child sexual abuse. But the judge still said that the mother shouldn't have applied the medicine and instead should have had Jack put it on himself, as if that was the real reason Jack ran away to live with Noah six years later. The judge had already made up her mind that Jack should stay with Noah and leave it up to Noah to make sure Jack saw his mother, which, of course, he never did. He had "won." Noah got to dominate Jack, the judge, and the mother. Case closed.

For those who understand parental alienation, this was a clear case of a highly aggressive father who for six years emotionally and repetitively told his son that his mother was the villain of their divorce while the mother said nothing about the divorce. Once Jack was living with Noah and not seeing his mother, these negative messages were repeated even more so—now in total isolation. This is a common problem with alienation when a child lives exclusively with the parent who is repeating such emotional messages in isolation without input from any other point of view.

That's why alienation gets worse with isolation with a bully, not better. Unfortunately, lawyers, therapists, and judges who do not understand the power of emotional repetition in isolation *suggest that an alienated child should be allowed to avoid the rejected parent until they feel comfortable seeing that parent again.* Of course, this rarely occurs because the alienation is coming from the parent the child is with, not the parent whom the child has rejected. This is a classic case of misunderstanding the PEP of a bully who keeps telling the bully's story of a fantasy crisis (the divorce, nonexistent abuse, or whatever), a fantasy villain (in this case, the mother), and a fantasy hero (the father), such as Noah told Jack and the judge who was quite impressed with the father's "protection" of Jack from his terrible mother.

Misunderstanding what was really going on, the judge inadvertently helped the father to prevent all contact of Jack with his mother for over two years with no end in sight. Apparently, Jack has no friends and no outside involvements (work, school, social life, etc.). He is isolated and under the control of his father and his bully's story even though he is going on twenty years old.

Sadly, millions of alienated children are misunderstood by professionals in this way, no longer have a relationship with one of their parents, and may never reconcile. They are instead living with and absorbing the bully's story every day with a bully parent, who is often domineering, vindictive, and intrusive.

While this example described the father as the bully, parental alienation was historically seen primarily as a gender issue (moms against dads) in the 1980s, but soon it became clear that mothers or fathers could become the rejected parent.[11] The reality is that alienation appears to be a product of unrecognized primitive emotional power, which can target mothers, fathers, grandparents, and other family members. The child absorbs one parent's primitive emotional power and turns it against the other parent. When whole families repeat these emotional messages to a child, it becomes almost impossible to resist absorbing them.

However, some professionals, including judges, are starting to understand this. As described in the prior chapter, after a thorough evaluation of the family—including ruling out child abuse or domestic violence by the rejected parent—some judges are ordering the child to return to the rejected parent and attend an intensive weekend program of activities together. It's too bad that didn't happen in this mother's case. She may never have a relationship with her son again.

HOW YOU CAN STOP THIS POWER

1. Open Your Eyes to the Pattern

Beware of any single source of information telling you of a crisis, an evil villain, and a hero (the bully's story). Check out differing sources of information. If you are in a position of power or influence, such as a judge or group leader, don't allow anyone to become isolated with someone who may be repeatedly telling a bully's story.

Each of the situations in this chapter contained extreme primitive emotional power. Yet in each situation, outsiders viewed the target's behavior as voluntary and mystifying. When people are receiving emotional messages of crises and villains repeated over and over again in isolation from any other source of information, the result is not surprising that people will believe absurdities and even become extremely rejecting or violent toward others in the service of their perceived hero—an obvious bully to everyone else. These are just three different examples of situations that millions of people have experienced with bullies, whether angry parents, political kidnappers, or even bullies claiming to be religious leaders. For most people, this power remains hidden or denied as they argue about the "issue" they see: an abusive mother, a revolutionary young adult, or a political statement. This pattern of behavior—this power—is hidden in plain sight for those who know to watch out for it.

2. Pull the Plug on the Bully

Bullies are always looking for others to hear their bully's story. The best way to pull the plug on a bully engaging in emotional repetition is to maintain a healthy skepticism. "Is that really true?" While you may not know the full story and may not be able to investigate it, by not automatically accepting what is being said, you are not adding to the bully's story and possibly the isolation of their target.

The power of emotional repetition is especially important to understand when people have become isolated with a bully, such as a domestic violence victim, alienated child, or victim of a workplace bully. Keep an open mind and consider that they themselves don't see what is happening to them because of this repetition.

Ask for the facts on which the information is based. If the facts don't seem likely to be true or seem minor compared to the severity of the accusations, consider the possibility that they are repeating a bully's story. Ask such questions as the following:

Who told you that?

What do other people say?

Is there another point of view?

How certain are you that this is true?

Do you have mixed feelings about the person—the alleged villain? (This is common with real relationships.) Or are your feelings absolute about the person?

Is a bully keeping the person isolated, so that you can't even ask questions?

You may need to withdraw your support from individuals or news sources that repeat misinformation. In cases involving divorce or some other family dispute, take a deep breath, remind yourself that this withdrawal is a form of compassion, and temporarily (and, if necessary, permanently) set a firm boundary between yourself and the bullying family member. With news sources, it helps to check out multiple sources from time to time and let go of those with questionable claims.

3. Set Limits with Credible Threats

Because of the power of emotional repetition, it's important for individuals and organizations to set limits on those who drive it in any setting. Watch out for the repetition of personal attacks, which can be especially destructive.

For example, family courts often give separated and divorced parents this clear warning: "Neither parent shall make disparaging remarks about the other parent in the presence of the child, nor allow others to do so." Similar warnings should be given to disputants by mediators and arbitrators, to members of boards by board chairpersons, and to political candidates by debate moderators. That is, candidates can criticize one another's policies, beliefs, or voting records, but they should be forbidden to say things like "My opponent is a monster," or "The other candidate hates you, your family, and our great country."

Remember, though, that unless these admonitions are combined with genuine, credible threats involving clear, specific, and painful consequences, bullies will ignore them. A bully who makes a highly emotional accusation should be immediately reminded of the limit that has been set ("We're not doing personal attacks here") and the conse-quences they will face (the meeting will be stopped; you will need to leave; I will need to end this conversation). On the first repetition of that accusation, they should immediately be subject to those conse quences. Otherwise, a bully gains momentum with their bully's story, and the repetitions will increase to the extent that reality may be lost for some or most of those hearing it. If you're in a position to add different, more accurate information, that can help.

4. Impose Serious Consequences

Interrupting the emotional repetition of a bully's stories often takes the involvement of authority figures who understand the need for consequences. Community members can be removed from meetings for violating standards of conduct and disturbing the rights of others. Debate moderators can shut down a candidate's microphone—or eject them from the debate. Citizens can boycott media that promotes a bully's stories for misleading the public. Furthermore, much of our legal system is designed to impose consequences on those who violate the standards of society and established laws.

For example, Alex Jones is a radio host and major promoter of absurd and easily disproven conspiracy theories. One such theory, which Jones emotionally repeated hundreds of times on his show, is that the shooting of twenty students and several adults at Sandy Hook Elementary School in 2012 was faked. Jones claimed, against all evidence, that no one died, and the children were all actors. The entire incident, Jones repeatedly insisted, was an effort to promote gun control.[12]

The power of this false emotional repetition was demonstrated by the fact that the grieving parents of the slaughtered children were harassed by Jones's followers and in some cases threatened with execution. It seems his followers were emotionally hooked by his bully's story of a fantasy crisis—fantasy villains—and him as the fantasy hero.

Out of loyalty to him, they were mobilized to rage against his fantasy villains—the parents of real children who died tragically.

His behavior ultimately reached the court system, and he was found liable to pay over $1 billion in damages to the parents for defaming them with his false stories. While he declared bankruptcy in hopes of avoiding that large a payment, the court denied him that escape route. If he liquidates his media business for a lesser amount, he will still owe the full penalty[13]—a powerful consequence for his bullying behavior.

5. Communicate Effectively About Bullies to Others

Explain to others the power of emotional repetition. Also explain how relying on a single source of information—whether it is a media outlet, a news feed, a website, a family member, a boss, or your company's CEO—can allow misinformation to flourish. If necessary, remind people that anyone can be taken in by the bully power of emotional repetition—not because they're stupid, but because our brains are wired to respond positively to this power.

The well-publicized story about Alex Jones has been educational for the whole nation. This is a good example of how his bully's stories mobilized some people's rage to attack the bully's targets even when the stories were blatantly absurd. People in general were horrified at this and wondered why anyone would attack grieving parents. But with enough emotional repetitions, there were people who believed them. That's why imposing consequences is so important to stopping such extreme bullying behavior and communicating to the world about the seriousness of these consequences.

6. Stand Strong with Others Against Bullies

The power of relentless repetition can be overcome by firm and resolute pushback from ordinary people working together. This is true even when people have been cruelly, vigorously, and constantly targeted by bullies.

For example, in the Alex Jones case, the reason it got to court was that the families of ten victims banded together and filed several lawsuits for defamation in Connecticut and in Texas. Some cases are still ongoing as of this writing. A jury recognized their pain and suffering by awarding the group of parents over $1 billion. This not only stops one person's endless repetitions of that bully's story but sends a message to anyone considering spreading bully's stories in such a hateful, public way. The parents stood together against their bully and succeeded.[14]

CONCLUSION

Repetition of emotional messages can be incredibly powerful, especially when the repetition occurs in isolation from any other different or more accurate messages. This can be lifelong relationship threatening (Jack's alienation from his mother may be permanent) and even life threatening (as in parents being threatened by Alex Jones's followers). We have seen how this can drive extreme behavior without people even realizing its source.

In the case of Patty Hearst, the jury and most people believed that she made a conscious decision to pick up a gun and rob banks for "the cause." However, if you understand the hidden power of PEP—essentially brainwashing—you can see how powerful such isolation can be when combined with emotional repetition. This doesn't mean that she should not have consequences for her behavior, as this would create a frightening world in which anyone could ask to be excused for their behavior. Her conviction seems appropriate, but the length of her sentence was shortened perhaps because of an intuitive understanding of the emotional repetition in isolation of a kidnapping victim.

In the case of Jonestown, the followers paid the ultimate penalty for absorbing Jim Jones's constant PEP talks. While family members tried to get their loved ones out of Jonestown before such an ending occurred, this can at least be a lesson for everyone else about following charismatic leaders to an isolated setting.

In the case of the angry son Jack, who became alienated from his mother, you can see how important it is to understand the source of the anger. Jack absorbed it emotionally from his favored parent's anger through the process of emotional repetition in isolation. This is why courts should never order or allow a child to be exclusively with one parent, unless a thorough investigation has shown that the child is truly at risk of physical, sexual, or emotional harm by having contact with the rejected parent, which is very rare. Supervised contact is almost always a better solution than no contact, so that a real relationship can be preserved and potentially grow when and if the family dynamics are resolved.

Throughout the rest of this book, keep an eye out for bullies' stories that are emotionally repeated, especially in isolation.

COMMON MISTAKE:
When people repeat what someone else says, that means it must be true.
If something feels true, it must be true even if the facts contradict it.

REALITY:
When people repeat what a bully says,
it often means they are emotionally hooked and uninformed.
When repeated often enough, false information can feel true.

CHAPTER 8

The Power of Negative Advocates

*One after another, she wrapped people around her
finger and persuaded them to do her bidding. The
first to fall under her spell was Channing Robertson,
the Stanford engineering professor whose reputation
helped give her credibility when she was just a
teenager. Then [several others and eventually] James
Mattis, George Shultz, and Henry Kissinger.*

—John Carreyrou, *Bad Blood: Secrets and Lies
in a Silicon Valley Startup*

ONE WAY BULLIES PROJECT AN IMAGE OF STRENGTH is by gathering *negative advocates* around them. Negative advocates are those seemingly reasonable people who advocate for bullies' negative thinking, negative feelings, and negative behavior. This makes bullies appear to have large-scale support while they tell their targets how isolated and weak they are. Usually negative advocates have been hoodwinked by a bully's stories, though they can also be bullies themselves.

Bullies constantly recruit negative advocates to help them persuade decision-makers and other influencers that the bully's bad behavior is normal and necessary. Most negative advocates are emotionally hooked but uninformed. They buy into the bully's story of crisis, villain, and hero (with the bully as the hero—*and* as the victim of the person or group they target). Because they see the bully as a victim, they feel that the bully badly needs their help.

This is all part of the bully's strategy and often motivates their negative advocates to work even harder than they do at persuading others that the bully's behavior is just fine. Negative advocates are often people with more credibility than the bully, such as professionals (lawyers, therapists, doctors, ministers, etc.) or respected family or community members. In divorce cases, bully parents regularly attempt to turn their kids and other family members into their negative advocates against the other parent and that parent's family.

The intensity of primitive emotional power is particularly effective at activating negative advocates. They often aren't even aware of becoming negative advocates, so they escalate their own energy and engage in the fight to protect the bully while attacking the bully's victims. They have become emotionally hooked by the bully's PEP. Negative advocates are much like codependents who try to protect the alcoholic or addict from the natural consequences of their problems. This is also known as *enabling* them to continue with their bad behavior.

Just as you need to question a bully's story, also question the apparent amount of a bully's power. Usually, what looks like power is mere showmanship. When multiple people firmly resist and challenge a bully's negative advocates, the whole bully's story is often revealed to be a sham and a scam.

PEP Is Contagious

What is the process by which other people get emotionally hooked by a bully? Research tells us that emotions are contagious. Since the emotions of bullies are intense, they tend to be intensely contagious. Here is how the process seems to work:[1]

3 Steps of How We Process Others' Emotions

OTHER PERSON'S EMOTIONS

1 ∘ EMOTIONAL CONTAGION
(your automatic reactions)

2 ∘ EMOTION REGULATION
(your conscious control, learned with age)

3 ∘ YOUR MOOD STATE
(your resulting positive or negative emotions)

Let's take an example of a condo association board meeting with a resident who is a bully we'll call Carlos. Carlos is opposed to a 5 percent increase in the monthly building management fee that the board has proposed. Of course, the owners are mixed about this increase, with most for it and some opposed. But Carlos is going to take it to the extreme and lead a loud, dramatic protest at the board meeting followed by a walkout.

Carlos tells several other owners that this is the end of the world as they know it. Even a 5 percent increase will eventually lead to 10 percent, then 50 percent, then 100 percent. He has all-or-nothing thinking, and he's very emotional about it. Here's how his emotions hook Rashid, one of his neighbors:

1. **Emotional contagion (automatic reactions):**
   Rashid hears Carlos's intense anger. He sees Carlos's angry face. They trigger the amygdala in his brain to also start feeling anxious and angry. The amygdala is the first part of the brain to sense danger and tell the body how to react: either fighting, fleeing, or freezing. This can happen in less than a fraction of a second, before we are even consciously aware of it. Some researchers call this *human Wi-Fi*—how we "catch" one another's emotions especially when we're anxious.[2]

2. **Emotion regulation (conscious control):**
   Rashid is on a fixed income and was already worried about his future finances. While he can afford the 5 percent increase, Carlos's intensity about more increases coming rapidly afterward feeds into Rashid's fears, and now he is really angry too. *How dare they threaten us with all these increases*, he consciously tells himself. Some call this *cognitive reassessment*, which allows us to consciously reinterpret the thoughts and emotions we actually accept from what others send our way.[3] In this case, Rashid accepts and increases Carlos's intensity with his conscious statement to himself. (Someone else might consciously decrease or reject this intensity.)

3. **Mood state (resulting emotion):**
   Now Rashid is just as angry as Carlos and ready to fight for him and with him. "You're right, Carlos! We have to fight this with everything we've got! When's the meeting?"

Rashid on his own was worried about his finances, but now he is enraged. Carlos has activated Rashid's primitive emotional responses of extreme fear, extreme anger, and possibly emotional loyalty to Carlos as his leader in this "necessary" fight. He "caught" Carlos's emotions without either of them realizing it. Rashid has become Carlos's negative advocate in a matter of moments.

However, when Carlos talked with Sabrina about his anger about the fee increase and tried to recruit her for a protest at the meeting, something very different happened:

1. **Emotional contagion (automatic reactions):**
   When Sabrina heard Carlos's intense anger about this, her amygdala sensed danger but saw Carlos as the danger. In a split second, she automatically was triggered to be angry and argue with him as she had argued with him in the past.

2. **Emotion regulation (conscious control):**
   Sabrina consciously reminded herself: *The building really needs some repairs, and the fee has never increased more than 5 percent over a ten-year period. But also, remember that arguing with Carlos is pointless, and I have better things to do right now.* With this thought, Sabrina's anger immediately subsided.

3. **Mood state (resulting emotion):**
   She calmly told Carlos, "I know you're worried about this leading to even higher fees, but that's not the history of this building—so I'm not protesting the increase. But I've got to go now, so see you later." And she hurried off before he could respond.

Conscious thoughts, like Sabrina's reminder to herself about not arguing with Carlos, can increase or decrease the emotions someone is experiencing, including those coming from a bully. Rashid absorbed Carlos's angry emotions, but Sabrina didn't. It makes a difference whether the listener is *predisposed* and/or *primed* to absorb a bully's intense fear, anger, or love/loyalty.

Predisposed Personalities

Rashid was predisposed to get angry, as he has a personality with a paranoid streak that easily becomes emotional. He fears that others are out to get him. He's been this way since he can remember. This makes him an easy target for becoming a negative advocate for bullies with intense emotions about almost anything—whereas Sabrina is a pretty calm person most of the time and it's hard to rile her up about things. This personality trait has helped her avoid unnecessary conflicts much of the time and made her several good friends.

We are all susceptible to getting emotionally hooked by the emotions of others, especially the primitive emotions of intense fear, intense anger, and intense love/loyalty. Our own personalities are predisposed to be more or less reactive to other people's upset emotions, especially if we have some history with them. This explains why Rashid was easily upset when he was around Carlos, but Sabrina was not. She appeared to have some natural immunity to his dramatic speech because of having a calmer personality. In addition, she had some history with Carlos and knew that he could get people worked up unnecessarily—but not her. Rashid has become a negative advocate for Carlos, whereas Sabrina has not.

Other ways we can be predisposed may be because of personal experience (e.g., a history of having to move because of cost increases), occupational knowledge (e.g., a real estate agent may have read about fees staying stable or going up in the area), or even childhood (e.g., being homeless for a little while). All these and other factors may predispose us to a strong or mild, positive or negative response to another person's intense emotions. Generally, being predisposed is more about our personality and life background.

Priming for Action

Priming can also influence whether we believe a bully's story and become a negative advocate. Priming is generally about recent events or conversations. They may prime us for gullibility and action—or caution. In the case of Jonestown, Jim Jones had tricked his followers into thinking they drank wine that was secretly laced with poison a few days before the real event. Then he told them there was no poison and that it was only "a test of their loyalty" to see how they would respond.[4] One wonders how many of them thought that was occurring again on the fateful day, or just went through the motions they had already learned.

In the case of Carlos and Rashid, Rashid was already worried about his finances, so when Carlos presented the 5 percent condo fee increase as a desperate crisis, Rashid easily jumped to the same conclusion. He easily became a negative advocate for Carlos and would go to the condo board meeting and totally endorse Carlos's angry statements without question. He would advocate for Carlos's bullying behavior. On the other hand, Sabrina already had a history with Carlos and was primed to resist whatever scheme or position he created. Therefore, she did not react with concern and told Carlos she would not participate in his planned public opposition to the increase. She did not become his negative advocate.

Anyone Can Become a Negative Advocate

Of course, all of us are susceptible to becoming negative advocates for people we are close to or even strangers who present us with bully's stories of intense fear and anger. Part of our human nature is to protect and defend one another against perceived dangers. This is our primitive emotional response system of caring and responding to others' panic or grief, as I mentioned in Chapter 4, which I interpret as simply love/loyalty. This caring response is activated especially when others present crises to us with a sense of urgency. Contagious emotions are one way that we have survived throughout history because they can lead to group action.

But this trait is also potentially dangerous because it leaves us vulnerable to becoming negative advocates for bullies telling us about their fantasy crises, their fantasy villains, and that they are fantasy heroes who have been done wrong by somebody else. We may be misled into arguments or even physical confrontations with the wrong people—the bully's innocent victims or people much more powerful than us. That's why learning about how easy it is to become a negative advocate is so important. Maintain a healthy skepticism about who you believe and who you follow.

The Case of Theranos

The more negative advocates a bully can acquire, the stronger and more persuasive he or she appears. It becomes easier and easier as negative advocates recruit other negative advocates. The more credible a negative advocate is, the easier it is for a bully to look good and credible. A good example in the business world is the case of Theranos, the blood draw start-up company that was going to revolutionize blood testing and make a fortune for those involved.

Anyone who is asked to invest in a new venture should learn from this example.

Theranos was founded by Elizabeth Holmes, a former Stanford University student. Holmes claimed that Theranos could accurately analyze many different aspects of someone's health from a few drops of their blood. But her company, Theranos, became a big con. It couldn't do any of what Holmes said, but she kept saying it anyway. She conned many wealthy and famous investors, recruited some of them for the Theranos board, and turned many of them into her negative advocates.

She presented herself as young, brilliant, and attractive. She dressed like Steve Jobs, the brilliant leader of Apple Computers, wearing black turtlenecks every day like he did. (He had said that he didn't want to waste any brain energy on deciding what to wear each day, so he bought many of the same outfit. Holmes claimed the same approach.) She also deepened the pitch of her voice to sound more authoritative. Remember the image of strength and sound of strength from Chapter 4.

As the investigative journalist John Carreyrou later wrote about her, "One after another, she wrapped people around her finger and persuaded them to do her bidding," including business, technology, and government leaders such as Rupert Murdoch (owner of Fox News), and Henry Kissinger and George Shultz (former U.S. secretaries of state). Each one enabled her to raise money, achieve public credibility, and hook in the next negative advocate. They were all apparently "bewitched by Holmes's mixture of charm, intelligence, and charisma."[5]

Until Holmes was busted for fraud, these many negative advocates gave her image a huge boost and helped her avoid consequences for running a business that was cheating on its blood tests and lying about the success of its testing devices.

While they may have been idealistic at first, when their employees pointed out many serious problems to them, Holmes and her business partner, Sunny Balwani, turned to viciously bullying their critics. An example of how her negative advocates protected her is what happened with George Shultz's grandson, Tyler Shultz, who landed a job with the company and tried to persuade them to voluntarily clean up their act. He sent an e-mail to Holmes with his concerns:

> I am sorry if this e-mail sounds attacking in any way, I do not intend it to be, I just feel a responsibility to you to tell you what I see so we can work towards solutions. I am invested in this company's long-term vision and am worried that some of our current practices will prevent us from reaching our bigger goals.[6]

Rather than working to protect the company and fix these problems, Holmes passed his e-mail on to her business partner, Balwani, who responded by e-mail calling Tyler "too junior and green to understand what he was talking about" and stating, "The only reason I have taken so much time away from work to address this personally is because you are Mr. Shultz's grandson. . . . The only e-mail on this topic I want to see from you going forward is an apology that I'll pass on to other people."[7]

Before we go further, let's consider whether Balwani was acting as a negative advocate for Holmes in writing this e-mail. It's not unusual that a negative advocate will take bullying actions on behalf of a bully to whom they are loyal, even though they are not ordinarily a bully. On the other hand, Holmes later claimed that Balwani, who was twenty years older than her, controlled her and that she was under his influence in how she ran the company.

Was she his negative advocate? Unlikely. He came to the company years after she had already been misleading pharmaceutical companies about the readiness of her technology. Later information indicates that this was a case of two bullies who found each other, so that neither made the other act like a bully.

Tyler immediately resigned after getting Balwani's e-mail. But then he got a call from his mother, who had received a call from his grandfather who had received a call from Holmes warning him that Tyler would not win if he continued his dissension against her.[8] Tyler was dumbfounded. He went to speak to his grandfather at his office. He explained everything and showed him the e-mails.

But his grandfather defended Holmes. "They're trying to convince me that you're stupid. They can't convince me that you're stupid. They can, however, convince me that you're wrong, and in this case I do believe that you're wrong."[9] This is a classic example of how a negative advocate can get emotionally hooked to totally believe and advocate for the bully and turn against his own family.

Once a negative advocate has committed to defending a bully, despite hearing contradictory information, they may remain stuck in that role. This seems to be a combination of emotional repetition and being on one side of a polarized dispute, which I explain more in Chapter 12. Briefly, once you have committed to a position with your "team," your confidence in the team's perspective increases and your ability to take in outside contradictory information decreases. Brain research tells us that this is a form of *confirmation bias*, in that once you have made a decision about what you believe, your neurons will continue to process information that confirms your position but that "disconfirmatory evidence processing is abolished."[10] Once again, as described in the prior chapter on emotional repetition, our brains aim for efficiency and therefore don't want to waste time and energy on matters that we think have already been resolved. Therefore, shaking negative advocates free from their favorable, but mistaken, beliefs about their "heroes" can be hard—when they are actually bullies.

But remember that different people have different personalities, with different responses to a bully's primitive emotional power. One person's primitive emotional response may be to accept and endorse a bully's behavior with excuses as a loyal negative advocate. Another may see the truth about what's happening and read the writing on the wall, finally pulling the plug on their support of the bully and never becoming a negative advocate. Remember, negative advocates are emotionally hooked. Without accepting that emotional hook, someone may be a supporter but not one who disregards reality, as described below.

HOW YOU CAN STOP THIS POWER

1. Open Your Eyes to the Pattern

When someone intensely defends someone who appears to be a bully, recognize that you may be dealing with a negative advocate—someone who is emotionally hooked and therefore may not listen to reason. Most negative advocates are not themselves bullies by nature, but some are. Ask them to give you details about the situation. Listen to see if they appear to have been conned by a bully's story. Have they caught the PEP of a bully with escalated emotions? Are they emotionally demanding that you do something on the bully's behalf?

Many bullies have an entourage of negative advocates who follow them into their battles, whether with the people around them, at work, in their communities (like Rashid with Carlos earlier in this chapter), or in their frequent legal disputes. Just picture high school mean girls or boys in gangs. Bullies need their negative advocates with them to protect them from the consequences of their negative actions.

Consider this tendency to always involve other people as a possible warning sign of a bully. Keep in mind that bullies demand loyalty from their negative advocates but don't care about them in return. It's very much a one-way street. It's also not unusual for bullies to abandon their negative advocates when they don't appear loyal enough.

Many negative advocates are family members who are used to defending their bully over many years and will not change their minds although other family members may want nothing to do with the bully. Some negative advocates are new to the situation as neighbors, friends, coworkers, and even professionals. They just want to help and may advocate for the bully because they are emotionally hooked but uninformed and believe that the bully has been treated badly. By giving such negative advocates more accurate and complete information, they may abandon—or even turn against—the bully. Be realistic. Some do and some don't. Keep your eyes open, be cautious, and don't be surprised.

2. Pull the Plug on the Bully

Whatever you do, don't become a negative advocate yourself! If you realize that a bully has roped you into becoming one, stop immediately—and blow the whistle on the bully as quickly as you can. If you sense that someone else is trying to emotionally hook you, step back. Double- and triple-check—from multiple, diverse sources—the story of a crisis, villain, and hero that you have been told. If you hear someone telling a story that could be a bully's story, ask yourself, *Is this really true? Or am I being told BS by one of their negative advocates?*

For example, in the Theranos case described earlier, some of the board members finally heard the information that the company was committing fraud with its promotion of false information and ineffective devices. Eventually, some of the board members resigned, most notably former U.S. Secretary of Defense General James Mattis. In 2021 Mattis testified against Holmes at her trial for defrauding investors. He pulled the plug on his support for her. She was eventually sentenced to over eleven years in prison for her convictions on four counts of investor fraud.

Did she care about the investors she had defrauded, the patients whose blood tests she faked, and others whose lives she tried to ruin along the way? Here's how investigative journalist John Carreyrou described her at the end of his book *Bad Blood:*

> With actions that ranged from blackmailing her chief financial officer to suing ex-employees, she had displayed a pattern of ruthlessness at odds with the portrait of a well-intentioned young woman manipulated by an older man. . . . A sociopath is often described as someone with little or no conscience. I'll leave it to the psychologists to decide whether Holmes fits the clinical profile, but there's no question that her moral compass was badly askew. . . . Her ambition was voracious, and it brooked no interference. If there was collateral damage on her way to riches and fame, so be it.[11]

Carreyrou seems to be discussing a bully with an antisocial personality (also known as a sociopath). Remember, bullies lack the brakes that most people have to stop themselves, and lack of remorse is one of the characteristics of someone with an antisocial personality. Therefore, it took a whistleblower, an investigative journalist, and the courts to stop her. While she was enabled for quite a while by her negative advocates, ultimately she was stopped when more than one of them pulled the plug.

3. Set Limits with Credible Threats on Negative Advocates

Although bullies' negative advocates are not usually bullies by nature, they often get coerced by bullies (or other negative advocates) into bullying behavior. This means that you need to set limits on negative advocates in the same way you would with a bully. You may have to threaten to withhold your friendship, end your cooperation or relationship, or even withdraw all contact with them. If a negative advocate is not inherently a bully themselves, such a threat can often be swiftly and profoundly effective.

For example, Barbara is an adult daughter who has had intense conflicts with her mother her whole life. She finally figured out that her mother has traits of borderline personality disorder, which explains why she acts like a bully and often screams at her daughter. She can't seem to stop herself. Barbara has built a life for herself two states away from her parents and has mostly cut ties with her mom. On the other hand, she stays in touch with her father, who recognizes that his wife has a problem, but will not confront her about it or pressure her to get help. Barbara and her dad secretly call each other on a regular basis.

At some point, the father starts getting a lot of pressure from the mother to reconnect her with Barbara. So Dad starts telling Barbara, "You have to understand your mother. You have to give her a break. She means well, she just can't control her anger and doesn't want to. She says she wouldn't be true to herself if she didn't express her opinions fully."

"Dad," Barbara said, "you know that's BS. Adults don't do that to each other. If you really want to help her, then you need to be part of some kind of intervention to get her some treatment for her problems."

"You know I'll never do that, Barbara," her father replied. "Just come and visit and start talking with her again."

Barbara doesn't want to go through that again. "Dad, if you're going to defend her behavior and even keep talking about her, I'm not going to call you. I spent too many years afraid of her anger, and I'm much happier now without her constant criticism and yelling at me. If you want to defend her and apologize for her and pressure me to talk to her, then I'm going to stop calling you. If you're willing to talk about anything else, then let's stay in touch. It's up to you."

Barbara has set limits with a credible threat with her father, who is the primary negative advocate for her mother. In some cases like this, the negative advocate bends and agrees to stop trying to get the mother and daughter back together. In other cases, the father just can't stop himself from being a negative advocate and the relationship with the adult child grows more distant and estranged.

Someday, with more public awareness about bullies, family members will set better limits on their bullies and no longer become negative advocates. Then they should be able to play a more positive role in pressuring them to get some form of treatment for their behavior. Since there are counseling treatments for borderline and narcissistic bullies, getting them into such counseling should become more of an option, as it is now for drug and alcohol treatment.

4. Impose Serious Consequences on Negative Advocates

Bullies usually need one or more negative advocates to succeed in their bullying. Fortunately, most negative advocates, unless they are natural bullies themselves, can be far more responsive to serious consequences than bullies.

For example, it's rare to see a prolonged, high-conflict court case without one or more professionals becoming a negative advocate (lawyer, therapist, etc.). Stopping multiple negative advocates in their tracks often results in stopping the bullies who recruited and encouraged them. This is how criminal prosecutors often work their cases. They get the lower-level offenders to give evidence about the higher-level criminals. The lower-level offenders, even though they were negative advocates when the going was good, are often less invested in the criminal scheme of the bully and want to avoid serious sentences, so they often cooperate with the authorities and testify against their bullies.

5. Communicate Effectively About Bullies' Negative Advocates to Others—Including Negative Advocates Themselves

Remind people who have been exposed to a bully's story that just because prominent folks—or large numbers of folks—believe or say something, that doesn't make it true. When you sense that someone has become—or is in danger of becoming—a bully's negative advocate, don't just shrug your shoulders. Speak up. Swiftly and firmly take a stand against both the bully and their negative advocate (or potential negative advocate).

For example, if it seems appropriate and safe, take the negative advocate aside and explain how they have become hoodwinked by the bully and their bully's story. Don't argue with them or blame them; just provide accurate information so that they can see how they have been misled. Once informed—especially if they are risking their own reputations—many negative advocates bail out on the bully. When they finally get it that the bully is about to be exposed, they realize they don't want to be associated with the fallout. This is what Tyler Shultz tried to do with his grandfather as he tried to explain how the company was in big trouble because of its many technical deficits. Unfortunately, George Shultz could not accept that his wonderful young CEO was doing anything wrong and continued to be her negative advocate even against his own grandson.

6. Stand Strong with Others Against Bullies and Their Negative Advocates

When even one or two negative advocates are resisted, confronted, and turned against the bully, other negative advocates may follow their lead. This is why the first and most effective step in stopping a bully can often be identifying and facing down their negative advocates. When fully informed, some back off or abandon their bully all together.

In general, ask yourself these questions if you are dealing with a possible negative advocate.

Is so-and-so serving as a negative advocate for a bully by

- Excusing their negative behavior as nothing important?
- Justifying their negative behavior by pointing fingers at others?
- Trying to convince you to tolerate the bully's behavior?
- Trying to convince you to support the bully and have you try to persuade others to do so too (i.e., trying to get you to be a negative advocate too)?
- Wanting you to be a character witness for the bully with others?
- Wanting you to bail out the bully—with financial assistance, by vouching for the bully to others, or fighting for the bully against his or her perceived enemies?

If so, then stand with those who are trying to stop the bully and their negative advocates. These dynamics can be subtle, but now you know what to watch out for. And don't let yourself become a negative advocate.

For example, Ghislaine Maxwell appears to have become a negative advocate for Jeffrey Epstein, the man accused of having sex with numerous teenage girls (discussed in Chapter 5). Why? Was she predisposed to becoming a negative advocate, like Rashid in the example earlier in this chapter? Would the girls set limits on her and help impose consequences by standing together someday?

Maxwell may be an example of someone who was predisposed personality-wise to be a negative advocate for someone like Jeffrey. She was the ninth child of a wealthy British businessman and apparently his favorite. She grew up being doted on. Her father may have been engaged in some criminal activities and he died as an apparent suicide when some of his actions were becoming exposed, including significantly stealing from his employees' pension fund.[12] Perhaps some antisocial personality genes or behavior ran in the family.

After ending a relationship with Epstein, she remained a very close friend and was eventually charged with recruiting, grooming, and helping him sexually assault teenage girls as young as thirteen. Many people described her as his enabler. Maxwell "walked the girls into a room where she knew that man would molest them," a prosecutor, Lara Pomerantz, said in the government's opening statement. "She knew what was going to happen to those girls."[13]

One of the high school girls Maxwell recruited for sex, Virginia Giuffre, would also become a negative advocate, recruiting other girls for Epstein and getting paid as a staff person. It appears that she, as well as many of the others, may have been primed somewhat for this because of coming from troubled homes and needing love and money (he typically paid them $200).

Eventually Maxwell distanced herself from Epstein and created a life of her own. But it was too late. He was arrested for a second time in 2019 and in jail awaiting trial when he allegedly committed suicide.

Maxwell hid for a while after Epstein's suicide but was finally caught and tried for her role as his advocate. Her argument at trial was that she was just a friend and knew nothing about his sex life. But there was too much evidence against her, with so many girls testifying against her, including Giuffre, the one who had become a staff person. Maxwell was convicted for recruiting the girls and sentenced to twenty years in a Florida prison. Several of his victims said that her involvement as a seemingly "nice" woman made them trust going to Jeffrey's house. This is often the role of a negative advocate for a bully who otherwise would not have been trusted.

But even negative advocates can go to prison when their victims stand together, as happened in this case. The court case against Maxwell happened primarily because the teen girls got together as adults and were willing to testify against her. One of the key witnesses was Giuffre, the teenager who had been a victim and temporarily worked for them. She had become a negative advocate, but not forever.[14] When negative advocates turn on bigger negative advocates, justice can be done.

CONCLUSION

Bullies frequently recruit negative advocates to agree with them, make them look better to others, help them avoid consequences for their actions, and sometimes do their dirty work. This is a concept also known as "enabling," because others enable the bully to keep on doing the bad behavior he or she is doing.

Look for negative advocates when you are wondering whether someone is a bully. Almost all bullies have them, often many of them. You can spot them because they take on the characteristics of a bully: blaming others, all-or-nothing thinking, unmanaged emotions (sometimes), extreme behaviors, and a drive to dominate or destroy you. Sometimes they are even more extreme than the bully in order to impress the bully.

Yet negative advocates can be stopped. They are not usually bullies themselves but people who have become emotionally hooked by the bully's intense fear, anger, charm, or false loving behavior. Sometimes you can turn around negative advocates by informing them of the whole picture and how it is not the bully's story they have been told. Sometimes negative advocates can change their perspective after being informed of what is really going on and become positive advocates to help calm down a bully and straighten them out a little. Sometimes negative advocates just bail out on the bully like Maxwell tried to do by developing a separate life, but it was too late. And sometimes the bully bails out on the negative advocate, like Epstein did by committing suicide.

In short, don't be a negative advocate and don't be intimidated by negative advocates. You can spot them, and you can stop them, along with their bullies—especially when you join forces with others whom they have harmed.

COMMON MISTAKE:

When people defend someone who has bad behavior and vouch for them, then the person must be okay and there's no need to check further.

REALITY:

When people strongly defend someone's bad behavior, it usually means they have become negative advocates who are emotionally hooked and uninformed or may be bullies themselves. You need to check further.

CHAPTER 9

The Power of Projection and Playing the Victim

Authorities investigating the killing of a veteran
Las Vegas journalist, Jeff German, said Thursday that
they found D.N.A. at the crime scene that matched a
public official who had been the subject of
Mr. German's recent reporting.

—"Authorities Say D.N.A. Links Las Vegas Official
to Killing of Reporter," *New York Times*

A BULLY OFTEN FALSELY ACCUSES OTHERS of being bullies and doing the bad acts that the bully is actually doing, sometimes in full view of everyone. Often the surprising level of detail in a projection-based bully's story makes it even more compelling. But the detail comes from their own behavior, which they project onto their target.

Projection is a concept that has been around for more than a hundred years, dating back to Sigmund Freud and others. The idea is that a person can't psychologically tolerate certain of their own thoughts, feelings, or behavior, so they "project" them onto other people like a movie screen and address them as though they belonged to that other person. This is usually an unconscious process of which they are totally unaware. Because of the power of projection, you can often predict the bully's future actions by what they accuse their target of doing right now.

For example, a person who feels angry at a loved one may not be able to tolerate this anger for unconscious reasons (fear of losing the loved one, a habit of repressing certain emotions, etc.). Therefore, he or she says to the loved one, "Why are you angry at me?" Loved one says: "I'm not angry at you." Projecting person says, "Yes, you are. I can feel it." And pretty soon the loved one starts getting irritated at being falsely accused and starts getting angry. "See, I knew it!" says the projecting person. If the loved one recognizes this projection, it can help them realize that the projecting person is mad at them for something or may be intending to do something for which you will get mad at them in the future. See if you can figure that out.

You can see the conflicts that projection often causes. The projecting person can't connect the dots back to their own feelings and behavior. This projection can carry a lot of emotional intensity against their loved one because of their frustration. But the loved one can't do something to make it better, because it's all occurring inside the projecting person's own head. While many people project occasionally, bullies do this a lot.

Bullies also often pretend to be the victim, consciously or unconsciously. "Playing the victim" can be particularly seductive in attracting negative advocates—family members, friends, and even professionals such as lawyers, therapists, and others—who just want to help a person in need. It is essential that you recognize this dynamic in others so that you don't get emotionally hooked into helping a bully by joining an attack on their real victim because you think the bully is *their* victim.

If you're the target of a bully and their negative advocate(s), recognizing when someone is playing the victim will help you understand exactly what is happening to you—and what to do about it. Don't become immobilized, and don't get angry at the negative advocates. Educate them if you can. If it's safe, show them how the bully is playing the victim and that's why they are so emotional about an often nonexistent problem they are attributing to you. If it's not safe, get help.

The Las Vegas Reporter

Let's look now at an example of a bully claiming to be a victim and projecting onto his true victim. This bully may have believed his own projections, which proved disastrous for his victim—and himself.

Jeff German was a journalist in Las Vegas for forty years, reporting on violent crime, mob chaos, and corrupt politicians. Robert Telles was the head of the small government office that administers estates for beneficiaries who are unable to handle them on their own. German got wind of tension in Telles's office and did some digging. Employees told him they "had been subject to bullying" and that the stress of working under Telles "had begun to affect their physical health." He demeaned them; gave them extra, unnecessary assignments; and even had tried to dig up dirt on them. One assistant retired after three decades "because of the situation."[1]

After these negative articles by German were published, Telles lost a reelection campaign to a top supervisor from his own office. "Typical bully," Telles wrote of German, criticizing his reporting. About two months later, Telles went to German's residence, convinced him to step outside, then stabbed him to death! Shortly afterward, Telles was arrested and put in jail with no bail. Authorities reported, "They found D.N.A. at the crime scene that matched a public official who had been the subject of Mr. German's recent reporting."[2]

In his trial for murder, Telles represented himself. Soon he got caught up in arguments about a police investigation that was ongoing before the killing occurred. He was reportedly involved in a scheme to flip houses that were being sold after being managed by his office. But Telles complained that *he was the victim* of police misconduct, claiming that "during the investigation into German's killing, police illegally tracked his phone and didn't properly request search warrants." He also claimed that he was framed.[3]

This case helps us understand how serious projection (that the other person is a bully) and playing the victim (police did it all wrong) can be. Someone is dead, and this court case is complicated by the defendant's perceptions that he is a victim of the police. He can't seem to look back at his own behavior and may never have been able to do so.

The case also raises the question of whether bullies know they are projecting and playing the victim or whether they really believe the stories they tell themselves. My experience tells me that they often really do believe they are victims, which is why arguing with them is pointless and may be dangerous.

Hate Crimes

This dynamic of projection and playing the victim appears to be prevalent in hate crimes. A bully projects onto a whole group (race, sex, religion, etc.) that they are acting badly, and the bully believes that he is their victim. Targeting a member of such a group can make it a hate crime.

One such example is the killing of twenty-three people and wounding of twenty-two others at a supermarket in El Paso, Texas, in 2019, a city that is 80 percent Latino. The gunman specifically said that he was targeting "Mexicans." It has been considered the largest anti-Latino attack in modern U.S. history. The FBI investigated it as one of the largest acts of domestic terrorism. In 2023 the gunman pled guilty to ninety murder and hate crime charges and received a sentence of ninety consecutive life sentences.[4]

The gunman wrote a manifesto showing that he believed in the "Great Replacement Theory," which had recently been circulated by some cultural leaders. This theory is that "white women are not having enough children and that falling birthrates will lead to white people around the world being replaced by nonwhite people." Those subscribing to this theory see it as a threat to their existence and blame it significantly on women working instead of raising families.[5]

This man's fear that somehow nonwhite people would hurt him justified in his mind the idea that he should hurt them. This seems certainly like a projection because no one had "replaced" the gunman, but his own actions ended the lives of so many nonwhite people and injured so many others. He did what he feared they would do to him. He also played the victim by claiming that he was losing out to nonwhite people when, in fact, he drove to another state to victimize them. This demonstrates how dangerous projection and playing the victim can be. Yet some cultural leaders in the media and politics appear to promote bullies' stories like this in order to get attention and power over others.

Most hate crimes are directed toward one individual, yet it is because of their group membership that they become someone's target of blame. For example, looking at just one year in one state, here are some of the statistics compiled by the California Department of Justice:

> Hate crimes soared in California in 2022, with year-over-year increases recorded in incidents targeting virtually every demographic group, according to a report released Tuesday. Overall, hate crime events—which officials say are likely under-reported—increased 20.2 percent in 2022, from 1,763 in 2021 to 2,120, figures from the California Department of Justice show. The numbers of such events have risen 145.7 percent since 2013.[6]

It seems clear that the idea of feeling like a victim and having the right to attack other people—to project one's own anger and sometimes violence toward others—is spreading in our current culture of bullying. Why? In looking at these statistics, the California State attorney general said, "Hate-filled rhetoric fills our social media feeds and dominates the news cycles. . . . It infiltrates our schools and our community gatherings. It seems to be at so many places; it's so pervasive."[7]

Yet it's important to understand that those who engage in such hate crimes are not ordinary people influenced by our culture. These are bullies whose restraints have been *released* by our culture. When cultural leaders project a sense of dangerousness onto a subgroup of people and then tell another group of people that they are going to be victims of this subgroup, it's not surprising that this can lead to violence.

Remember from Chapter 4: Bullies make it personal. They attack your person, not just your ideas or behavior. Theories like this one create a fantasy crisis and then point the finger at their fantasy villains. This activates primitive fear and rage—often unconsciously—which then can mobilize murderous action by someone who wants to be a (fantasy) hero. When messages of projection and playing the victim are repeated enough, they aren't just words—they are activating primitive emotional responses that seem crazy but are actually quite predictable when you understand these dynamics. That's why most people restrain themselves from using such words.

Internet Bullies

One of the easiest places to project all your negative thoughts, feelings, and behavior is the Wild West of the Internet. There are no consequences most of the time, and you can find like-minded people who can share feeling like a victim with you. Yet has the Internet made all of us into bullies?

While it seems like everyone is becoming more hostile online, two researchers have found otherwise. Across eight different studies, they found that "being online did not make most people more aggressive or hostile; rather, it allowed a small number of aggressive people to attack a much larger set of victims." They also identified that small group of people as "status-driven individuals who are drawn to politics and are equally hostile both online and offline." But they explain that online discussions *feel* more hostile because their aggressive behavior is more visible online.[8]

In other words, online bullies are most likely this small group of aggressive "status-driven individuals" who lack the normal restraints of most people on the Internet. Most of us tend to blame ourselves when there is a conflict and try to figure out what to do differently. Bullies blame others, not themselves. Since this doesn't solve problems, they just keep blaming and blaming, with the Internet making this super easy for them.

If we hold bullies responsible and set limits on them, it will change the whole culture. That's one of the main themes of this book. You can't do it all alone. But be aware that when people try to set limits on bullies, they play the victim. They insist that they (or they and their cronies and followers) are being victimized by terrible fantasy villains (which could include you), who might then appear to be bullies to the uninformed observer. The more people understand these dynamics, the more effective we can all be.

HOW YOU CAN STOP THIS POWER

1. Open Your Eyes to the Pattern

When a person tells you that someone else is acting very badly, recognize that they could be projecting. When someone claims to be a victim of someone else, recognize that they could be playing the victim. Don't just take them at their word. Instead, here is a way to regularly think about such claims: Consider three possibilities, especially if they want you to take action against their alleged villain(s). I call this the "3 Theories of the Case."

3 Theories of the Case

1. The allegation of bad behavior is true.

2. The allegation of bad behavior is not true. The accuser is the one who is acting badly and who is likely projecting their own behavior onto the innocent person, who is not acting badly.

3. Both are acting badly—that is, the situation involves two bullies who are trying to dominate or destroy each other.

By keeping an open mind with these three theories, you are less likely to inadvertently become a negative advocate for anyone—especially someone who is projecting or playing the victim. Think it through if someone wants you to take extreme urgent action because of what *they say* someone else said or did. Consider how credible the person is who is telling you this. If you know the person is very credible, then do what you can. Otherwise, maintain a healthy skepticism.

In many situations, things are not very clear. Therefore, consider these three possibilities before taking action on someone else's behalf. If you are doubtful or unsure, it can help to say to yourself or out loud, "You might be right. I wasn't there. I'll never know. While I can see your frustration [or fear or anger], I would need to know a whole lot more before I would take any action in this situation."

Give yourself time to figure out if anyone in a dispute may be projecting or playing the victim. These questions may help:

Does anyone have a history of lying or exaggerating?

Does anyone appear disproportionately angry, sad, or helpless?

Does anyone regularly avoid responsibility for their own actions?

Does anyone regularly blame others for what appears to be their own behavior?

Does anyone repeatedly present himself or herself as a victim in life?

Can anyone else shed some light on what it going on? Can they confirm the story?

2. Pull the Plug on the Bully

After looking into a potential bully's story, as suggested, if you figure out that a bully wants you to help them by projecting or playing the victim, then withhold or withdraw your support.

For example, in one family court case, a wife alleged that her former husband had been violent with her every day for a week. She submitted a declaration with plenty of detail to this effect. The judge issued a restraining order against her husband, which included removing him from the family residence. At the next hearing, the husband provided evidence that he had been out of the state when the alleged abuse occurred. The wife's attorney asked for her detailed declaration, which was entirely false, to be removed from the file, and the restraining order was dropped.

As the case progressed it became obvious that *she* was a bully, not him. Rather than accepting her behavior, he and his attorney assertively explained to the judge that her stories were false and provided useful evidence to expose them. While it would have been tempting to just move on to other issues, they felt it important to speak up so that there would be no momentum for future false allegations, of which there were many. They pulled the plug on her behavior by exposing each false statement until the court clearly understood what was happening and imposed financial penalties on her for lying.

3. Set Limits with Credible Threats

Make it clear to the bully that if their dramatic story turns out to be partly or wholly untrue, you will act swiftly and vigorously to hold them accountable. This might involve blowing the whistle on them to their boss (or their boss's boss), or reporting the bully to an ethical board, or filing charges against them. Decision-makers should consider all three theories of the case and hold people accountable if their stories turn out to be false.

For example, laws have been passed to restrain Internet scammers from falsely claiming that they are victims of crises and that people should send them money. Such fraudulent behavior can earn them fines or imprisonment under federal laws, such as 18 U.S. Code Section 1030, "Fraud and related activity in connection with computers." Is this a credible threat? See below.

4. Impose Serious Consequences

Bullies must always be severely (and, whenever possible, swiftly) punished for making false or misleading accusations or important statements, so that they are dissuaded from such further behavior—and so others are protected. Claiming crises in which they are victims can be one of the most effective ways of misleading unsuspecting people and getting their money.

For example, the "grandparent scam" was a nationwide scam that involved calling people in their seventies and eighties and telling them that they needed to send money to keep their young adult grandchild out of jail. In one case, an eighty-seven-year-old woman was tricked by a young woman pretending to be her granddaughter "saying she needed nine thousand dollars bail money after a serious car crash." Then, the next day, the young woman demanded another $42,000 "or she would face manslaughter charges and several years in prison." The older woman was supposed to keep all this secret and not discuss it with anyone. But a week later the young woman demanded another $57,000 because the "granddaughter" had broken the "gag order" that they "falsely claimed a judge had made ordering her not to discuss the case or her payments with anyone."[9]

Altogether, eight con artists swindled over seventy people across the country out of more than $2 million over the Internet. The first person to be sentenced received nearly four years in prison and has to pay restitution of over $400,000. The judge called the case "heartbreak-ingly evil." The case, which made national news, was investigated by the San Diego Elder Justice Task Force.[10]

This is a good example of how bullies can take advantage of anyone. In this case, the bullies were playing the victim for cash. Fortunately, there are now agencies starting to help set limits and help the courts impose consequences for such people. Remember, bullies can't stop themselves and will use modern means for newer and more dramatic fraudulent schemes. They lack a conscience in most cases, and they can reach across the country and around the world, so that not many people need to be involved in these scams to impact dozens or hundreds of unsuspecting victims. But law enforcement and other agencies are joining forces to catch these bullies, so that more are now getting caught and facing consequences for their bullying behavior. Still, everyone needs to learn about these bully behaviors so that, as much as possible, they don't get conned in the first place.

5. Communicate Effectively to Others About Bullies

Most people are unfamiliar with the power of projection or don't realize when it's happening. Furthermore, most simply cannot imagine that a bully would accuse their own victim of being the bully. This would seem outrageously cruel, and it is. But that doesn't stop bullies— it often appeals to them.

Explain to others—especially decision-makers, such as managers, police officers, judges, and school principals—how the power of projection works. Encourage them to consider that projection may be involved whenever someone makes extreme or detailed accusations about someone else. Otherwise, they can easily get emotionally hooked by a bully's story and come down hard on the bully's target. This is the complete opposite of what actually needs to be done. It also further isolates the bully's victim, who then feels even more alone and helpless.

For example, suppose a coworker, Rafael, comes to you complaining that another member of your work group, Latanya, is not doing her share of the work on a current project with a deadline coming up. "She's really not pulling her weight," he says. "I can't carry the whole team on this project, even though I understand it better than anyone else. Either she's too slow or too stupid to know what she's doing. Would you tell our supervisor that she's holding us up? I've got an important meeting to get to."

What would you do? Keep in mind that Rafael and Latanya and you are all equal members of this team. Ideally, you should consider the 3 Theories of the Case. First, maybe what Rafael is saying is true, and it would be appropriate for you or Rafael to tell the supervisor. If you're wise about office politics, you would usually want to tell Rafael to talk to the supervisor himself. Why get caught in the middle, especially when you don't know the details of the situation?

Second, you should consider the possibility that Rafael is the problem, not Latanya. Rafael sounds like he has a superior attitude with some of his comments: "I understand better than anyone else." "She's too stupid." "I've got an important meeting." This all might be true, but if you were really going to get involved, you would need to check out whether Rafael has a reputation for being arrogant and whether his statements are accurate or exaggerations.

Third, consider the possibility that both Rafael and Latanya are being difficult. Do all this before taking a position on what's happening—and if possible, don't take a position at all. If you do take one person's side, and one of them is a bully, you will be setting yourself up to become part of a conflict that may not have an end in sight.

The 3 Theories of the Case is such a simple and self-protective approach. You are encouraged to communicate this approach to everyone you care about. Tell them about projection, playing the victim, and not jumping to conclusions. It's one of the best ways to avoid getting stuck enabling a bully or fighting a bully unnecessarily.

6. Stand Strong with Others Against Bullies

When friends, family members, coworkers, or community members accuse others of horrible behavior, look into whether the accused is truly acting badly or if the accuser is acting badly. Keep an open mind. Let people know you are seriously considering the 3 Theories of the Case without jumping to conclusions. Once you figure it out, stand strongly with those who are setting limits on bullies or otherwise stopping them. The following is a good example of handling a public dispute,

Middletown, Ohio, is a small city of about 50,000 people. Marlon Styles was hired as the superintendent of their city schools in 2017 and brought an optimistic and creative energy to the community. However, at an August 2021 school board meeting he became the target. Comments were made objecting to the mask policy of the district, which started out voluntary but became mandatory temporarily when COVID-19 cases suddenly increased. Someone said, "Currently, this room, this meeting, is our battlefield. Right now, what is at stake is the physical and mental health of our children. . . . These masks are being forced on our children."[11]

Then it became more personal about Superintendent Styles, who is Black. He had recently explained a six-year strategic plan at an earlier board meeting and mentioned the term "culturally responsive discipline" in his presentation. This earned him the wrath of the Keller family, who claimed that Styles was bringing "woke CRT ideology" to the district instead of education. Kent Keller warned, "It's indoctrination. . . . You've awoken grassroots parents, mobilizing a movement to bring back common sense and stop division in this country."[12]

Soon after these comments, the enraged group got up and walked out of the meeting. Styles didn't respond to those comments. Later, a video clip started circulating of him saying "culturally responsive" and "equity." He made his own video to explain what all those words meant and invited the angry parents to come to his office and talk about the facts. But that wasn't enough, so he asked for help from his friends who were religious leaders in the Middletown Area Ministerial Alliance. He asked them if the comments at the previous school board meeting were "representative of our community." They all said no.

Interestingly, the complaint that Styles was "creating division" appears to have been a projection. It is really easy to absorb those kinds of statements as being about the "other side" of a dispute if you are not thinking about it. These kinds of words should trigger a healthy skepticism and the 3 Theories of the Case.

The feedback from the ministerial alliance was to "keep the main thing as their main thing. In this case: the kids. Remind them that, no matter the disagreements over theology or pedagogy or even public health, *all* belong."[13]

At the next school board meeting, members of the alliance asked for time during public comments. After some initial angry comments, they took their turns. One after another, they spoke of the strengths of Middletown, the resilience of students, and their commitment to support their institutions and their leaders. Black and white citizens spoke about considering the most vulnerable, hiring local youth, and naming a new wing of the school to honor a young white student who had died from child abuse—to raise awareness. These leaders and other "positive gossipers" attended the next eight school board meetings, "widening the frame" to put important context into each of the discussions.

Eighteen months later, Mr. Styles retired from the district and now advises other superintendents on creating "learner-centered environments." His main advice: "I realized . . . that you can ask for help. I decided to take action by stepping back and leaning into the community leaders whose life work is to serve others. . . . Every school community has a quiet majority. Authentically and genuinely reach out to them."[14]

By standing together, it is possible to overcome the bullying behavior of a few unrestrained individuals. When you are blamed for being divisive or inappropriate, rather than arguing with that projection, demonstrate how unifying and open to viewpoints you really are.

CONCLUSION

As these examples have shown, projection is a common occurrence with bullies. Now that you know about this, you should be able to spot it fairly easily. Always ask yourself: Is the criticism they are saying true about another person, or is it a projection of what they are thinking, feeling, or doing themselves? Sometimes this will help you predict what they are actually planning to do in the future.

The fact that they can't see that they are projecting their own behavior is a big problem, because bullies honestly believe that others are thinking, feeling, and doing what the bullies themselves are actually thinking, feeling, and doing. This can make them more dangerous toward those whom they are projecting onto, who often have no idea why they are being attacked. It's not really about them; it's about the bully's personality. Always keep projection in mind as a possibility whenever you hear a dramatic story of a crisis, a villain, and a hero so that you don't get emotionally hooked and inadvertently become a negative advocate with the bully against their victims.

Playing the victim is also common for bullies. Some do it unconsciously because of their projections, and some do it consciously when they are intentionally conning people. They are good at getting sympathy from this action. Therefore, it's always good to consider this possibility when someone tells you that they have been treated terribly by someone else and you start feeling bad for them. Remember that their primitive emotional power often triggers primitive emotional responses inside you that are neither rational nor helpful. Get the facts.

Many of a bully's stories include projection and playing the victim. Keep in mind that they often come to believe their own (false) bully's stories, even though they sometimes deliberately and strategically concocted those stories in the first place. Projection operates unconsciously for many bullies. Don't be surprised that they won't see it even though it may be obvious to everyone else.

Most of all, don't get drawn into arguing with them and telling them that they are projecting or playing the victim. Remember, they lack self-awareness and can be highly defensive. Keep that in mind when you develop your own strategies for dealing with this power.

COMMON MISTAKE:

When someone says somebody else is hurting them, this is always true and they need protecting without question.

REALITY:

When bullies blame others for being hurtful, they are often projecting their own behavior onto others and playing the victim when they are actually the perpetrator. Check it out.

CHAPTER 10

The Power of Surprise Attacks

"Madness and scaremongering continues,"
Mr. Polyanskiy wrote on Twitter. "What if we would
say that US could seize London in a week and cause
300K civilian deaths? Would it feel right
for Americans and Brits? It's as wrong
for Russians and Ukrainians."

—Russian deputy ambassador to the United Nations, two weeks
before invasion of Ukraine, denying any such plans

BY NOW YOU KNOW THAT MANY OF THE POWERS OF BULLIES are hidden in plain sight. All put together, they are the PEP formula that works on our primitive emotions beneath general awareness. However, bullies catch most people by surprise, and that still may happen to you, because they are skilled at surprise attacks. Developing a healthy skepticism may protect you from most of these surprises.

In general, people don't realize that *anyone* can become the target of a bully. They think that happens only to weak people or people who are used to being victims. Most people operate assuming that everyone in their lives will be reasonable and follow the rules. This leaves them unprepared—and disoriented—as a result when a bully targets them.

Bullies use surprise attacks to immobilize their targets, preventing them from understanding what is happening and organizing a strong response. A surprise attack shuts down most people's logical thinking and triggers our primitive emotional responses of doing whatever it takes to survive. This usually means fleeing, freezing, or submitting. Rarely do people fight back when caught by surprise, which works to bullies' advantage. Surprise attacks are one of the most common primitive emotional powers in the PEP formula.

When caught by surprise, many targets simply submit to the bully because the bully quickly gets into their head. Some few fight back, but the bully is usually more prepared, more powerful, and more experienced. Since bullies don't restrain themselves, they are willing to break the rules to get what they want. Worse, today's technologies have enabled bullies everywhere to anonymously attack targets anywhere in the world. Everyone needs to have a healthy awareness of this possibility, without becoming immobilized, so that they are less likely to be caught by surprise.

Swatting

Swatting is a term that describes calling emergency services to harass someone by sending out a SWAT (Special Weapons and Tactics) team for a fictitious emergency. It has been used by bullies in a variety of scenarios. The following are two examples of people who have engaged in swatting with tragic consequences—and gotten caught.

Mark Herring was a grandfather who loved technology and became enthusiastic about social media faster than most. He joined Twitter in 2007 and, living in Tennessee, he grabbed the handle "@ Tennessee." Over the years, he got several offers to sell his Twitter handle for thousands of dollars. But he wouldn't budge.

Then a young man named Shane Sonderman decided to lead a plot to bully Herring into giving up his beloved Twitter handle. Previously, Sonderman had bullied at least five people in efforts to force them to give him their social media handles, and if they didn't, he organized various ways to harass them. Once he sent a firetruck to a woman's parents' house and said afterward, "did your parent's enjoy the firetrucks? . . . i plan on killing your parents next if you do not hand the username on instrgam over to me."[1]

Sonderman acquired Herring's contact information and posted it on the Internet. In April 2020 a coconspirator of Sonderman (a teenager in the United Kingdom) called the police pretending to be Herring. He claimed that there was a murder of a woman and pipe bomb threat at his address. The police sent out a SWAT team and surrounded his house. They demanded that he come out with his hands visible. When Herring came out and saw all the police pointing guns at him, he suffered a massive heart attack and died.[2]

Herring clearly never imagined having a SWAT team surround his home, pointing their powerful weapons at him. Who could have imagined such a thing? It was so shocking, it killed him. And it must have been shocking to the police too! Could they have imagined that they would be used for such an evil scheme?

But this isn't the only such case. Did you know that this has been going on for years?

While this was apparently first used to harass celebrities, it has grown in recent times. In 2017, Tyler Barriss, a man known to friends as a "professional swatter," made a 911 call to police in Wichita, Kansas, claiming to be inside his home with a gun and hostages. He gave the address of Andrew Finch, who was uninvolved and was surprised by the police showing up at his home. As he answered the door unarmed, a police officer thought he was reaching for a weapon and shot and killed him.[3]

Barriss apparently has a long history, making dozens of swatting calls. In 2019 he pleaded guilty to fifty-one federal charges related to such calls and was sentenced to twenty years in prison. This was longer than the ten years in the sentencing guidelines but was considered appropriate given the seriousness of this relatively new crime.[4] But perhaps it was too short if he has a bully personality pattern that will last a lifetime. Barriss's conviction might make you think that he didn't really win. But he will be out someday, most likely with the same bully personality, able to live the life that his victim will not.

After the killing of Herring, Sonderman was convicted of conspiracy and sentenced to just five years in prison. His coconspirator was a British teenager who was not even brought to the United States for trial because he was a minor. He bullied a stranger from around the world, without consequences!

Sonderman's lawyer said that his five-year sentence was fair and that Sonderman had expressed remorse for his actions that led up to Herring's death, as well as remorse for the other victims of his harassment.[5] Yeah, right! A little late for that remorse, you might say. Do bullies even have real remorse? That's actually a good question that needs to be addressed.

Remorse? What Remorse?

Let's go back to the three personality disorders described in Chapter 3 that most bullies are likely to have (remembering that not all those with these personality disorders are bullies, but most bullies have one or more of these personalities). Those with antisocial personalities lack remorse. It's one of their characteristics, and someone as cruel as Shane Sonderman may fit into this category, which doesn't bode well for his future. This is usually a lifelong pattern that has become hardwired by adulthood if not from birth.

On the other hand, bullies with narcissistic personalities lack empathy but usually do not purposely violate the law and recklessly endanger the lives of others. They usually are more interested in dominating others and being seen as superior than in destroying them. Some of them are able to change somewhat.

Likewise, bullies with borderline personalities primarily have a problem of lack of control over their emotions. They often have remorse if their intense anger has harmed someone, especially someone they care about like a spouse. They may buy flowers and apologize and say they'll never do it again. But then their feelings of insecurity may start building up again, and their abusive behavior may return in a moment of fury over some slight, large or small. Having remorse isn't enough for them to control their emotions. They have to learn emotional self-control and self-regulation, which a few do but most don't. However, some may learn this in therapy that is designed to help them manage their emotions.

This is the general pattern of many perpetrators of domestic violence, often known as the *cycle of violence*, with three basic steps: internal buildup of emotional tension, outburst of rage (verbal or physical), then a period of remorse. Those with this borderline pattern don't intend to harm those they love, but sometimes their emotions are so intense that they seriously injure or kill their partners in a moment of rage that they soon regret.

On the other hand, other perpetrators of domestic violence may have the antisocial personality pattern. They too may seriously injure or kill their partner but lack the ability to feel remorse about it. You can often spot this pattern from their insensitivity to anyone and willingness to harm others for sheer pleasure and dominance—and willingness to completely lie about it. Notice if they ever show remorse when they have not been caught. Unlikely.

Overall, knowing about these patterns of behavior may help you avoid situations earlier so that you are not caught by surprise after you make a commitment. If you see a pattern of lack of remorse, lack of empathy, or lack of self-control, don't ignore it. If you hear hints of violence in your partner's words or attitudes, get help in analyzing whether you are at risk.

The Wedding Night

Domestic violence almost always starts with a surprise attack, often six to twelve months into the relationship. Sarah and John had a whirlwind romance. He was perfect for her. Very romantic and charming. He treated her to a trip to the Bahamas and Hawaii. He really made her feel special. This was really nice, because a year before, her boyfriend of three years had dumped her, and her father had recently passed away. She was looking to find her soul mate. John seemed to fit the bill. He shared her interests in bird-watching and pickleball (although he wasn't very good at it). In some ways he seemed to be her knight in shining armor. Within six months they were married.

But on their wedding night it all changed. He slapped her after something she said. It caught her by surprise. "What was *that* about?" He said, "That was nothing. Forget about it. But things are going to be different now." He said he was never really interested in bird-watching and pickleball. In fact, he didn't even like to travel. He said he was in charge now and wasn't going to listen to any more of her whining about her father passing away. He was all that she should need now, and he slapped her hard on the butt (where it wouldn't show) to make it all clear. A surprise attack!

This is an example of the kind of stories we received when I co-wrote the book *Dating Radar* with my colleague and cofounder of the High Conflict Institute, Megan Hunter. In an online survey with over three hundred results, many people told us that they found out that their dating partners were bullies only after they made a major commitment to the bully, such as marrying them—some right away, some after a few weeks, and some after a year or two. They had been deceived by charm, fake compatabilities, and appearing to be a knight in shining armor or a fairy-tale princess to take care of them.

Here are three examples of survey comments that we received from women and some men with similar stories of being surprised:

- "It started on our wedding night. He told me he was on his best behavior while we were dating and now that we were married he could let his true colors show. I thought he was being sarcastic. He was not."
- "I knew on our honeymoon."
- "He seemed to change most after our engagement and changed even more dramatically than that immediately after getting married. It was during our honeymoon, those three

days following our wedding, that his behavior took a turn for the worse and I realized I'd just made the greatest mistake of my life."[6]

For reasons like this, we recommend in *Dating Radar* that people who are dating wait a year before making a major commitment, such as getting married, having a child, or buying a house together. Usually, if their partner is a bully, the warning signs of bullying behavior appear within six to twelve months.

Coercive Control

As mentioned earlier in Chapter 4, coercive control in intimate partner relationships may only involve a few incidents of surprise violence to intimidate their partner into long-term submission. An abuser may only hit their partner once a year, but the fear of being hit lives on every day for the victim/survivor. Many spousal abusers establish a pattern of controlling their contact with friends and family members; controlling their finances, such as demanding to know how every penny is spent or not even letting the target have money; controlling their physical health, such as demanding that they eat certain foods or limited amounts and even making them weigh themselves several times a day while the bully watches; unwanted and rough sex; even coming to the target's workplace unannounced and being disruptive. Simply the threat of future violence over time is sufficient for the bully to gain control over every aspect of the target's life.

Over time, the effect of their abuser's threats and demeaning messages about themselves (verbal emotional abuse) weakens their self-esteem and makes it harder to leave, not easier. The effect of their PEP automatically makes them defer to their abuser in an effort to survive. Then, many victims criticize themselves for accepting this behavior, and people around them may criticize them as well for their "poor choices," without realizing how they are an unconscious survival mechanism. *Why do I put up with this?* It may not make sense until you understand that the bully has primitive emotional power over their victim.

Keep in mind that in primitive days people often had no choice of leaving a violent partner, who may also have helped her find food to eat, protected her from dangerous animals, and held off other dangerous human beings. In small tribes and communities, there was often nowhere to run and hide. This seems baked into most people's unconscious automatic survival responses. Submitting to bullies may have helped our ancestors survive as long as they did, but now we need to understand this response and help people manage it and overcome it—rather than criticize them for having it.

The Invasion of Ukraine

For bullies, part of their PEP formula is to deceive and distract. Antisocial bullies are the best at this, as they have no conscience or rules of honesty restraining them. They will say whatever works in the moment. Just as a pickpocket will point up at something in the sky to distract you while stealing your wallet, most bullies will distract you when they are preparing surprise attacks—if you express suspicions, they will try to override those with strong words. ("I would never deceive you! How dare you say such a thing!"). Russia's invasion of Ukraine is a classic example.

To put this in context, it helps to think back to the catastrophic withdrawal of American troops from Afghanistan in August 2021. The U.S. government had planned this for a while and announced a gradual total troop withdrawal in April that would last until September. This was to be the fulfillment of a deal made with the Taliban by the prior administration. As of August 10, it was expected that the U.S.-supported government would fall to the Taliban in thirty to ninety days. Instead of fulfilling the deal, the Taliban rushed in and took control of the entire country in five days, on August 15.[7]

The Taliban quickly created chaos, killed many of those who helped the government, and reversed all the progress that women had made in twenty years. The Afghan president fled the country, and the current U.S. president was mostly blamed for terrible planning and being caught by surprise by bullies. *Didn't he know who he was dealing with?* people wondered.

Fast-forward to February 2022. In this context, Russian president Vladimir Putin told the world that his military was just doing training exercises as he amassed 200,000 troops near the Ukraine border. His deputy ambassador to the United Nations, just two weeks before the invasion, had written on Twitter, "Madness and scaremongering continues. What if we would say that US could seize London in a week and cause 300K civilian deaths? Would it feel right for Americans and Brits [sic]? It's as wrong for Russians and Ukrainians."[8]

Some people call this *whataboutism.* "Don't look at me. What about what *you're* doing?" say the bullies. Don't be distracted. Remember, the issue's not the issue; the personality is the issue. You don't have to defend your caution around bullies. Be suspicious. Check things out. If there is a bully involved, their goal is to dominate or destroy by any means necessary, including surprise attacks. With this possibility in mind, the U.S. president publicly revealed that intelligence showed that Russia was planning to invade and take over Ukrainian cities.

When they did attack on February 24, 2022, it shocked and surprised the world—including most Ukrainians and most world leaders. But this time the U.S. president wasn't caught by surprise and quickly organized a coalition to help Ukraine fight back. Perhaps he always knew that Putin was a bully, or perhaps the catastrophe in Afghanistan was fresh in his mind.

Surprise Attack on Israel

In October 2023, members of Hamas—the governing party for the Gaza section of Palestine next to Israel—engaged in a brutal surprise attack on Israel which was designed to provoke an extreme response. They killed approximately 1,200 people, mostly civilians, with many beheadings, of all age groups, and sexual assaults, then took about 240 hostages. Israel responded with a brutal attack on all of the Gaza Strip, forcing the evacuation of over one million Palestinians and, as of March 2024, killing more than 30,000 (the majority of whom were women and children), in their efforts to destroy Hamas.

Events like this will keep happening by "surprise" after this book is published, but the principles relating to bullies will remain the same. Bully leaders like to fight and dominate or destroy their targets. Generally, the people of their nations or territories are not interested in fighting and dominating and destroying. As a retired Israeli Army general and critic of the Israeli government said after their attack on Gaza was underway, "Our peoples should both be led by sensible majorities, but both peoples are being led by their extremists."[9]

In terms of bully dynamics, the attack on Israel should not have been a surprise if you considered the reality that no people or group of people are satisfied to be losers or second-class citizens in a win-lose relationship. When two peoples live side by side, as is the case with Israel and the Palestine territories, and one dominates the other, as is also the case, there will always be efforts to overthrow the status quo.

Yet the Israel leadership deceived themselves. Just a few months before the October surprise attack, their prime minister, Benjamin Netanyahu, said, "I think my record speaks for itself. The last decade in which I led Israel was the safest decade in Israel's history. But not only safe and secure for Israelis, also safe and secure for Palestinians."[10] Instead, it appears that this situation was a ticking time bomb that Israel should have anticipated, given its long-term win-lose relationship with the Palestinians next door.

HOW YOU CAN STOP THIS POWER

1. Open Your Eyes to the Pattern

Be prepared for surprise attacks. Pay attention to words that suggest someone's desire to create a win-lose relationship with you. Is there a pattern of lack of remorse, lack of empathy, or lack of self-control by such persons? If someone threatens to do something extreme, pay attention to the possibility that they may actually carry through with their intentions. Remember that bullies have narrow patterns of repeated behavior. The more you spot these patterns, the less likely you are to be caught by a surprise attack. People are easily distracted by what bullies say, so they don't see or pay attention to what bullies are actually *doing* and *have done*.

For example, every national leader should study and should have studied the *pattern* of surprise attacks by Vladimir Putin since he became president of Russia in 1999. In 2000 his troops invaded the rebellious Chechnya region in the south of Russia and essentially leveled the entire big city of Grozny over the next ten years as the way to gain control over the rebel resistance fighters. Then in 2008 he conducted a surprise invasion of the former small Soviet Union country of Georgia, carving out a section loyal to Russia.[11]

In 2014, after the people of Ukraine threw out the Kremlin-friendly president, Putin lined up troops along the Crimean Peninsula of Ukraine who wore no identification (known as "little green men") and whom Putin denied knowing anything about. Then they invaded, took over Crimea, and Putin annexed the peninsula as part of Russia. In 2015 Putin lent a hand to the murderous dictator of Syria by helping him level rebellious regions in the same manner as he had done in Grozny.[12]

With this knowledge, the invasion of Ukraine in 2022 should not have been a surprise. Bullies have narrow patterns of repeated behavior. We need to open our eyes and find the patterns.

2. Pull the Plug on the Bully

Never keep bullying a secret. Get help by talking to someone—*anyone*—who feels trustworthy. Discuss the situation with them and look at your options together. Don't isolate yourself, which is easy to do when you have been caught by surprise. As quickly as possible, remind yourself that you don't deserve to be bullied, and that this can happen to anyone. Therefore, it's perfectly reasonable that you would want to get help and approach the problem as one of stopping the bully rather than blaming yourself or keeping it to yourself.

For example, a new supervisor took over a work group that previously had had a popular manager for several years. The new supervisor was intimidating, had wide mood swings, publicly blamed others for her own mistakes, treated her staff unequally, and made one employee, Anita, her target of blame. Anita had worked in the department for many years and was two years from retirement. In the mornings, she would try to avoid the supervisor and tiptoe into her office sight unseen. She didn't want to quit her job, but everyone was walking on eggshells around this supervisor. No one knew when there would be a surprise attack of blame. Anita didn't know if she could last two more years.

Anita sought consultation on how to manage her supervisor. It was recommended that she not avoid the supervisor but instead try to greet the supervisor each morning with a friendly statement showing empathy, attention, and/or respect—an *EAR statement*.[13] The employee learned to engage her bully supervisor in frequent conversations, getting on her good side and not acting intimidated. She also asked for a meeting with her union rep and the supervisor to clarify expectations—and subtly set limits for the supervisor by implying that someone was looking over her shoulder, so she'd better behave. Within a month, Anita had become her supervisor's favorite employee. She didn't let her boss shut her down or cause her to internalize the boss's PEP. She pulled the plug on the bully's power.

3. Set Limits with Credible Threats

In organizations, tell others what the expectations are and that there will be swift and clear consequences if any bullying occurs. Have the entire organization reinforce these standards and expectations. Post policies before surprise attacks occur. If and when they do, be prepared for the bully's endless (and bogus) excuses and attempted distractions. Every organization needs to create and maintain a strong reputation for setting limits and following through with serious consequences if they are violated.

For example, one university had to deal with a science researcher who repeatedly made surprise attacks against at least five of her co-workers. Ms. Weigert repeatedly insulted people, made "racially and ethnically insensitive remarks," and "created a threatening atmosphere." One colleague feared that she would physically harm someone. Ms. Weigert's supervisors gave her several warnings, both verbal and written, explaining that if she "did not change her behavior immediately, further disciplinary action could be expected." But instead of changing her behavior in any way, Ms. Weigert used a classic bully move: She declared herself the actual victim. She falsely claimed she had disabilities and filed a federal complaint. However, her bullying behavior continued.[14]

Ms. Weigert was then fired, quite properly. Predictably, she filed a lawsuit against the university. But in court she never provided any proof of a real disability. The university won the lawsuit because it had properly set limits with a credible threat of termination, which it then acted upon.[15]

4. Impose Serious Consequences

As described earlier in this chapter, domestic violence is one of the most common forms of bullying. It almost always begins with a surprise attack—generally within a few months to a year into a relationship. The bully usually distracts from or denies the violence, and a pattern develops and continues. Often, the victim becomes stuck in the situation. But nowadays, our courts have begun to understand the importance of consequences in cases of domestic violence.

For example, courts are starting to impose jail sentences or admission to treatment programs on bullies, in addition to issuing restraining orders on them, for such behavior. The recommended serious consequences include jail time and/or a twelve-month batterer's treatment group program that meets at least once a week. Perhaps 70 percent of spousal abusers actually do improve their behavior after such a yearlong program, according to one group leader.[16]

The ideal is for this consequence to be ordered as soon as possible. In reality, many people stay in relationships with domestic violence and cover it up so that it can go on for years without others knowing about it. It is going on in every community, but most people don't see it and therefore don't know how serious and widespread this is.

5. Communicate Effectively to Others About Bullies

Relationship professionals—such as counselors, lawyers, doctors, and ministers—need to ask specific questions of their clients to see if bullying is occurring in their lives. Human resources professionals and upper management need to educate everyone in their organizations about bullying and what to do if it occurs.

For example, as described earlier in this chapter, when Vladimir Putin was gathering his army for the invasion of Ukraine and claimed it was just for military exercises, the U.S. government announced to the world what he was doing. While the Ukrainian government was publicly downplaying any threat, the head of the Ukrainian Air Force quietly moved most of its jets away from the airfields, which were some of the most likely places for a surprise attack. These announcements may also have given European allies a chance to begin preparing military support and a safe haven for refugees. At the time, the U.S. president was criticized for being an alarmist, but he turned out to be right.

6. Stand Strong with Others Against Bullies

The immediate united response of democracies against the "surprise" Russian invasion of Ukraine is a classic case of standing strong and responding effectively to a surprise attack by a bully, especially by the United States and much of the Western world. Some world leaders said that it was Russia's private business since so many Ukrainians spoke Russian and Ukraine used to be part of the Russia-led USSR. But others realized that such an aggressive action by a bully government could be the first step to invasions of other countries that were part of the USSR and possibly more of Europe. By standing strong with the Ukrainians, powerful consequences were put into place (economic sanctions, trade restrictions, military equipment support, and worldwide social isolation) that significantly restrained Russia's efforts to take over the whole country of Ukraine.

Even small countries like New Zealand joined in the fight against this bully. A few weeks after the invasion, Prime Minister Jacinda Ardern of New Zealand spoke with Volodymyr Zelenskyy, president of Ukraine, about how her small country of only five million people could help. She offered what money, equipment, and training they could.

Here is how she described their conversation in an interview:

> He said to me, "It's not about small, and it's not about big. It's those who react and those who don't, and you have reacted." And that just says it all. It's not about size. It's about values. And in these moments, standing together, regardless of whether you're on the other side of the world or not, and showing that this is not a conflict that we're going to let happen in the shadows. We will speak up. We will speak against it and stand together until it ends.[17]

This is how you stop bullies. It's too bad that we still have to worry about countries invading other countries, given the potential threats to all of our existence that can be caused by the acts of one bully.

CONCLUSION

Bullies use surprise attacks to quickly gain power over others, no matter whether they are in a family, a community, or another nation. They can be highly successful because most people never consider this possibility for themselves and therefore are totally unprepared. These attacks may be so shocking that they cause a heart attack or violent overreaction, as in the swatting incidents. It may cause such fear in domestic violence victims that they start walking on eggshells, losing energy and self-esteem while they live in fear of the next surprise attack. Even national leaders can be caught by surprise when they trust other leaders—even those with a history of bullying and brutality, such as the Taliban and Vladimir Putin.

It helps to reflect on whether you are in a win-win relationship with a bully. If so, don't be surprised when the bully will try to turn it into a win-lose relationship. Examples of this are the wedding couple described earlier, as the husband sought to turn their equal relationship into one in which he was in charge.

Likewise, if you see a win-lose relationship with a bully already on top, don't be surprised to find out that it is an unstable situation and sooner or later the loser is going to make efforts to fight back, possibly with a surprise attack. Examples of this are the women who took Harvey Weinstein to court and won after he sexually assaulted them. This may also describe the relationship of Israel with the Palestinians, who fought back with a brutal surprise attack on Israel, which was followed by an assault on the Palestinian territory. As win-lose relationships are always unstable, there will always be predictable "surprise attacks." The only solution appears to be creation of an equal, win-win relationship, such as the retired Israeli Army general recommended.

There are more bullies in the world now than we have been used to seeing for decades. Maintain a healthy skepticism and watch for patterns of behavior that lack remorse, empathy, or self-control.

The past is the best predictor of the future. Eyes need to be wide open. But bullies are good at denial and distraction. The biggest lesson here for spotting them is to look at the patterns of behavior and ignore the words of bullies. The biggest lesson for stopping them is to pull the plug on the bully by speaking up, getting help when you need it, and standing with others who you see are being bullied.

COMMON MISTAKE:

You can't predict when a bully will attack you by surprise.

REALITY:

If you recognize warning signs of bully behavior,
you can often predict, prepare for, or avoid surprise attacks.

CHAPTER 11

The Power of Bullies as Leaders

*From a young age Boris Johnson longed to
be World King—but the gods are mocking him.
The Prime Minister blusters, equivocates and
flounders. At a time of crisis, he has failed
to learn what it means to lead.*

—Jason Cowley, *The New Statesman*

MOST BULLIES ARE DRIVEN TO BE LEADERS—of their families, their
work groups, their communities, their nations—not so they can provide any actual leadership, but to dominate or destroy as many people
as possible. They have a very different agenda from most leaders who
want to work *with* others and want to *earn* their respect by leading
them in successful efforts for the benefit of the group. Bullies seek to

dominate others and demand their respect by controlling them and humiliating them for the bully's own benefit.

Until you recognize this significant difference, you may innocently contribute to a bully's drive for power and inadvertently defend the bully's behavior when others begin to resist it. Boris Johnson—who, from his youth, according to friends and biographers, "longed to be World King"—is a good example of this.

> Johnson inhabits a pagan world of gods, heroes, portents and prophecies. His pre-Christian sensibility enables him to transcend the burdens of conscience that constrain mere mortals, freeing him to create his own destiny, in the manner of all great men.[1]

In other words, Johnson appears to have a classic *ancient* bully personality. His main skill may be the primitive art of getting attention by making up bully's stories, as described in Chapter 6, rather than real leadership skills for the modern age. He may have been born this way. Many of today's bullies appear to have been born with an innate drive to be the alpha male (or female). His "pre-Christian sensibility" seems to have provided the same lack of conscience as many of the bullies described in this book and other historical bully leaders.

My theory is that such bullies emerge from the part of the human personality gene pool that goes back many millennia, when the times demanded ruthless manipulators to gather people tightly together and follow the bully's dictates in the absence of real knowledge of science, history, and collaboration. While our cultures, legal systems, and political systems, such as democracy, have evolved dramatically over the last thousand years, our biology and personalities have not.

Primitive Emotional Leadership

Bullies as leaders start to make sense when you look deep at human history. As I mentioned in Chapter 4, modern humans (Homo sapiens) first appeared around 200,000 years ago. Until we developed speech about 60,000 to 70,000 years ago, we communicated with emotions instead of words: facial expressions, grunts and groans, hand gestures, and other body language.[2] Who has the greatest images of strength and sounds of strength today? Our bullies. Who still communicates primarily emotionally? Our bullies. Their primitive emotional power is now on full display as bullies try to dominate the modern world.

Until 10,000 to 12,000 years ago, we were hunter-gatherers living in communities of a few dozen to about 150 people, half of whom were children.[3] Then we started developing agriculture and living in villages of several hundred people. About 5,000 years ago, we started creating written languages and forming cities and large empires with hundreds of thousands of people, such as the Egyptian kingdom ruled by the pharaohs, the Qin dynasty of China, and the Roman Empire with millions of subjects.[4]

What made it possible for so many of us to live together? In his book about the history of human beings, titled *Sapiens,* Yuval Noah Harari has a theory that makes sense. "The secret was probably the appearance of fiction. Large numbers of strangers can cooperate successfully by believing in common myths."[5]

Who would create and enforce these common myths and related rules? While we don't have conclusive proof, bullies would have been perfect for the job. For example, the psychologist Erich Fromm describes the ancient leaders of these empires as examples of malignant narcissism. He includes many extremely powerful and vicious leaders as fitting into this category:

> The Egyptian Pharaohs, the Roman Caesars, the Borgias, Hitler, Stalin, Trujillo—they all show certain similar features. They have attained absolute power; their word is the ultimate judgment of everything, including life and death; there seems to be no limit to their capacity to do what they want. . . . This Caesarian madness would be nothing but plain insanity were it not for one factor: by his power Caesar has bent reality to his narcissistic fantasies.[6]

In other words, it may be that the Caesars' extreme personalities are what it took to unite such a huge empire. The result was good, in that we have learned that large societies can be more efficient, creative, hardworking, and powerful than villages and small towns on their own. However, the price of getting to these large, stable societies could have been massive death and destruction, and there was no promise that management was efficient. But somehow it appears that these bully personalities played a productive role in building large empires that organized the world ultimately for the better in the present. Nowadays, we already have a world of nations, large and small, such that these bully personalities pose more of a threat to society than work to build society.

Thus, in primitive times, these strong, aggressive, dominating leaders—kings, queens, and even village chieftains—appear to have had the necessary emotional power and myths to hold groups of people together. Their myths—stories actually—didn't have to be true. Everyone just needed to believe in the same stories in order to coexist.

These ancient leaders appear to have dictated who a group's enemies and friends were, and the group's rules. When leaders said go to war, people went to war. When leaders said stop fighting, people stopped fighting. The leader was everything, in order to survive in a dangerous world. The village or kingdom was held together by strong (and vigorously enforced) loyalty to the leader. In these early times—before the scientific method, written history, codified laws, or any concept of democracy—the only thing holding a group together was loyalty to its ostensibly great, all-wise leader. Even if the leader was totally wrong about things, it was more important that the group stuck together by remaining loyal to the leader.

Such systems were structured in a very rigid, top-down manner at all levels of society. This dominance hierarchy appears to be a universal trait of all mammals. There is always someone above (except for the very top leader, as long as he or she lasts) and someone below. Win-lose relationships were constantly forming and re-forming with a king (sometimes a queen) at the top of the heap. Dominate or be dominated. The person or group with the most primitive emotional power at the time ruled. The leader's emotions—the *image of strength* and *sound of strength*—were essential. So bullies often became the leaders—until they were overthrown by a bigger bully or more effective leader.

Setting Limits on Kings and Queens

But something started to change in a big way for humans less than a thousand years ago, starting with the written document known as the Magna Carta issued in 1215 in merry old England. It reined in the king's powers and made the written law a "power in itself." It was the result of an uprising of "the leading men of England." While the king or queen still held the most power, he (or she) was now somewhat restrained.[7]

The American Revolution went a few steps further, by creating a constitution in 1789 that laid out all the fundamental laws and rights for the whole country, *totally independent* of any king or queen. It replaced a king with a president who would be elected for a set term. Legislators and judges and states would share power with the president in a system of checks and balances. Regular elections at all levels replaced the need for wars or revolutions to overthrow a monarch, who at times might be a bully. Just vote them out sooner or later.

This flexibility through regular elections was built in on a regular basis, potentially bringing long-term peace that would allow most of the population to enjoy life, liberty, and the pursuit of happiness. Included were mechanisms to revise the U.S. Constitution, which has led slowly (painstakingly slowly for many groups) to the inclusion of almost all citizens in the voting process at present.

The point is that constitutional democratic government made it clear that society could be more efficiently organized with the creativity and decision-making of numerous people, based on knowledge generated by science and written history, so that the country wasn't dependent on a single monarch to make all the important decisions—based a lot on whim and guessing. No one could possibly play that role for thousands and millions of people in modern society.

The most effective cultures became the ones that made the wisest use of their human resources, so that constitutional democracies have increased since 1789, with many countries adopting constitutions modeled after the U.S. Constitution. The end of World War II in 1945, in which democracies beat several dictatorships, brought a rapid increase in countries becoming democratic.

With democracy, nations learned to restrain their bullies—at least the worst of them. Criminal laws, civil laws, moral sanctions, and well-established standards for behavior moved bullies more and more toward the fringes of society. Good citizenship, self-discipline, and requirements for respectful behavior mostly kept bullies out of leadership roles.

Bully Leaders Are Back

Our current world culture has launched bullies again to the forefront of society. Starting in the late 1990s, the number of democracies around the world leveled off. Around 2004, several democracies started backsliding to a single ruler—generally termed an *autocrat* (and typically a bully)—who despite strong opposition changed their countries' constitutions to allow an autocratic form of government.[8]

One of the best examples of this is Vladimir Putin. After the fall of the Soviet Union in 1989, Russia seemed headed in the direction of a democracy, with elected government officials and legislators. Many of the former member countries of the Soviet Union also moved in a democratic direction when it dissolved. But when Putin was appointed as president in 1999, he quickly proceeded to chip away at the democratic government so that he could become the supreme ruler. In *The Future Is History: How Totalitarianism Reclaimed Russia*, Masha Geffen writes, "[By 2002,] in just two years, Putin had greatly weakened the power of elected officials by creating federal oversight over governors and giving the federal center the right to fire elected governors; reversed judicial reform; and monopolized national broadcast television in the hands of the Kremlin."[9] While there were outbursts of resistance along the way, when he ordered the invasion and destruction of Ukraine, as a former member of the

Soviet Union that was becoming democratic, no one could stop him.

How did Putin succeed? By telling bully's stories with lots of emotional repetition, especially through the media that he controls, and a lot of projection and playing the victim. He at first said that the reason for the February 2022 invasion of Ukraine was to protect Ukrainians from their "Nazi rulers"—clearly a fantasy crisis. Yet this had special meaning in Russia because of the Nazi treatment of Russians in World War II. However, it was hard to maintain this argument since Ukraine's high-profile president, Volodymyr Zelenskyy, was Jewish. This was a good example of bully's stories as BS.

As the West and NATO countries became more active in supporting Ukraine's resistance to the Russian invasion, Putin changed his fantasy crisis to that of Russia's very existence being threatened by the West and NATO. Since he controls almost all the information that Russians see, his bully's stories have been largely effective. After a year and a half of the war, despite a failed surprise attack and significant losses of Russian soldiers, his status as a hero has gone up, not down. They see him as the protector against chaos and insecurity because he has convinced the population that the West poses an existential threat to them. By August 2023, eighteen months after he started the war against Ukraine, the percentage of Russians "who overtly admire Putin has grown from 8 to 19 percent, and 68 percent of Russians now say they want him to be reelected, a significant jump from 48 percent of Russians before the war." Also, support for official institutions (which he dominates) has grown, "including the cabinet, regional governors, parliament, and even the ruling party, United Russia."[10]

By activating fear that Russia's very existence was in danger, intense anger at the West, and love/loyalty for him as their hero—a complete bully's story endlessly repeated in the isolation of controlled news—he has used the full PEP formula to his advantage. While outsiders may be astonished at how the people of Russia have been misled, those on the inside of the country apparently thoroughly support a terrible war against an innocent nation. Understanding bullies as ancient leaders using primitive emotional power helps explain the feelings Putin has activated in Russia.

Leaders at All Levels

It's not just national leaders who are succeeding with the use of primitive emotional power. Bullies now get the most attention in our culture, and their behavior is described and talked about repeatedly in detail in our media. Their *images of strength, sounds of strength,* and *words of strength* dominate the 24/7 news, movies, TV, radio, social media, and therefore our own conversations. Their primitive facial expressions and body language are shown repeatedly in close-ups on our screens. The sounds of their aggressive speech, hype, and personal attacks fill the airwaves.

If there was a training program for bullies as leaders, it would look a lot like our current media-saturated culture, with its *culture of fear, culture of blame (anger),* and culture of heroes. We now see overwhelming problems everywhere that make us extremely anxious and susceptible to bullies as leaders—as long as they are *our* bullies.

Our Primitive Emotional Responses

It isn't just the bullies who are acting on ancient impulses now. It's all of us. Primitive emotional power triggers primitive emotional responses within us. Just as the Russian people have been conned on a large scale, PEP can also grab us at the individual level. Many identify with the bully and become his negative advocates. Others become fighters who instinctively oppose the bully. Decision-makers (some-times elder family members, workplace managers, courts, voters) get easily emotionally hooked into seeing the bully as a victim who needs to be helped. So, out of ignorance and being manipulated, they often get a gut feeling that they should punish the true victims on be-half of the bully who is playing the victim. Bullies are like that: they know how to use their PEP to confuse and dominate people.

According to a poll in 2022, "About one in three Americans prefer strong unelected leaders to weak elected leaders."[11] Bullies who are skilled at image but lack leadership skills can easily manipulate this preference to gain power. Thus, the struggle between having rules and laws versus having one supreme leader is not over yet. Unfor-tunately, as we have seen, world culture has reversed in this regard in this century. Technology has weakened our social connectedness, and modern media has helped bullies move from the fringes of so-ciety into positions of power and cultural influence again.

And what do bullies do with all the power that they acquire? They eliminate any challengers, and they throw away the existing laws and rules. Why? Because bullies want to make the rules up as they go. Remember, as ancient leaders their job was to get attention and enforce loyalty in order to hold the kingdom together and build larger kingdoms. They wanted the rules to be whatever they chose at the time and not imposed on them by others. Their complaints are, "I feel too controlled. I want to take my shackles off. I want total freedom." But in the modern world, we need fixed rules to be most productive and to get along in a complex society. Now we need the rules in order to restrain bullies, not to remove the rules. We need to understand that they will, by their very nature, want to dominate or destroy those around them, yet we can still set limits on their behavior. In short, if there are no rules, only bullies will rule.

But bullies are not always winning these leadership struggles. The following are two examples of bully leaders and how they were stopped in recent years—because they couldn't stop themselves.

The Bully Mayor

In the small community of Sequim, Washington, a few QAnon-supporting residents quietly were elected to the city council un-opposed and took control of the council. They told "everyone who would listen that they represented the silent majority of the county." They appointed a mayor, who proudly claimed to have brought freedom to the city, wearing a T-shirt that read, THIS IS THE USA. WE EAT MEAT. WE DRINK BEER. WE OWN GUNS. WE SPEAK ENGLISH. WE LOVE FREEDOM. IF YOU DO NOT LIKE THAT, GET THE F**K OUT.

Soon this mayor and his city council forced the resignation of the popular and competent city manager, because he criticized the mayor "for urging the listeners of a local radio show in August 2020 to check out the QAnon conspiracy theory." Then the mayor and city council passed a nonbinding resolution condemning the county public health officer's emergency COVID mandates. Soon afterward, anonymous threats were made on the public health officer's life.

The mayor and his supporters "claimed to be nonpartisan and accused critics of being outside agitators," which appears to have been a projection. (Remember, bullies project their own thoughts, feelings, and behaviors onto others.) In fact, the mayor and his supporters appear to be the ones who were partisan and had recently come from outside the community. The majority of residents "reacted in horror to his [the mayor's] bullying persona and far-right antics." A majority community movement arose, from progressives to "moderate conservatives." They organized a massive get-out-the-vote, door-knocking campaign to throw out the mayor and his cronies in the next election.

In the end, all five opposition candidates won 65 to 70 percent of the vote, the mayor and city council were out, and the community and public conversations significantly calmed down. Standing together, a whole community succeeded in fighting back.[12]

Always keep projection in mind as a possibility whenever you hear a dramatic story of a crisis, villains, and a hero. It may be the exact opposite of what you are being told.

The City Council President

Bullies aren't just dominant in small-city politics but also in some of our biggest cities. Nury Martinez, president of the Los Angeles City Council and a Latina woman, resigned after an audiotape was leaked with her making racist and other disparaging comments in a conversation with two male council members and Ron Herrera, president of the Los Angeles County Federation of Labor. Apparently, the men made no objections to her comments and at times made their own derogatory racist statements.

The focus of this secretly recorded discussion was "strategies for ensuring that council districts would be redrawn so that Latino leaders would have key blocs of voters within their districts, as well as 'assets' like airports that can enhance an officeholder's political influence and fundraising ability."[13]

Over two days, protesters packed the council chambers demanding their resignations before any council business could proceed. Other politicians, even at the national level from their own party, called for those involved to resign. Martinez and Herrera resigned, but the other two councilmen did not, saying their silence during these remarks should not exclude them from serving. (Perhaps they were negative advocates by remaining silent? See Chapter 8.)

Once again, a bully's story, projection, and playing the victim seem to be involved in their actions. Apparently these politicians believed there was enough of a crisis caused by other terrible politicians that they were justified in severely manipulating the redistricting process in a bullying manner, because they had been victimized in prior voting maps. While being treated unfairly may have been the case in the past, bullying others should not be the solution in the present. The result of the protests was an investigation into the redistricting process and a call for a "fully independent" body to be in charge of future voting maps.

Creating new win-lose relationships to make up for past win-lose relationships will never be stable. No one wants to be the loser, so there will always be another surprise attack waiting around the corner unless win-win relationships can be enforced, such as by independently drawn voting maps. The built-in temporary nature of elections is one of the best ways to maintain stability and restrain bullies. That's why the complex modern world works better with democracies instead of kings and endless wars.

HOW YOU CAN STOP THIS POWER

1. Open Your Eyes to the Pattern of Bully Leaders

Most bullies want to be leaders, usually from an early age, so that their patterns of behavior are often obvious for years. Yet most people disregard these patterns, thinking the person is simply being ridiculous or has good competitive energy. Others don't realize that these bullies are showing patterns that will ripen into domineering or destructive behavior as leaders—until they are in charge. This also happens in small groups and families.

Think of the coworker who volunteers to be the leader of a group project that no one else wants to lead. Then he or she turns out to be a bully. They try to dominate and abuse everyone. Often, they do little or no actual work themselves and then they take credit for all the team's accomplishments.

Look at Brian Mitchell, who kidnapped Elizabeth Smart. He wanted her to be the first of many submissive "wives."

Look at the examples in cities, such as the mayor in the small community of Sequim, Washington, or the president of the city council of Los Angeles. They both saw themselves as leaders who needed to dominate their citizens with us-against-them thinking.

Look at the many major historical figures who were bullies—Hitler, Stalin, Mao, Ceausescu, Castro, Zuma, Amin, Pol Pot—and the many national leaders today who are full-blown bullies: Putin, Xi, Maduro, Modi, Orban, Kagame, Erdogan, and many others who have taken their democracies and turned them into autocracies with one bully leader. They tell bully's stories with surprising success because our media culture now rewards them by publicizing and endlessly repeating their stories as if they were true. And we repeat them too. This isn't how it should be in modern society. We have to recognize how we are playing a part in our new world of bullies so that we can stop.

2. Pull the Plug on the Bully Leader

Boards of directors, voters, and others need to become more assertive about pulling the plug on bullies in leadership positions in business, organizations, and politics. They should see the pattern and avoid putting bullies in positions of power, no matter how charismatic they may be. The bully will hurt everyone in the long run, so if they do mistakenly give the bully power, the sooner the better for pulling the plug.

For example, this brings us back to Boris Johnson, the British leader at the beginning of this chapter. He was enabled and tolerated by the Conservative Party that appointed him in 2019. Finally, his colleagues pressured him to resign in 2022. Until then, they had been his willing negative advocates. Eventually, however, his bullying behavior and false statements (such as denying participating in parties he banned for everyone else during COVID) and his approval of other's bad behavior (covering for a known sex offender) caught up with him. Even many of his longtime supporters demanded his resignation.

3. Set Limits with Credible Threats on Bully Leaders

Leaders need good supervision so that they cannot do too much damage. Organizations should be able to put bullies on probation, with the threat of being fired if they don't improve. All organizations should make it relatively easy to remove dangerous leaders before they engage in too much destruction and consume huge amounts of organizational time and energy before the organization realizes what is happening. Sometimes, by making a credible threat of consequences if they keep behaving badly, some bullies will stop.

For example, Dr. Collins was a co-owner of a surgery clinic. He eventually sold his interest in the clinic to the other partners but remained on as a senior surgeon. However, he proceeded to use his authority to sexually harass many of the female nurses and staff. Complaints came to the clinic administrator about his use of inappropriate language in the presence of employees and patients. There were complaints about him bringing "pictures of breeding donkeys" to the office to try to hook the female nurses and staff into conversations about sex.

One day, he took a gun out of his pocket and pointed it at the chest of one of the female employees. The partners "made the decision to suspend Dr. Collins, place him on probation, and require anger-management classes. . . . [He was warned] that his employment would immediately be terminated if he did not follow said terms, or if any more incident reports were made." With this warning, they set limits on him. We'll find out soon if that was enough.[14]

4. Impose Serious Consequences on Bully Leaders

If necessary, impose consequences when limit setting and threats are not enough. Removal from leadership positions, criminal penalties, and public humiliation should all be options for bully leaders. No leader should be above the law or allowed to destroy a good organization.

For example, not surprisingly, in the example of Dr. Collins, he did not change his behavior. Instead—as bullies typically do—he tried to legally challenge his suspension. (Remember Ms. Weigert in Chapter 10, who sued rather than improve her own behavior when limits were set on her.) As the clinic had threatened if he didn't change his behavior, a decision was made by a 3-1 vote of the shareholders to terminate his employment. (The one vote in his favor was Dr. Collins Jr., his son. Perhaps he was his father's negative advocate.)[15]

5. Communicate Effectively to Others About Bully Leaders

Everyone needs to become educated about bullies in all aspects of life today, including leadership, so that they do not fall prey to bully leaders masked as heroes. Teaching people to watch out for bully's stories is a good place to start. Can you spot the fantasy crisis? Can you see how the fantasy villain was picked? Is this really a hero? Most people enjoy being able to spot claims of a fantasy crisis and fantasy villains and realizing that this person is a fantasy hero. Regardless of the issue, the bully's personality is the problem, and they won't be able to stop themselves. Explain to others that bullies will eventually need them to set limits and that it's better to avoid giving the bullies power over others in the first place.

For example, a university men's rowing coach had a reputation as a bully, which was not spotted or believed by the administration. Brian Lilly Jr. was a rowing student who had overcome juvenile rheumatoid arthritis as a child and grown into a top-ranked rower. But Lilly and others were constantly berated by this coach, who used emasculating terms, petty insults, and sudden outbursts that left the students walking on eggshells. Lilly reached out to other coaches and athletic department staff about the rowing coach's abusive behavior, but nothing was done. Other team members complained. After Lilly complained to the coach about another student's sexual misconduct and assault against several female students, the coach demoted him from a top-ranked boat to the fourth boat, which also included the student whose conduct he was concerned about. Eventually, after months of criticism and being retaliated against, Lilly committed suicide.

His parents filed a lawsuit against the university "hoping their personal tragedy will further the broader conversation about the mental wellness of collegiate athletes and rein in abusive coaching." Their lawyer said, "He was an abusive bully who subjected his rowers to terrifying temper tantrums, mean-spirited insults, and countless mind games. [He] did not care to build this kid up; he used his power to break Brian down."[16]

However, it's important to note that the rowing coach has also filed a lawsuit to clear his name and for wrongful termination by the university. So while it's important to educate others about the existence of bullying and bullies, it's also important to avoid jumping to conclusions about any specific case without a thorough investigation, which appears to continue at the time of writing. The main point is that coaches and universities are in positions of power and leadership over students, who are at a vulnerable age when bullying can quash a person's self-esteem and future career. More education of educators needs to be done to rein in bullies who take advantage of these positions of power.

6. Stand Strong with Others Against Bully Leaders

Don't get stuck arguing about logical or ideological perspectives. Bullies are opportunists who rarely have consistent values, beyond gaining power for themselves. This is 100 percent about personalities —bully personalities. The issues are not the issue. Arguing about issues just diverts people from setting limits on bullies.

For example, it's sad that Brian Lilly Jr. felt the need to speak up for others who were being bullied as well as for himself. If enough people would do that on a regular basis, there would be much less bullying, and others like Lilly would have a better chance at living.

Work with others to set limits or establish rules or laws that will stop bullies in their tracks. Much of our criminal court system is already designed to do that, and our civil courts play a role as well. We just need those involved to have the full knowledge of bully dynamics so that they don't underestimate their dangerousness and ability to manipulate decision-makers.

CONCLUSION

Bullies appear driven from birth or early childhood to be leaders. They try to build hierarchical groups—families, work groups, communities—that they can dominate. In primitive times, having a dictatorial leader may have been practical and led to larger and larger communities and empires. The bully leader was the source of all knowledge and decisions, and the social glue that held the group together through universal loyalty. This usually worked until smarter or stronger bullies came along and violently overthrew them and created a new hierarchy. Given their role in prehistory, *bullies aren't evil; they're ancient!*

But in modern times, we have many sources of knowledge, the scientific method for understanding reality, and democracy for making the best use of most people's creativity, collaboration, and labor. Emotional intelligence helps us get along and work together as equals. We don't need rigidly hierarchical organizations led for a lifetime by kings or dictators anymore. This means that we don't need bullies to be in charge. In fact, we need to prevent them from being in charge and having the opportunity to destroy the existing social standards, rules, and stability. Sure, we can improve society, but it must be done peacefully. In our nuclear age, humanity cannot survive anymore the endless, violent rise and fall of dictators.

On a personal level, it helps to understand this drive to dominate or destroy, and to know that bullies don't even understand it themselves and can't stop themselves. Bullying in families (child abuse, domestic violence, parental alienation) should not be hard to stop, but I know from forty years' experience that these are often intractable problems because they are misunderstood, even by many professionals. We have the knowledge and the treatment methods. But we also must remember that some people's personalities really are different and committed to dominance and destruction and may need legal restraints, including prison. We should not be naïve about this and tolerate people being abusive in their family relationships.

In the workplace and in communities, knowledge of this drive to dominate or destroy can help protect employees and community members sooner rather than later after too many naïve chances have been given. It's very common in organizations to tolerate bullies for far too long, simply because people don't recognize their patterns from the start and keep hoping the bullies will change on their own. Once again, we must remember that some people cannot stop themselves and we cannot avoid involvement as innocent bystanders. As the cover of this book shows, we can and should help one another out.

COMMON MISTAKE:

People who want to be leaders should be encouraged to do so without question.

REALITY:

Bullies are usually driven to be leaders from childhood, so they can eventually dominate or destroy others. They should never be put in positions of power over others. Questions should be asked about the patterns of behavior of would-be leaders.

CHAPTER 12

The Power of Polarization

*Siblings in a narcissistic family are . . . pitted against
each other through competition and comparison.
Since the narcissistic parent requires that all family
members focus their attention on them, closeness
between siblings is considered a threat.*

—Karyl McBride, *Will the Drama Ever End?*

FEW PEOPLE RECOGNIZE that the same process of *polarization* now
occurs regularly around the world, at three different levels: in families, in groups, and in politics. Polarization in all of these settings
is mostly an *emotional* process, more than a logical or ideological
one. Human logical disagreements will always exist. They are simply
problems to solve. They help us consider more than one option or
approach, which helps us learn over time what works best. In equal
relationships, we have many ways of negotiating solutions to our

differences, large and small, such as taking turns, seeking more information, compromising, or trying out both options.

Polarization is *personal*. Intense polarization—the frightening kind that can turn into violence—is more than a difference of logical opinions. It's a form of primitive emotional power. It causes people to say that you, your positions, and your group are totally wrong, inferior, subhuman, or should not exist. You feel it emotionally, in your gut. The other side's point of view feels truly life-threatening, and its members may say life-threatening things that reinforce this fear perhaps in a seemingly joking manner, but such jokes have serious implications. While polarization may have logical *contributing* causes, the intensity of it is emotionally driven primarily by bully leaders. They make it personal to get the people they polarize to fight one another so that the bully can gain power or keep power, like a narcissistic bully parent. Most secure parents know much better than to pit their children against one another.

Likewise, polarization is not driven by ideological disagreements themselves. Friends and family have argued about politics for centuries. But from time to time, bully political leaders turn minor differences into intensely emotional "us-against-them" narratives. It's about good people versus evil people, patriots versus traitors, believers versus infidels, or the deserving versus the undeserving. When people accept this false us-against-them distinction, they naturally increase the polarization—and the risk of violence.

Bullies can polarize people over anything: money, age, looks, values, nationalities, medical treatments, safety precautions, election results, and even food options (Google "Cracker Barrel Impossible Burger"). The more this primitive emotional power is repeated, the more intense the polarization. Thus, polarization grows or diminishes based on the leaders of the family, the workplace, the community, or the nation. It comes from the top down.

This is especially true in nations with bully leaders. For example, I was traveling once in Cambodia and visited the Killing Fields, where in the 1970s the Khmer Rouge slaughtered 25 percent of the Cambodian population. Pol Pot, the brutal dictator, had turned the poor and farming people against the urban government and professional people in a sweeping effort to destroy any possible opposition to his power. Our guide had our group of twelve sit at a picnic table as he described the ways that one person after another was executed on these grounds. Then, he looked at me, pointed, and exclaimed, "You would be dead!" I asked why. "Because you wear glasses! That's a sign that you were assumed to be in the elite classes, as in the government or universities." Polarization can be fatal.

Polarization Comes Down from Bully Leaders

It isn't immediately obvious that intense polarization comes from primitive emotional power, which can leave ordinary people upset and bewildered, wondering what they did to cause it. However, intense polarization doesn't come from the bottom up. People don't walk around polarized without a bully leader to instruct them in us-against-them. People often get this backward. *I didn't realize we were so polarized. What have we done to cause this?* That's what bullies want you to think as they deny actively doing any such thing.

In reality it isn't "we" who have caused this. It starts from the top and the bully's story. Using emotional repetition, the bully creates intense fear, which triggers intense anger at the bully's target. Remember, emotions are contagious. The bully defines the crisis, the villain, and the hero (all fantasies). Then, when people repeat the emotional messages they have heard—often word for word—the polarization grows.

We don't have to participate in this. If a leader were to instruct a group on tolerance and unity, polarization would be at a minimum. Most people have the ability for both adversarial thinking and cooperative thinking. A leader brings out the best or the worst.

The bully leaders are the ones who bring out the worst of our adversarial thinking, with detailed instructions from their bully's stories of the terrible crisis, the evil enemy, and the hero (the bully, of course). In all these situations, bullies exaggerate the smallest disagreements or negative emotions and magnify them into major us-versus-them, win-lose, high-conflict, heroes-versus-villains disputes. Once people are emotionally hooked, they often follow by repeating this and making it worse, as explained below. Our part is in what we watch, listen to, and repeat. We didn't cause the current polarization, but we can cause it to grow even worse with our own naïve actions.

Polarization's Primitive Purposes

As we saw in the last chapter, bully leaders are always talking—telling their bully's stories—and always demanding loyalty above everything else. In primitive times this helped keep people together for stronger group action and survival, since people didn't have science, maps, and detailed written history to guide them. Oddly enough, it seems that polarization probably had at least two functions: for humanity to survive and to thrive.

Polarization to survive. Let's take a prehistoric community and a leader named Leif. Leif is one of the early speakers and leaders. He says, "Follow me. Let's go over that mountain over there to a land where everything is perfect and wonderful. I'm perfect and wonderful, so you should follow me, of course." Leif is big and strong and loud and charismatic. He's also very likely a bully, with a core group of intensely loyal followers and many people he has alienated. Half the people cheer Leif and agree to follow him. They are predisposed from birth or how they were raised in childhood to follow strongman leaders.

But the other half of the people are natural-born or raised skeptics. "No way! Leif is nuts! He's a jerk. He'll ruin your life. Don't follow him!" The group argues and splits down the middle. They have nothing to base their opinions on except personalities, and an image of strength, sounds of strength, and words of strength. No one knows what's over the mountain. But Leif has an intense personality that appeals to some and turns off others. Here's their chance for half the group to split off from his dominance. He leads his group over the mountain and down into the next valley. A sudden storm comes and floods the valley, and Leif and his followers all drown. But fortunately, half the group stayed behind and they survive. Humanity will live another day.

Or, on the other hand, Leif and his followers find that the next valley has rich soil and lots of animals to hunt, and they survive and thrive. Suddenly, those left behind are hit with a winter snowstorm that is so intense that they all freeze to death. Fortunately, Leif and his group went ahead. Humanity will live another day.

This seems to be a realistic occurrence over and over again in the history of human beings. If you connect the dots back to the origin of Homo sapiens, humans started out in eastern Africa approximately 200,000 years ago and then spread from Africa to Europe and Asia starting about 60,000 years ago. About 12,000 years ago, humans came to North America, over the Bering Strait when it was frozen in the Ice Age, and then to South America. To cover the earth took thousands or millions of little group decisions: "Should I stay, or should I go?" Bully leaders were probably significant in causing these polarizations and leading one side to the benefit of humanity. (Sometimes the bully's supporters and sometimes the bully's opponents were better off.) Narcissistic bullies would have played a big part as they always want to show how their way and their idea are superior to the status quo.

Polarization to thrive. Bullies may have also played a big role in helping humanity thrive, creating the progress we know today. The vast majority of us have empathy and respect for one another, and we experience remorse if we upset or harm someone. This is what makes it possible for us to mostly get along with a large number of people. Everyone puts on their own brakes. Thank goodness!

But a small percentage of us are bullies, who tend to lack empathy, remorse, and self-control. By pushing us into fighting one another—mostly physically in primitive times—they may have kept social change built in as part of our human relations. By dominating or destroying one another based on the effects of polarizing personalities, fundamental questions for groups may have been resolved. By polarizing a community into two groups, one "side" dominates or destroys the other "side," based on which side's approach was more successful. Whether the result of any battle was for better or worse may not have been obvious for a while, but overall it appears that humans moved mostly forward and rarely stood still.

Over time, wars seem to have promoted some good ideas and eliminated some bad, gradually benefiting humanity, but with many mistakes and much destruction along the way, leaving much room for future improvement. For example, the U.S. Civil War eliminated slavery after increased conflict between slave states and free states. Of course, there have been many steps backward and forward since then, and there is still room for much more progress. World War II settled the question of whether Europe would be better off with one dictator (Hitler) or many countries mutually respecting one another's boundaries. The outcome of WWII also ended the Nazi's genocide of Jews, gays, and others and made the United States a world leader. Again, there have been many steps forward and backward since then but with general progress up to the present.

Bully leaders always try to target vulnerable or small groups of people, but social values and democracies have progressed over the years to stop them more often in modern society and prevent them from driving us into war. Bullies are becoming a risk to us all today, with nuclear weapons and modern media, which can spread bully polarization quickly throughout a population before its dangers become obvious.

Today you can see polarization whenever a bully is present in families, work groups, and politics. It's almost uncanny how society reaches a roughly 50-50 split. It's as if it's in our social DNA to take opposite sides of an issue and fight in some form until it becomes clear which side is going to be more successful at solving the problem or destroying the other side. In modern times, we have made progress in limiting our fights to talking, reasoning with one another, negotiating, and voting on issues rather than resorting to violence on a large scale. However, in our new world of bullies, such progress appears to be backsliding.

Polarization in Families

Most parents try to treat their children equally, so that they grow up confident with good social skills for a world of people who generally treat one another equally. They don't pit one child against the other. However, families with a narcissistic bully for a parent can permanently destroy relationships between siblings. "Siblings in a narcissistic family are . . . pitted against each other through competition and comparison. Since the narcissistic parent requires that all family members focus their attention on them, closeness between siblings is considered a threat." This can continue into adulthood as long as the narcissistic parent is alive and beyond.[1]

In other words, the narcissistic bully parent creates a polarization within the family between siblings so that they will focus their attention on the bully and dislike one another. Sadly, this often becomes a permanent polarization in the family into adulthood, as this example demonstrates for two brothers, now in their fifties, as one of their therapists describes:

> The boys were pitted against each other, one the scapegoat and one the golden child. They were constantly compared, ended up being very competitive, and remain so to this day. Carl, the scapegoat, told me this: *I can see the dysfunction now and I don't blame my brother, but I also can't seem to forge a closeness with him. He seems to have taken on some of our dad's narcissistic traits and sees me as the "failure" of the family.*[2]

This is a good example of the family polarization that many therapists deal with when their clients grew up with one or two parents who were bullies—in this case, most likely their father was a narcissistic bully as described by the son.

In divorce cases, this family polarization can become even more intense, as described in earlier chapters. The bully parent often takes one or more of the children onto their side and *alienates* the children against the other parent. In other cases, a bully parent turns against one or more of the children, physically or just verbally, and causes *estrangement* between the child and that bully parent. In both scenarios the bully creates a polarization that can then involve numerous other people, who become emotionally hooked into taking sides.

Family members and friends angrily line up against one another on behalf of their preferred family member in extreme polarization, driven most of the time by one high-conflict parent. As mentioned in Chapter 6, this can reach the level of tribal warfare. It can include a child developing hatred for one of their parents, and for the grandparents on that side of the family, and even for the family dog, which the child once loved, because his or her primitive emotional responses have been hijacked. Some of these family polarizations last a lifetime.

Polarization at Work

Polarization in the workplace is sometimes called *splitting*, as a work group splits in half over how to do the work. In some hospitals and substance abuse treatment programs, this process is commonly known as *staff splitting*, turning groups of coworkers into two teams that grow to strongly dislike each other. For example, staff become split over the care of a patient with a serious personality disorder. Typically, half the staff become angry with the patient for their hostile and inappropriate behavior, and the other half become angry with those staff members and defend the patient. Marsha Linehan, the developer of dialectical behavior therapy for borderline personality disorder, explains that staff splitting is attributed to the patient but is really the responsibility of the professionals who allow themselves to engage in arguing over the treatment plan or one another's behavior.[3]

This seems to occur because the patient tells some staff members that they are the "good guys" and not at all like the terrible other staff who they say are the "bad guys." The patients feed stories to each "side" about the other. This is usually an unconscious process driven by their personality. Since emotions are contagious and patients with borderline personalities tend to have intense emotions, staff tend to absorb the patient's split perspective and start getting angry with one another—which can become quite loud and personal at times. Since I've worked in psychiatric hospitals, I have seen and experienced this dynamic in action.

Linehan goes on to say that staff shouldn't allow themselves to get hooked into splitting but recognize that this is happening and work at integrating the opposite concerns into one cohesive treatment plan. For example, staff on one side of the split may recommend going easy on the patient and being more supportive while the other side wants to set limits and raise expectations. A deeper look at the patient's problems may lead to a more refined plan, which includes being more supportive *and* setting limits with higher expectations in some areas of behavior but not others, for step-by-step progress.

Polarization in Group Decision-Making

Group decision-making in the workplace and in business can be very vulnerable to the emotions of polarization. Research on group decision-making in business explains how group members can influence one another, create groupthink and polarization, and make bad decisions. In analyzing why a single group can fail to make good decisions, business researchers Sunstein and Hastie explained groupthink as follows:

> As people gain confidence, they usually become more extreme in their beliefs. The reason is that a significant moderating factor—their own uncertainty about whether they are right—has been eliminated. With respect to group polarization, the key point is that agreement from others tends to increase confidence and, through that route, to increase extremism.[4]

With such confidence, mistakes can be made about who to hire, which investment to pursue, and whether a new policy will really work. "When individuals are leaning in a direction that is mistaken, the mistake will be amplified by group deliberation."

When the group has been organized around a bully leader who speaks in terms of us-against-them, the group pressure toward polarization can be even greater and emotionally reinforcing. If the group is operating under misinformation or believing in a fantasy crisis-villain-hero story, it will be particularly resistant to new, more accurate information; such information that comes from outside the group may be interpreted as an attack on the beliefs of their leader and therefore a personal attack on their leader, who must be defended rather than doubted. This takes us into the increasingly polarized field of politics.

Polarization in Politics

Modern politics worldwide is often organized around two or more groups or parties that disagree with each other over which policies a government should implement. In elections, they make their case for and against each other's policies, then the voters decide. While these opposing groups would ideally be working with the same accurate information, the group process can interfere. Polarized groups tend to have an emotional relationship with their leaders and become predisposed to their viewpoints, such that decisions are made based on each leader's beliefs and defending the leader rather than objective information.

Sunstein and Hastie also studied the impact of accurate media information on a predisposed political group in 2009. Alaska governor Sarah Palin initially said that the Affordable Care Act (also known as Obamacare) would create "death panels" to decide the fate of sick patients. When credible media sources corrected her, something strange happened:

> The correction actually backfired among Palin supporters with a high degree of political knowledge. After receiving the correction, they became *more* likely to believe that the Affordable Care Act contained death panels. Ironically, the correction intensified their original belief. The study suggests that if members of an out-group support some proposition, their very support might entrench the preexisting beliefs of the in-group.[5]

In other words, when there is intense polarization, the members of each opposing group will not change their opinions with new information—no matter how accurate—that comes from someone identified with the other group. Instead, it is purely interpreted at the primitive emotional level as an attack on their leader and themselves, and therefore rejected. This appears true for all political persuasions.

Once an *anti-community* is established—based primarily on what and who it is against—nothing from the other "side" can get in.

In the early 2000s, Sunstein and Hastie, plus a colleague, did an experiment with citizens from two cities in Colorado: Boulder (known for being predominantly liberal) and Colorado Springs (known for being predominantly conservative). They organized groups of approximately six citizens who held the political leanings of their cities and asked them to address three hot topics at the time: climate change, affirmative action, and same-sex civil unions. First, they had them write their opinions individually. Then they had them discuss each issue with the goal of reaching a group position on each topic.

The result after their deliberations was that the Boulder group became more liberal and the Colorado Springs group became more conservative. This happened in two ways: First, as a group they became more extreme after their internal discussions. Second, they became more extreme than their anonymous pre-deliberation individual views. The researchers concluded, "There's a big lesson here. Group deliberation often makes not only groups but also individuals more extreme, so much so that they will state more-extreme views privately and anonymously."[6]

We see this increasing in politics today, as groups experience emotional repetition in isolation from each other and reinforce their polarized views more and more over the years. Bully leaders tend to promote this for close bonding with their followers, which they enjoy. But over time, the risk of violence increases.

In an increasing number of countries today, the top leader is a bully whom almost half the country supports and defends, no matter what the bully does, for the reasons just described. Meanwhile, almost half the country adamantly opposes the leader. These two sides constantly fight with each other. Emotions escalate. Some people on both sides start hating each other and thinking of each other as the evil enemy. It becomes very personal and therefore can eventually lead to violence—physically eliminating the evil enemy.

For example, the former country of Yugoslavia was an amalgam of six smaller countries that were bonded together during World War II under the leadership of Josip Tito. After Tito died in 1980, the federation slowly fell apart, officially ending in 1992. While the six smaller countries had mostly gotten along, after Tito's death the president of Serbia, Slobodan Milosevic, a classic bully leader, worked long and hard to create maximum polarization.

Among Serbians, Milosevic resurrected old nationalist grudges and incited dreams of a "Greater Serbia." He rallied his fellow Serbs against their old allies: the Slovenes, the Croats, the Bosnians, and the Albanians. Because Milosevic tightly controlled the media, especially radio stations, he used them to divide the people who had formerly lived side by side. As one of his associates later said, "He creates disorder and manages to convince people only he can resolve it."[7]

HOW YOU CAN STOP THIS POWER

1. Open Your Eyes to the Pattern

Polarization is about emotionally seeing the other side as evil people rather than about undesirable behavior or a disagreement. Recognize that polarization is an emotional process, not a normal result of differences of opinion. Looking to see the reality, rather than the emotional fantasy of the other side, can be very eye-opening.

For example, in his book *Why We're Polarized*, Ezra Klein explains some of the misconceptions that political parties in America have about each other that promote further polarization. He found some surprising results from a 2018 survey, which he says show that both parties are more similar than different and that the levels of animosity don't match the levels of difference. Both parties are majority white, middle-class, heterosexual, middle-aged, and nonevangelical Christians. But here is what they believed about each other:

> Democrats believed 44 percent of Republicans earned over $250,000 a year; it's actually 2 percent. Republicans believed that 38 percent of Democrats were gay, lesbian, or bisexual; the correct answer is about 6 percent. Democrats believed that more than four out of every ten Republicans are seniors; in truth, seniors make up about 20 percent of the G.O.P. Republicans believed that 46 percent of Democrats are black and 44 percent belong to a union; in reality, about 24 percent of Democrats are African American and less than 11 percent belong to a union.[8]

It seems to me that the polarization comes from bully's stories and emotional repetition in isolation. With our eyes open, we need to look at how we can pull the plug on our fantasies about each other, which leads us to our next strategy.

2. Pull the Plug on Bullies' Polarization

Manage your own emotions in discussions of differences. Pay attention to your breathing when you are around people who disagree with you. It can calm your extreme thoughts. Look for commonalities. Recognize that polarizations are highly dangerous. Learn and teach conflict resolution skills. Refuse to see others in all-or-nothing or personal terms. Ask questions and listen. Find the good in each other. Override your primitive emotional responses to become more extreme from group discussions. Allow yourself to look at and listen to a variety of news sources and friends. Don't allow yourself to become isolated only with like-minded people.

For example, in 2019 some researchers created an event in which 526 voters from around the United States representing the full political landscape came together for a long weekend at a conference center in Texas. They talked about difficult political topics in terms of proposed policies in small groups, getting to hear each other's concerns and personal stories behind their concerns. Their ID tags and the policy proposals did not mention political parties. The outcome was a willingness to see each other as ordinary people, with real experiences and feelings as the source of many of their opinions. The study concluded, "Voters at the event on both the left and the right appeared to edge toward the center. . . . In fact, some people did change their minds." And some of them formed new friendships even though they disagreed on policies.[9]

The point here is that talking in small groups and one-on-one seems to overcome the political polarization that people have from a distance when they just talk to people in their own group. Since polarization is an emotional process, fed by bully leaders on one or both sides, it's not that hard to pull the plug when people speak directly to each other rather than through their leaders and groups. The concern about hopeless polarization is misplaced. The problem is emotional repetition in isolation, not policy disagreements, and the need to set limits on bully leaders who promote unnecessary polarization.

3. Set Limits with Credible Threats

Refuse to be part of extreme or extended arguments. If you have a position of authority, make it clear that you expect everyone to treat one another with respect. Set limits when you see polarization arising, such as between individuals or groups in families, the workplace, and even legal disputes. Don't allow emotions to take over. Require civility when addressing differences.

For example, the divorce between two famous actors, Alec Baldwin and Kim Basinger, was a high-profile, high-conflict media circus. The actors fought over their only child, their daughter, Ireland. In 2007 a voicemail surfaced that recorded a very angry Baldwin yelling at his then-eleven-year-old daughter for not answering a call from him. Amid the very public hubbub over this voicemail, with attacks and defenses for each side through their friends and lawyers, the public became polarized, with many fathers siding with Baldwin and many mothers siding with Basinger. (It is, of course, possible that both actors were bullies, at least when it came to their child.)

As the battle reached a fevered pitch, the judge in the case held a hearing. She sternly warned both parents to stop discussing their custody dispute in public. There were no further public announcements, and thereafter both parents quietly shared the responsibility of raising their daughter. Ireland is now an adult who reportedly has a happy relationship with both of her parents.[10]

4. Impose Serious Consequences on Polarizing Behavior

Once enough people realize that the polarizing behavior of bully leaders is the current biggest threat to humanity (especially in our world of nuclear weapons and high-emotion media), we will impose serious consequences sooner rather than later on such behavior. In the previous century, historians say that only three bullies were responsible for over 100 million deaths from wars and starvation: Hitler, Stalin, and Mao Zedong. In this century, the weapons of mass destruction are far stronger, and the weapons of high-emotion media are much more powerful. We must find ways to restrain or arrest bully leaders who attempt to promote polarization before they get very far. Imagine how different our world would be if Hitler, Stalin, and Mao had been stopped in their early days.

For example, Slobodan Milosevic, the former bully ruler of Serbia mentioned earlier, was the primary cause of 200,000 deaths and "the eviction of millions from homes in a practice that became known globally as ethnic cleansing." But eventually his own negative advocates tired of his extreme behavior and spoke out against him. Ultimately, they turned him in to the International Criminal Court in The Hague in the Netherlands. He was tried for war crimes and died in prison in 2006.[11]

5. Communicate Effectively to Others About Bullies' Polarization

Explain to others that polarization is an emotional process, not a primarily cognitive one. It is almost never the result of disagreements about real issues, which are normal. Intense polarization is personal, about whether people should even exist or not. It can ultimately lead to violence and war. We need to educate our children—and one another —about the history of polarization and violence, in other countries and in the United States. This requires multiple approaches, including classroom civics education, public service announcements on television, ads on billboards and web pages, the making of historical documentaries, and the creation of relevant content for YouTube and TikTok. This education must never stop, as each new generation needs to be alerted to the hidden powers of bullies—who can arise in each generation and poison whole populations—and to the methods that can reliably stop them.

For example, in his profound 2022 book, *This Is the Voice*, John Colapinto explains the difference between voices that divide and voices that unite, in all types of situations. He also provides a solid—and

easy-to-communicate—neurological explanation of how bullies' polarizing messages work:

> It is the demagogue (in public speech) or the abusive
> bully (in private) who privileges the limbic brain above
> the cortex, who tunes his voice to atavistic roars and
> growls, gasps and shrieks, who weaponizes the voice
> in ways that appeal primarily to the listener's emotion
> centers, thereby activating her primal, irrational, animal
> instincts of fear, envy, anger, resentment, vengeance.[12]

This description describes exactly how primitive emotional power
works by triggering the listener's primitive emotional responses.

6. Stand Strong with Others Against Bullies' Polarization

Boycott conversations and public commentary that emphasizes
polarization rather than unity and tolerance. Don't elect bully leaders
who use polarization to gain power. Stand with others who use emotional messages for *positive* purposes to unite people, not those who
use primitive emotional power to divide people. Encourage those who
use *positive respectful emotional power (PREP)*. We're ready for it.

For example, the apartheid government of South Africa was ruled
essentially by bullies from 1948 until the early 1990s, discriminating
against Black South Africans on a massive and severe scale. Nelson
Mandela and his compatriots stood strong against these bullies' polarization for decades, eventually forcing the resignation of its white leader,
F. W. de Klerk, in 1994. Extreme violence was predicted when apartheid
fell. However, when Mandela succeeded de Klerk as president, he stood
against all bullies, white and Black, from the political right and left.
Polarization was built into apartheid, but Mandela brought a peaceful
transition to the country by motivating a wide range of citizens using
unifying language. This included a big role for Bishop Desmond Tutu,

who led a Truth and Reconciliation Commission that further promoted unity and peace rather than polarization.

CONCLUSION

Polarization can occur anywhere, especially in families, groups, and politics. Bullies tend to polarize whatever social situation they are in. It seems almost hardwired as part of their primitive emotional power to enable them to dominate or destroy others. They see the world as us-against-them and emotionally pass that perception on to others.

The most intense polarization comes from the top when the bully is a leader who defines both sides of the polarization with their bully's story (the villain's group and the hero's group). In these situations, the people in each opposing group often blame themselves for the polarization when they really should set limits on the bully leader. This problem is widespread. Also, people repeat the bully leader's talking points, which adds to the polarization rather than reduces it. This is now "our" world of bullies because of the part we play in repeating polarized messages. We must work hard to avoid this.

What can be done? The research on groups talking is very revealing. When those within two opposing groups talk within their own group, they grow more extreme in their points of view. Yet when people talk together with those with opposing views, they tend to soften their views and empathize with each other instead of hating each other. This gives us a clear direction for all who are concerned about reducing intense polarization.

The average person doesn't create polarization. Bully leaders do. Of course, a bully anywhere in the organization could essentially become a bully leader, such as the example of a patient at a hospital causing staff splitting. But the average person or group member can resist polarization and not cooperate with it, which is especially important in today's world, where the repetition of false and exaggerated news travels faster than the truth. The risks of escalation in a world of nuclear weapons and artificial intelligence is far too great to ignore. Yet this chapter showed many examples of people overcoming polarization. We know what to do. We just need to get enough people to do it.

COMMON MISTAKE:

Polarization is caused by issues and different points of view.

REALITY:

Polarization is primarily an emotional process taught
top-down by bullies who make it personal, defining people on the
other "side" as stupid, immoral, less than human, or so
evil that they should be eliminated.

CHAPTER 13

How High-Emotion Media Promotes Bullies

"These are young guys who feel like losers, and they have an overwhelming drive to show everybody they are not on the bottom," he said. "In the case of the Buffalo shooter, it was about trying to impress this community of racists he had cultivated online."

—Frank T. McAndrew, professor of psychology, Knox College, on the motivations of mass shooters

THE BIGGEST CHANGE DRIVING US BACKWARD into this new world culture of bullies is the development of high-tech, high-emotion media. Using primitive emotional power (PEP), the media repeatedly hooks our brains with constant messages of fear, anger, and love/loyalty. This locks us into watching, listening, and participating, such that we're often unable to stop. The intense emotional repetition of bully's stories can lead to primitive emotional responses, including violence at every level of society.

As each new media invention (from radio to TV to social media to AI) enters the information highway, it has no values or limits—essentially, no restraints. However, values and limits are necessary in all healthy human relationships. Where there are no rules, only bullies will rule. Combining their unrestrained personalities with unrestrained media puts us all at risk. When the powers behind modern media don't set limits, we have to set our own to protect ourselves and our families—especially our children.

With all this going on in the background of our daily lives, it is no wonder that we are more susceptible to bullies today and their emotional manipulations. Their exaggerated behavior fits right into the culture and throws off our radar of who we can trust and who we cannot. By activating our most primitive emotional responses, our judgment is poorer and our tolerance for bad behavior is much higher. This appears to be especially true when bullies use fear to isolate us and persuade us to trust them and no one else.

There are three key ways in which this high-emotion media influences all of us, and we need to understand them in order to put on the brakes. High-emotion media

1. Trains young adults in the details of how to be bullies.
2. Creates a culture of fear and blame, driving people to seek bullies for security.
3. Increases polarization, which can lead to accepting extremism and violence.

Training Young Adult Bullies

One of the most disturbing current trends in bullying is mass shootings at schools, stores, malls, and almost anywhere. A significant number of these shooters are young men between eighteen and twenty-one years old. News reports indicate that "six of the nine deadliest mass shootings in the United States since 2018 were by people who were 21 or younger, a shift from earlier decades."[1]

Apparently, these young men have not found a place to fit in and have been following the media portrayal of mass violence online to give themselves a sense of power and dominance in their unhappy lives. While most public discussion of mass shootings focuses on gun control and mental illness, little attention has been paid to the impact of emotional repetition in the media influencing the young people who become mass killers.

For example, as the expert at the beginning of this chapter explained, "These are young guys who feel like losers, and they have an overwhelming drive to show everybody they are not on the bottom," he said. "In the case of the Buffalo shooter, it was about trying to impress this community of racists he had cultivated online. In the case of the kid in Uvalde, it was about going back to the place where you felt disrespected and acting out violently."[2]

This analysis further supports my concern that many people who feel stuck in the loser position of win-lose relationships will revolt in one way or another, sooner or later. No one wants to be a loser. Much of today's young adult bullying appears to be an effort to compensate for *being bullied* or *feeling like they were losing out* after endlessly watching grievance-based media repetition. For an adolescent who has felt like a loser for years, it's not hard to imagine that being a powerful mass shooter, if only for a day, is very appealing. They haven't yet developed the self-restraint that comes with brain development in the mid twenties, which usually leads to productive adult lives.

Now bullies can find one another online and gain confidence for remaining stuck in their negativity and immaturity, just as the last chapter explained about polarized groups talking among themselves. Finding such a group—an anti-community—makes them more confident and extreme. Titania Jordan, who works for an online safety company monitoring violent content, says, "It's a way for them to show strength if they are bullied or left out. It's just a part of the narrative now in all these cases—there's always a social media component."[3]

Watching the news about mass shootings can have a contagious influence on anyone who feels powerless or depressed. Unfortunately, news broadcasters glorify the emotional drama with endless coverage of students rushing out of the school building with their hands over their heads in a panic and the wailing of parents and police sirens. Since videos are one of the most effective ways of providing training these days, showing videos of mass shootings— sometimes as they are happening and always in detail afterward—is one of the best trainings for the next generation of mass shooters.

Do we really need to have our media overemphasize these events in such a manner?

What Can We Do About This?

As a society we need to set stronger limits on news about bullies, because this targets our lower brains without our even realizing it. For the sake of free speech, the news about mass shootings should be written about in print media rather than presented on screens in living color. Print media doesn't have the same hidden access to our lower brains that visual and sound media have.

Also, saying a shooter's name and showing his picture can be very motivating, so these should also be withheld. When reporters ask what the motive was, they should instead ask what media the person watched and what social media platforms inspired them. While modern news and dramas on our screens may be entertaining for adults, they can serve as *training* for the next generation.

Young men and women require challenges and opportunities to belong. We need to promote healthy activities and outlets through our media more than images of dominance and destruction. And, of course, our families and communities need support for providing in-person group activities to all young adults (sports, music, live drama, and so forth) so that they don't become isolated full-time with negative media and social media. Cultures reap what they sow.

A Culture of Fear and Blame

Since the turn of the twenty-first century, media competition (radio, TV, Internet, and social media) has created an intense and widespread culture of fear and blame. This environment benefits bullies. If we are constantly in a state of fear and told that all our problems are caused by evil people, then we will be more willing to look for heroes to solve our problems. For example, two terrorist events were studied to see their impact on our minds and bodies. In 2001 television repeatedly broadcast the 9/11 attacks on the World Trade Center in New York. Constant media exposure to these traumatic events "was associated with high risk for probable posttraumatic stress disorder (PTSD) and other negative emotions." The fear of future terrorism that this television exposure triggered apparently caused acute stress and impacted cardiovascular health.[4]

In a 2020 study, similar health outcomes were described following the 2013 Boston Marathon terrorist bombing, with a surprising result comparing media exposure to actual presence at the bombing: "Likewise, 6 hr or more of daily media-based exposure to the Boston Marathon bombings (BMB) was associated with higher acute stress than was direct exposure to the BMB."[5] Even fictional exposure to increasingly graphic images of violence can have the same emotional impact of creating a generalized sense of fear. The study reports, "Triggering fear and anxiety also may activate attentional biases toward threat-related stimuli (bloody images; etc.), making it difficult for more anxious people to disengage."[6]

In other words, if the goal of today's media, regardless of form, is to capture people's attention and keep them engaged, then primitive emotional power is the way to do it. Just exaggerate these events and people will believe the world is on the edge of collapse; the feeling then develops that strongman leaders are needed, and bullies are eager to promote themselves as our heroes.

As Daniel Goleman, the man who made us aware of emotional intelligence, observed, "People who feel threatened and anxious are especially prone to catching other people's emotions."[7] Bullies intuitively know this.

But it's not just fear. We're primed to think in terms of villains too. Nowadays we have been taught to believe that all problems are crises, and all crises are caused by identifiable evil villains. Yet today's problems are much more complex than simple crises and usually need a lot of people to solve them—maybe all of us—such as with climate change and worldwide viruses. But for bullies to gain power, they need simple villains to activate our primitive rage. Otherwise, who wants to be a follower? And who would follow a leader with no history of leadership skills and organizational support?

As such, bullies must generate feelings of extreme fear and rage as a shortcut to leadership: "There's a terrible crisis caused by evil people, and trust me, only I have the skills to solve it." High-emotion media prepares us for that. The plots in the most popular movies and television series contain a terrible crisis, an evil villain, and one or more heroes. In this century, Marvel Comics and DC Comics graduated to a home on the big screen and a never-ending supply of bully's stories with all three parts: crisis, villain, and hero. Police shows with the same crisis-villain-hero script have dominated TV ratings for decades. They grab our attention, and our brains are very comfortable with them.

But it's not only the dramas, which most of us understand are fantasies. The daily news—which we count on to describe real life—is also structured around crises ("Breaking News!"), villains (some foreigner or big government or big business or school shooter), and the daily hero. Even the *New York Times*—the most widely read newspaper in the United States—has been found to tilt unnecessarily negative since the 1960s and more so in the new century.[8]

No wonder that people worldwide are so anxious. Sure there are problems to solve, but bullies gain power by making up crises or turning real problems into crises. It doesn't help that TV news then provides us with easy fantasy villains to associate with these fantasy crises. Fox News has been the most watched cable news channel in the United States since 2015.[9] In a book describing its popularity, *The Loudest Voice in the Room*, Gabriel Sherman wrote, "On Fox News, the tedious personages of workaday politics are reborn as *heroes and villains* with triumphs and reverses—never-ending story lines."[10]

High-emotion media doesn't usually look for depth. Instead, they ask "How do you feel about so-and-so?" They want to show fear, anger, and tears rather than facts.

The reality is that if the "crisis" and the "villain" are automatically accepted as true, people will give the fantasy hero their power. Since many people (one out of three in America[11]) are predisposed personality-wise to emotionally prefer strongman leaders, a fantasy hero can seem very appealing—especially one who is a good storyteller in a culture of fear and blame. Their targets of blame can be anyone who fits well into the storyline, and the bully's negative advocates will attempt (and sometimes succeed) to destroy them.

But bullies are not heroes—they are all about image, sounds, and words. In a high-emotion media culture, bullies just *look* like heroes. The real heroes are the problem-solvers who collaborate to find solutions in the boring world of reality and complex problems—such as developing a vaccine for COVID.

Belief in bully's stories repeated thousands of times through modern media has misled whole populations throughout the past hundred years, people who didn't realize what was happening until it was too late—misled by storytellers using state-controlled radio, movies, and television. Emotional repetition in isolation via high-emotion media has made one person's widespread control of a country possible like never before.

This may explain why, after sixty years of steady progress up to 2004, democracies worldwide have since been backsliding toward authoritarian governments with single rulers who turn out to be bullies. In 2022, for the first time since 2004, Bertelsman Stiftung's Transformation Index, which studies nations using several factors, "counts more autocratically governed states than democracies. Among the 137 countries surveyed, only 67 are still democracies, while the number of autocracies has risen to 70."[12] As you will see, this tracks closely with the rise of social media.

What Can We Do About This?

Watch out for media use of the bully's story in its portrayal of real life and news as compared to its programs of fiction and fantasy. Unfortunately, these narratives are getting confused these days as the same media are getting used for both purposes. Ask yourself these questions, which I suggested with individual bullies in Chapter 6:

1. **Is this really a crisis?**

   Is this a totally made-up crisis or a real problem that requires a wide range of people working together to get it right rather than a single hero? Get your information from a variety of sources. Be aware that your primitive emotional fear system is manipulated by much of the media to get you to watch or listen, and especially social media, which has fewer controls. Don't repeat what you have heard until you have verified it with a credible source. If you repeat what a credible source says, tell your listener who the source was so that they can check it out too. Don't get a reputation for spreading false information.

2. **Is this really an evil villain?**

   As described earlier, check out the source of your information. But also maintain a healthy skepticism that the alleged "villain" is really a totally evil person. When people talk that way about other people, it is often an exaggeration and shows their own all-or-nothing thinking. Consider the possibility that many of today's problems are not created by a single villain but rather by multiple factors, such as climate change and worldwide human viruses.

3. **Is this really a hero?**

   Get some background on who you are seeing and hearing through the media. Are they problem-solvers or storytellers?

There aren't many people who are good at both. Do they speak in dramatic, emotional tones, like fictional TV characters? Or are they a source of reliable and useful information?

Increasing Polarization

The polarization research described in the prior chapter explains that opposing groups talking within themselves will always become more extreme as a group and also as individuals. If their whole purpose is to completely reject the other group, or to make it personal and hate the people in the other group, then it's anti-community—they desire to eliminate the other group and no outside information can get in, no matter how credible.

For example, Hitler was the first to use the radio and newsreels for emotional repetition of his shrill voice and images of strength in isolation; no one else had used these new media this way.[13] He successfully gained power by railing in these media against the small Jewish population in the 1930s, which was less than 1 percent of Germany, with disastrous results.

In the 1950s Joe McCarthy was the first to weaponize the arrival of television by teaching fear of and hatred for communists in the U.S. government and Hollywood. He used intense emotional repetition of his face and voice in isolation—no one else had used TV this way—until he couldn't produce any proof and was censured by the Senate.[14]

In the 1990s there was the demise of the Fairness Doctrine,[15] which required balanced viewpoints by all radio and television stations licensed by the federal government. This change allowed them to broadcast one-sided news and views to their audiences, which included the establishment in 1996 of Fox News (leaning right) and MSNBC (leaning left).[16]

In 2004 Facebook got started, in 2005 YouTube began, and in 2006 Twitter and smartphones were launched, with algorithms that fed more and more extreme views to keep their users online.[17] According to the Global Media Statistics website, over 60 percent of the world's population uses social media as of 2023, which explains its powerful emotional influence worldwide.[18]

The correlation of the rise of social media since 2004 with the backsliding to more primitive autocratic governments makes sense. Unlike radio and television, the Internet and social media provide intense *interactive* communities of like-minded people who can share and reinforce one another's extreme thoughts about outsiders—as anti-community—without restraint. In a sense, there are no adults in the room of many social media platforms, so the most primitive thinking can gain strength and reinforcement. This can reinforce the simple thinking and beliefs of large numbers of people. By spending many hours a day living in the fantasy world of crises, villains, and strongman heroes, it's not surprising that many people no longer believe in the real world of democracies with leaders who can handle complexity, compromise, and collaboration.

In addition, modern radio, television, and visual social media—in contrast to the information provided by most newsprint, books, and mild-mannered announcers—emphasize extreme faces and extreme voices, which hook our right brains unconsciously while turning off our left brains' thinking processes (see Chapter 4). For example, the amygdala (alarm center) in the right brain is particularly sensitive to "nonverbal facial expressions," which are processed "very rapidly and below the level of consciousness."[19] And bullies have the most emotional faces and voices.

Unfortunately, with today's competing media, polarization is easy as people can tune in to their own favorite radio and television stations and other sources, such as podcasts, and find their own favorite celebrities or talents to feed them only what they want to hear. This means a lot of emotional repetition in isolation.

The result of this in the United States is the following, as described by Ezra Klein in his book *Why We Are Polarized,* when reporting on a study about how Democrats and Republicans see each other: "The more interested in politics people were, the more political media they consumed, the more mistaken they were about the other party."[20] He goes on to say that political reporting emphasizes outrage. "We are outraged when members of other groups threaten our group and violate our values. As such polarized media doesn't emphasize commonalities, it weaponizes differences: it doesn't focus on the best of the other side, it threatens you with the worst.[21]

Over time this widening polarization can become a dangerous situation for any group, community, or country.

For example, in Rwanda in 1993, a radio station was founded and controlled by members of the ruling regime, which was dominated by the Hutu ethnic group. It preached hatred for the minority ethnic group, the Tutsis. It became nicknamed "Hate Radio." In 1994, after a year of broadcasting negative stereotypes, over 800,000 members of the Tutsi ethnic group were slaughtered by members of the majority Hutu ethnic group, primarily with machetes.

After this occurred, an International Criminal Tribunal for Rwanda was established, which tried and convicted two radio journalists and one print journalist for their primary roles in promoting the killing of Tutsis. In delivering their life sentences, one of the three judges stated,

> You were fully aware of the power of words, and you
> used the radio—the medium of communication with

the widest public reach—to disseminate hatred and violence. . . . Without a firearm, machete or any physical weapon, you caused the death of thousands of innocent civilians. . . . The power of the media to create and destroy fundamental human values comes with great responsibility. Those who control such media are accountable for its consequences.[22]

In its judgment, the court acknowledged the importance of freedom of speech by distinguishing "between the discussion of ethnic consciousness and the promotion of ethnic hatred."[23] This addresses the issue of making it personal, which is the dividing line between solving problems in terms of behavior and promoting the domination or destruction of a whole person or group of people—what bullies (with their ancient personalities) are intent on doing as compared to the vast majority of modern citizens.

As I mentioned in Chapter 12, the bully leader of Serbia, Slobodan Milosevic, also controlled the media, primarily radio, in the 1990s war between the former parts of Yugoslavia. He also clearly used it to sow division between ethnic groups and was tried in a UN International Criminal Tribunal for the Former Yugoslavia for his role in driving the conflict and causing the deaths of 200,000 people.[24]

The rule of law is necessary to set limits on bullies such as these and provide realistic consequences. These international criminal courts seem to have done a reasonable job in permanently stopping the bullies from driving these national catastrophes with the use of their high-emotion media. While they are after the fact, in the long run it is hoped that such tribunals will serve as a brake on future rulers who are tempted to eliminate one group in order to gain control over another.

What Can We Do About This?

There seem to be two general ways that high-emotion media can be managed so that it is not used to promote polarization and violence against individuals and groups of people.

First, set limits on hate speech as compared to ethnic consciousness, as the Rwanda tribunal distinguished. Hate speech attacks people for *who they are*, not for any particular behavior, and lays the groundwork for their possible elimination. Ethnic consciousness, on the other hand, can recognize differences and tell stories of how a group may have been poorly treated in the past. When there is more widespread understanding of the primitive emotional power of hate speech, maybe governments will restrain their own use by recognizing that hate speech can become a clear and present danger to the lives of others, even a year or more after disseminating it.

The U.S. Supreme Court has interpreted the First Amendment as allowing restrictions on speech that presents such a "clear and present danger."[25] However, this has been generally viewed as an *immediate danger*. I leave it to others to sort out where these lines should be drawn, but time and events are likely to tell us that it needs to be more tightly drawn as our modern media technologies become more and more powerful. As occurred in Rwanda, the dangerous messages were building for over a year before they (inevitably?) ripened into extreme violence.

Second, since polarization grows when there is no contact with the people and ideas of an opposing group, a solution would be to require the inclusion of opposing viewpoints when opinions are being expressed on media outlets. As mentioned previously, the name for this in the United States was the Fairness Doctrine, which was the law of the land from 1949 to 1987. It required radio and television stations that were licensed to use the airways by the U.S. government's Federal Communications Commission to present both sides of editorial opinions and both opposing candidates for office. This way listeners and viewers were exposed to two points of view, at least, and less likely to be manipulated and polarized by hearing just one side.

The rule was eliminated after cable and satellite television stations argued that it shouldn't apply to them and that it was too restrictive of freedom of speech.[26] Given our understanding now of how one-sided media enables bullies to dangerously increase polarization, it would be beneficial for this doctrine to be reenacted.

CONCLUSION

Most people know that the Internet has shortened our attention spans. But our high-emotion media has also shortened our ability to reflect and think, resulting in an overemphasis on intense emotions that have been internalized worldwide without us understanding why—which has made us anxious, angry, and susceptible to bullies as self-promoting "heroes." This chapter has attempted to explain why and what we can do about it.

This knowledge should help us disengage from overexposure to today's media by limiting our consumption to what is really necessary. We have to realize that what we watch and what we repeat can make us part of the problem or part of the solution. This awareness should also motivate us to find a healthier balance and more realistic interactions with real human beings. After all, you get more of what you pay attention to. This brings us to the last chapter and the future.

CHAPTER 14

Toward a Win-Win World

*Almost every week we get e-mails from parents,
managers and professionals telling us how our
New Ways simple skills have helped calm a family or
workplace situation. And how their skills will help
them keep the peace going forward.*

—Megan Hunter, CEO, High Conflict Institute

THE WORLD IS NOW AT A CROSSROADS in a struggle over the structure of our social relationships. That struggle is between bullies with an intrinsically win-lose outlook and reasonable people who want a win-win approach to relationships and problem-solving. Win-win must win.

We have lots of hope. Knowledge is power, and there are skills for turning win-lose interactions into win-win ones. We can learn to spot bullies and stop their bullying behavior at the individual level and together as a society. We have the knowledge. We just need more people to share it, learn win-win skills, and restrain bullies before they gain too much power over us in all our relationships.

Unfortunately, adult bullies and their primitive emotional powers (PEP) have been making headway around the world in recent years, bringing win-lose relationships and an increase in violence with them. The trend in this direction seems to be growing. In large part this is because bullies as cultural leaders have learned to harness technologies that promote massive repetition of primitive images of strength and sounds of strength through face and voice communication, which can activate fear, anger, and love/loyalty in us beneath the level of consciousness. Bullies at all levels of society have been learning and acting on this, from family violence to workplace bullying on up to the highest levels of nations preparing their citizens to bully other nations.

Yet we know what to do. Here is a quick summary from these chapters of how to spot bullies and stop them at the individual level:

Spotting and Stopping Bullies

PRIMITIVE EMOTIONAL POWERS	HOW TO SPOT BULLIES	HOW TO STOP BULLIES
Unrestrained Personalities	Spot efforts to form win-lose relationships. Recognize that they can't stop themselves.	Don't tolerate win-lose relationships. Steer clear or get help.
3 Primitive Emotions	Spot their efforts to induce fear, anger, and love/loyalty in you.	When you spot these efforts, guard yourself from getting emotionally hooked.

Spotting and Stopping Bullies (continued)

PRIMITIVE EMOTIONAL POWERS	HOW TO SPOT BULLIES	HOW TO STOP BULLIES
Making It Personal	Spot attacks on your whole person, such as demeaning comments, threats to reputation, and implied threats of physical harm.	Recognize that they are not problem-solving but trying to gain dominance over you.
Bully's Story (BS)	Spot their fantasy crises, villains, and heroes.	Expose the bully's story as false or gross exaggeration.
Emotional Repetition	Spot the repetition of bully's stories about you or others.	Explain to others that emotional repetition is why people believe the bully's story, not because it is true.
Negative Advocates	Spot bully's emotionally hooked negative advocates.	Steer clear of them or inform advocates of true information.
Projection and Playing the Victim	Question whether accusations better fit the blamer than the accused. Question whether an alleged victim might actually be the perpetrator.	Expose projections as about the bully, not you. Expose how they are playing the victim to gain negative advocates.
Surprise Attacks	Spot their use of primitive emotional powers as soon as possible before they gain power over you.	Anticipate surprise attacks. Maintain a healthy skepticism. Expose their bullying patterns.

Spotting and Stopping Bullies (continued)

PRIMITIVE EMOTIONAL POWERS	HOW TO SPOT BULLIES	HOW TO STOP BULLIES
Bullies as Leaders	Spot their drive to be dominant over others wherever they are.	Don't give them power over you. Don't help put them in positions of authority over others.
Polarization	Spot their efforts to create us-against-them conflicts and have people fight each other. Spot their all-or-nothing thinking about people in your family, community, etc.	Expose their efforts to create us-against-them groups. Keep contact with those on the other side. Listen and keep an open mind.

© 2024 Bill Eddy

What Can We Do Together?

This marriage of bullies and high-emotion media is now dominating our world culture—a situation that will continue to escalate until both can be sufficiently restrained. This isn't just social media; it's all forms of highly repetitive visual and voice media that promote bully dynamics (TV, cable TV, streaming movies, etc.). As human beings with primitive emotional responses buried deep within us, we are bound to get emotionally hooked beneath our level of consciousness by bullies' PEP. Many of us are becoming immobilized, polarized, or joining the bullies in attacking their targets. But we have the knowledge to overcome this reaction if enough people participate in setting limits and learning new skills.

We can effectively manage technology and our social relationships, but to do so we need to learn new methods of restraining bullies on a worldwide basis. Problems can—and must—be solved without making them personal and without making them about dominating or destroying other human beings.

If humanity is to survive this struggle, we need to do four things (at least)—and we can. We have already begun. The following gives me a lot of hope:

1. Provide coaching and training for bullies and those around them.
2. Emphasize mediation and negotiation to resolve disputes.
3. Develop positive respectful emotional power.
4. Create a worldwide emphasis on restraining bullies.

Provide Coaching and Training

We need to teach as many human beings as possible—ideally, everyone—individual conflict resolution skills for self-restraint and win-win solutions. Just as importantly, we need to educate our children, our leaders, and ourselves about what bullies do, how and why they often succeed, and how to spot them and restrain them. Here are some points of progress:

Overcoming Domestic Violence. Many treatment groups are available for those who are violent with their intimate partners (dating partners, living-together partners, married partners), primarily for men but a few for women. David Wexler of Relationship Training Institute developed a group treatment method over the past thirty years called the STOP method. He has been training leaders for this method around the country for decades. Wexler says that about 70 percent of men who go through this program with weekly meetings for a year demonstrate more empathy for their partners, stop their violent behavior, and treat their children better as well—because they don't want them to become perpetrators or victims of domestic violence. But about 30 percent do not learn these self-management skills and need further restraints, such as long-term restraining orders, time in jail, or both.[1]

Overcoming Child Abuse. Physical child abuse is one of the easiest behaviors to change with the right approach, positive support, and repetition of positive behaviors. One of many programs is the Parent-Child Interaction Program (PCIP) for parents who have had their two- to seven-year-old children removed from the home because of abusive behavior. PCIP teaches parents how to interact with their children nonabusively with minute-by-minute coaching in weekly sessions over a period of fourteen to twenty weeks, after which they usually get their children back home permanently. They find that abusive parents often have nothing positive to say to their children, so that part of the treatment is learning to give their children positive feedback as well as refraining from hitting or otherwise abusing them. Follow-ups one and two years later have shown the long-lasting success of learning these self-management skills.[2]

Child sexual abuse by adults is much harder to treat as it may be hardwired for years into the person's brain development during their own early sexual development in adolescence. However, some treatment programs are finding success in treating juvenile sex offenders, which is the best time to turn around the beginnings of such abusive, bullying behavior. Such programs emphasize cognitive behavioral therapies and relapse prevention for the individual offender. However, these treatments also need to involve the culture in which an adolescent is raised (family, peers, school, community) to be most effective.[3]

Overcoming High-Conflict Divorce. Approximately 20 percent of divorces (including unmarried couples with children who separate) are considered "high-conflict" because of ongoing bullying behavior by one or both parents, including fights over the children, polarization of relatives, and repeated use of family courts. These cases often involve a child who resists or refuses contact with one of the parents primarily because of abuse or alienation. Family counseling and parenting programs can teach skills to reduce these conflicts, including our High Conflict Institute method called *New Ways for Families,* which teaches both parents a set of win-win conflict resolution skills (managed emotions, flexible thinking, moderate behavior, and checking yourself rather than blaming others) in counseling, an online class, and coaching with the online class. Some of our surveys indicate that about 80 percent of high-conflict parents improve their ability to coparent and stay out of court.[4]

Retraining Difficult Employees. The question of whether to fire or keep bullies or "toxic" employees is an important question that many organizations have studied, including two researchers at Harvard Business School. Their definition of toxic workers includes behavior that is harmful to the organization, its property, and its people. They suggested that some such employees may need to be fired, but with others the organization should try "coverting them to average employees."[5]

I developed a new coaching method (*New Ways for Work*) with my colleague from the High Conflict Institute, L. Georgi DiStefano, to coach such employees so that they may be able to remain with their organizations as more productive workers and managers. This doesn't change their personalities but can take the edge off their interpersonal behavior, which some high-tech companies call "sharp elbows." Coaching in specific areas is a rapidly growing field, with physician coaches, executive coaches, and others. Taking a coaching approach, many highly skilled but difficult employees are able to keep their jobs although others cannot change enough and are moved out of their organizations.[6]

Organizational Training. Teaching simple skills for work groups or whole organizations is another way that groups can manage their internal behavior to restrain bullies from harming an organization's culture. For example, our *BIFF Communication Method* (basically *brief, informative, friendly*, and *firm*) for e-mails, text messages, and letters[7] has been adopted company-wide by several organizations. In one consultation case we had, a high-tech company asked us whether to fire or keep a manager who was sending bullying e-mails to her employees. We suggested that they give her three coaching sessions in using the BIFF method and see if she could change enough to keep her position as a manager. The outcome is confidential but giving people a "chance to change" is one of the themes of our coaching and trainings. After a group training, general team communication often improves, and sometimes particularly difficult employees decide to retire or leave the organization on their own. In either case, bullying behavior is stopped.

Nonprofit organizations, churches and other faith-based institutions, volunteer groups, social groups, higher education, and health-care facilities all need to pay more attention to redirecting bullies within their groups. Ironically, these types of groups attract more bullies because they tend to be more friendly and tolerant, yet they are also some of the last to realize that they are dealing with a bully.

Teaching Emotional Intelligence. As I briefly mentioned earlier in this book, primitive emotional power is the flip side of emotional intelligence, which helps people have equal, win-win relationships. The goal of primitive emotional power (PEP) is to gain dominance over others in win-lose relationships or to destroy them. There are no equal relationships formed with PEP. It comes from our primitive roots when dominance hierarchies were the way of life: eat or be eaten; kill or be killed. People who used PEP were safer because they dominated or destroyed those who were a threat to them—but it only lasted until another bully dominated or destroyed them. In a win-win world, emotional intelligence (EQ) skills are very helpful and practical. Some bully leaders can perhaps be taught EQ skills, so that they are more effective and personally satisfied in the win-win world.

Emotional intelligence skills emphasize self-management, self-awareness, social awareness, and relationship management. In an article for Harvard Business School Online, Sabrina Landry explains the importance of EQ, "It is one of the most sought-after interpersonal skills in the workplace. In fact, 71 percent of employers value emotional intelligence more than technical skills when evaluating candidates."[8]

Daniel Goleman, the person who popularized EQ starting in the 1990s, said in an interview, "The most effective leaders are all alike in one crucial way: They all have a high degree of what has come to be known as emotional intelligence. It's not that IQ and technical skills are irrelevant. They do matter, but . . . they are the entry-level requirements for executive positions."[9]

Since the numbers of bully leaders appear to be increasing, society as a whole needs to learn the skills of emotional intelligence. Since EQ has been around for over three decades, it's not hard to find a course or someone who is teaching these skills. They need to be more widely disseminated, not just to high-level employees and business leaders. The more that people in general recognize the signs of PEP, the more the principles of EQ make sense and can be more widely taught to slow bullies down and perhaps turn some of them around.

Emphasize Mediation and Negotiation

We need to improve our mechanisms for conflict resolution—especially in our legal and political systems—to reinforce the use of win-win solutions rather than win-lose solutions. This is already happening in the American legal system, where more than 90 percent of civil disputes headed for court are settled without a trial. Mediation is now required as a first step in many family disputes, such as those over the custody of children in a divorce. Mediation methods such as restorative justice are being taught to some children and teenagers in trouble. We also need to ensure that all conflict resolution professionals learn how to manage bullies in their training and practice.

Mediating with Community Bullies. Many bullies who practice theft, intimidating people, stealing cars, and so on start out acting that way as teenagers and end up in prison. Many organizations are attempting to redirect them as soon as their bullying gets them into trouble in the community. One such organization, National Conflict Resolution Center (NCRC) based in San Diego, California, has for several years made significant efforts at disrupting the school-to-prison pipeline. They also create guidelines and programs for civil discourse, help colleges with civility programs, and assist communities with their mediation services for individuals and group conflicts.

Victim-offender mediation programs for teenagers—and some young adults—help bullies face their victims in a dialogue, as well as other consequences, for nonviolent offenses. By meeting their victims and discussing the pain the bullies caused, and getting to know each other as human beings, bullies are often able to turn their lives around and become more cooperative citizens.

Mediation of All Forms. Mediation is becoming a common method for resolving conflicts at all levels of society with win-win outcomes, from community disputes to divorce mediation to workplace conflicts to labor-management disputes to international conflicts between nations. A neutral mediator helps two or more sides in a dispute talk together, make proposals for settling their differences, and reach their own agreements. A mediator does not decide for the parties, like an arbitrator would do in a legal dispute. To agree, both sides must be satisfied enough to stop fighting. Thus, mediation promotes win-win solutions.

Mediators have to be well trained to be able to facilitate such agreements without dictating them. NCRC is one such organization that does a lot of mediation training. The Academy of Professional Family Mediators is an organization that promotes training and continuing education for divorce mediators and other family disputes.[10] The Association for Conflict Resolution is a broad international organization that holds workshops and conferences to promote the use of mediation and other negotiation methods to professionals.[11]

Training Professionals in Dispute Resolution. More universities around the world are providing master's degrees in dispute resolution (MDR). More law schools are also offering mediation courses to their students, because they are likely to represent clients in mediations or facilitate mediations themselves someday. The win-win world is expanding. This is becoming a popular career interest for many young professionals.

Develop Positive, Respectful Emotional Power. We need to encourage, support, and train people to respond to bullies using positive respectful emotional power that unites people rather than divides and polarizes them. For example, teaching methods of communicating with empathy, attention, and respect (EAR statements) can often calm an upset person and turn a win-lose conversation into a win-win one.[12]

Likewise, teaching written communication that is brief, informative, friendly, and firm (*BIFF Responses*) when responding to a hostile e-mail, text, or letter can avoid or defuse conflicts. Also, teaching how to make proposals and respond to them respectfully can turn

around many win-lose arguments about the past by focusing the discussion on what to do in the future.

For the past fifteen years, we have taught these three communication methods (EAR, BIFF, 3 Steps for Making Proposals) to turn
win-lose interactions into win-win experiences. I am still occasionally amazed that they really work and help resolve conflicts that once
were hopelessly escalating before these approaches were used. It is
possible to shift win-lose situations into win-win solutions. The key
to each of these methods is to shift a bully's emotions and behavior
into contributions to joint problem-solving.

Create a Widespread Focus on Restraining Bullies

Throughout this book I have emphasized that the main problem
with bullies is their unrestrained personalities. They can't stop themselves. Therefore, society needs to restrain them but at the same time
get the benefit of their creative ideas and energy.

People in charge of public settings should deny bullies the opportunity to engage in personal attacks, use intense blame, invoke a fantasy crisis, or demonize a fantasy villain or group. This should apply
to all media, at public meetings (school boards, homeowners' associations, neighborhood and ward meetings, city councils, etc.), and
at workplace gatherings. These are reasonable limits to free speech.

We need to recognize that bullies have benefited society in surprising ways by pushing us to change. Most of us don't like to rock
the boat and don't want to upset one another. Our strong empathy
helps us care about one another and get along in the status quo. But
bullies—with their lack of empathy and self-restraint—overcome
our mutual caring and push us to change. In the process of following
or pushing back, we become polarized into groups that then go their

separate ways or fight until one dominates the other—for better or for worse.

In this process, through trial and error, bullies appear to have slowly pushed society forward—but with many errors and at a huge price: loss of life, loss of freedom, and loss of long-lasting peace as each new bully overthrows the previous status quo and dominant bully. We have to realize that this push-pull win-lose model of progress is unsustainable in our world of nuclear power and pervasive high-emotion media. The tools of our collective destruction are already in place and need to be restrained.

The better solutions are in spotting bullies and restraining them earlier, since they cannot stop themselves. Bullies aren't evil; they're ancient. We cannot afford them as bullies in the modern world. Just look at the three bullies who killed over 100 million people in the last century: Hitler, Stalin, and Mao.[13] Three bullies caused wars, death, and massive destruction—while none of them owned nuclear weapons at the time. Bullies are the greatest threat to humanity today—individually and collectively. They need to be restrained, individually and collectively.

CONCLUSION

Bullies have unrestrained personalities. They have ancient personalities that use at least ten primitive emotional powers (the PEP formula), operating beneath our conscious awareness, to hook our brains and get us to submit to their dominance or help them dominate others. These powers are the same, whether bullies use them in your family, your workplace, your community, online, or in the larger world. Just by becoming aware of these ten powers, you should be able to spot bullies a mile away. We all need to develop a healthy skepticism—and know what we are looking for.

Don't let them deceive you. Don't be caught by surprise. There usually are warning signs of these ten primitive emotional powers. By joining with others, it is possible to stop bullies, as I have shown with numerous examples. The more people who understand this, the better it is for everyone. No one should suffer a bully alone.

In this book I have tried to show how our technological progress has inadvertently weakened our families and communities, weakened our restraints against bullies, and strengthened bullies' emotional powers. They are able to manipulate us because we crave the sense of community and power that they appear to represent. Polarized groups have the most intense sense of community within them. Yet polarized groups are anti-communities, built primarily on who they are against. While seeming to satisfy deep emotional needs of their members, they shut out important information and can become dangerous.

Bullies are all about creating images of strength, sounds of strength, and words of strength—all exaggerated by massive high-emotion media—rather than being real leaders and problem-solvers. We have to recognize this as early as possible if we are going to stop them. They love to take a sledgehammer to rules and laws, so that they can be in charge without restraints. But when there are no rules, only bullies will rule. We can't survive that.

We have to watch out for their bully's stories of fantasy crises (instilling fear), fantasy villains (activating anger), and fantasy heroes (inspiring love/loyalty) for whom we would do anything, including becoming violent. You can practice spotting bullies' stories by just watching the news and other people in your community. Plenty of examples are out there.

Bullies don't make the connection back to their own behavior as most people do. They don't connect the dots. Most of us have the flexibility to occasionally look for our own part in our difficulties so that we can change to make our lives better. We generally have the ability to realize that people respond to us in negative ways when we are negative toward them. Yet bullies misconnect the dots and find odd ways to blame others. They truly lack self-awareness, and you can't give it to them. They will just fight you on it and make things worse. Just make the connections for yourself and don't buy the way that they misconnect the dots of responsibility to the wrong people: their targets of blame. They do this to mislead other people and gain power over them.

In the struggle this century between win-lose and win-win, we cannot allow win-lose to triumph. Win-winners must guide the way into the future, which includes having to spot and stop bullies as soon as possible. We know what to do. We just have to get enough people together to restrain bullies while getting the best out of them. Bullies push us to do better, but they can't stop themselves and their methods. We don't need to eliminate them or their ideas. We just need to restrain them and manage our conflicts so that no one gets hurt as we compete for better ideas to help us all thrive. Let's replace our new world of adult bullies with a long-lasting win-win world of ideas, solutions, and cooperation. Ultimately, we're on the same team.

40 Predictable Behaviors of High-Conflict Personalities

EXCERPTED WITH PERMISSION from *5 Types of People Who Can Ruin Your Life* by Bill Eddy (New York: Tarcher-Perigee, Penguin/Random House, 2018).

Since high-conflict people tend to treat all their relationships as inherently adversarial, there are at least forty things you can generally predict about them, once you know about the four primary characteristics of *all-or-nothing thinking, unmanaged emotions, blaming others,* and *extreme behaviors.* This is regardless of where the person lives, their age or race or gender, their social class, their level of intelligence, or their occupation. They:

1. Won't reflect on their own behavior.
2. Won't have insights about their part in problems.
3. Won't understand why they behave the way they do.
4. Won't change their behavior.
5. Won't seek counseling or any form of real advice.
6. Won't understand why they succeed in the short term (when they are initially charming and persuasive) and why they fail in the long term (when reality sets in).
7. Will become extremely defensive if someone urges them to change.

8. Will claim their behavior is normal and necessary, given the circumstances.

9. Will lack empathy for others although they may say the right words.

10. Will be preoccupied with drawing attention to themselves.

11. May be preoccupied with the past, and/or with defending their own actions and attacking others.

12. May have a public persona that's very good, covering a negative personality in private.

13. May call others crazy when it's suggested that they are being inappropriate.

14. May bully others but defend themselves by saying that they were bullied.

15. Will be preoccupied with blaming others, even for very small or nonexistent events.

16. Will have lots of energy for blaming others, since they don't spend it on self-reflection.

17. Will have targets of blame who are intimate others or people in positions of authority.

18. Will focus on a single target of blame, and try to control, remove, or destroy that person or group.

19. May assault their target of blame financially, reputationally, legally, emotionally, professionally, or physically.

20. May engage administrative or legal procedures against their target(s) of blame.

21. Will constantly seek negative advocates to assist in blaming others and defending themselves.

22. Will easily turn against their negative advocates when they don't do as they're told.

23. Will demand loyalty from others and tell them what they need to do.

24. Will not be loyal themselves, claiming they were betrayed.

25. May be very secretive, yet demand full disclosure from others, including confidences.

26. May breach confidences about others when it serves their purpose.

27. Will truly wonder why so many people "turn against them" over time.

28. Will turn on family and good friends in an instant; may (or may not) later try to repair the relationships.

29. Will have few, if any, real friends over time. Only a few family members will stick by them.

30. Will not be happy most of the time, except when people totally agree with them.

31. Will have high-intensity relationships, starting with intense attractions but ending with intense resentments and blame.

32. Will have unrealistically high expectations of their allies, which will inevitably be dashed.

33. Will sabotage themselves, working against their own self-interest.

34. Will create many of the problems that they claim they are trying to solve.

35. Will project onto others what they are doing or thinking themselves.

36. Will lack self-restraint, even when it's in their best interests to restrain themselves.

37. Will do things impulsively, then sometimes regret it (and other times not regret it).

38. Will ask for many favors yet will not reciprocate them.

39. Will respond to requests with unrelated demands, often ignoring the request altogether.

40. Will "split" those around them into all-good and all-bad people, triggering many conflicts.

APPENDIX 2:

Glossary

*Terms with an asterisk are author's original terms to help in explaining bully dynamics.

Adult bully:

For the purposes of this book, an adult bully is defined as someone who has the personality pattern of a high-conflict person (blaming others, all-or-nothing thinking, unmanaged emotions, and extreme behaviors), plus a drive to dominate or destroy another person or group.

*Anti-community:

An emotionally tight-knit community of two or more people intensely polarized against another group, with the desire (expressed or hidden) to treat that other group as evil or eliminate them. Examples are a parent and child engaged in alienating behaviors during a divorce against the other parent and their relatives; members of a political party who view members of another party as evil; an online hate group against those of other ethnic backgrounds; a country invading a neighboring country with the goal of eliminating it as a separate country. Once an anti-community has formed, logical information coming from outside the anti-community will not be considered valid, and exposure of bad behavior by a leader or member of the anti-community will bring intense group support, not criticism, for that leader or member.

*BIFF Response:

A BIFF Response is usually given in writing in response to someone's angry or misinformed e-mail, text, letter, or online comment. It stands for *brief, informative, friendly,* and *firm*. It helps keep the communication from escalating into personal attacks. For more on this method, see https://highconflictinstitute.com/communication/how-to-write-a-biff-response/.

*Bully's story (BS):

This is the story of a *fantasy crisis, fantasy villain*, and *fantasy hero* that bullies universally use to gain power over their victims and to attract negative advocates to attack their victims. This activates the unconscious primitive emotional responses of fear, anger, and love/loyalty in the bully's victims and negative advocates. The Internet, movies, news, and social media have all increasingly emphasized the story format of crisis-villain-hero as the way to view all problems in today's world, which has primed us all to follow bully leaders who tell bully's stories.

*Culture of fear and blame:

Most media and cultural leaders today contribute to this culture of fear and blame by competing to share images, sounds, and words of crises to grab people's attention on a 24/7 basis. By simplistically presenting all problems as caused by evil individuals, bully leaders often paint an all-or-nothing picture that distracts from the reality of modern problems that have many causes and need many solutions.

Dominance hierarchy:

The term used to describe the top-down social structure of all mammals, with the one on top dominating those below him (or her) in terms of leading the group to food, eating first, having sex with whomever they choose, and often having to fight to maintain their status. Those up and down the hierarchy—especially primates like chimpanzees and humans—may regularly fight for a higher-status position.

*EAR Statement:

This is a statement made to calm an upset person, especially one who is angry with you. By making a statement that shows empathy (I can see how frustrated you are), attention (tell me more, I'd like to understand), and/or respect (I respect your efforts to solve this problem), you calm most people in less than a minute. For more about this method, see https://highconflictinstitute.com/divorce-coparenting/calming-upset-people-with-ear/.

*Emotionally hooked:

When a bully's primitive emotional power unconsciously engages (or "hooks") a person's primitive emotional responses (fear, anger, and love/loyalty) in a way that immobilizes them or mobilizes them to become a negative advocate against another target of the bully. This explains why negative advocates can be so angry at someone they don't even know for no logical reason and refuse to hear any factual information from them.

*Fantasy crisis:

This "crisis" is a total fabrication or exaggeration of a real problem that bullies use to trigger a primitive fear response in their victims or negative advocates. This fear primes them to believe in the bully's fantasy villain as the cause of the crisis to get them to give their power to the bully as the fantasy hero to save them from the crisis.

This crisis rarely gets close examination as the bully shifts the focus to the fantasy villain as the target of blame and the bully as the fantasy hero.

*Fantasy hero:

Bullies present themselves as "heroes" to their victims and negative advocates to gain power over them. Using images of strength, sounds of strength, and words of strength, the bully can seem like a hero, especially based on their story of a terrible (fantasy) crisis and an evil (fantasy) villain, whom they promise to dominate or destroy. By keeping their potential victims and negative advocates emotionally focused on a fantasy crisis (inducing fear) and fantasy villain (inducing rage), they are accepted at face value as the heroes they say they are without being challenged.

*Fantasy villain:

This "villain" may be totally fabricated or may have some vague relationship to the *fantasy crisis*, but regardless, they are totally blamed for it by the bully as *fantasy hero*. This *target of blame* serves as a distraction and focus of anger or rage. This person could be the victim, who the bully blames as causing all their own problems. More often the villains are people who cannot defend themselves or are caught off guard and do not even try.

*High-conflict person or personality (HCP):

Someone who has a personality pattern of blaming others, a lot of all-or-nothing thinking, unmanaged emotions, and extreme behaviors. Many but not all HCPs have a personality disorder.

*High-emotion media:

Modern media emphasizes images of conflict, crisis, chaos, and fear, along with faces and voices dramatically telling extreme stories to grab people's attention by preying on their unconscious emotions. To get more attention, high-emotion media promotes the faces and voices of high-conflict people or bullies. People who are more emotional absorb other people's emotions more easily. Today's high-emotion media is also high-tech media, so it can provide emotional repetition worldwide at an intensely high level. This primes us for a bully's stories and polarization.

Hyperbole (hype):

A purposeful exaggeration usually not intended to be taken literally. As used in this book, this term describes a bully's exaggerated statements with primitive emotional power that can immobilize a bully's victims or mobilize a bully's negative advocates while being denied by the bully as meaning anything serious.

Illusion of truth effect:

When false information is repeated enough times, it starts to feel true. This is because our brains are very efficient and assume that something is true if it is repeated a lot by others. Also known as *illusory truth*.

Love/loyalty:

As used in this book, this describes the devotion of a bully's victims or negative advocates toward the bully. This is usually powered by the bully's expressions of love and loyalty toward the victim or their negative advocates, but the bully just wants their love and loyalty and is unlikely to reciprocate it. This is one of the three primitive emotional powers that bullies regularly use along with fear and anger (rage) in order to dominate or destroy their victims or targets of blame.

*Negative advocate:

A person who advocates for a bully or other high-conflict person (HCP) by justifying their bullying behavior or assisting them in attacking their *targets of blame*. A negative advocate enables a bully to continue acting badly, such as a codependent person does with an alcoholic or addict. Negative advocates—such as a respected family member, lawyer, or therapist—often have more credibility than bullies or HCPs. They inadvertently help a bully in courts and other settings to avoid consequences for their behavior. However, they often abandon the bully when they become fully informed about the bully's behavior, so bullies are constantly recruiting new negative advocates.

Parental alienation:

This occurs during and after many divorce and separation cases when a parent bad-mouths and interferes with the other parent's relationship with a child, with the result that the child resists or refuses contact with that other parent. This contrasts with a child resisting or refusing contact with a parent because of that parent's own abusive behavior or otherwise negative parenting, which is known as *realistic estrangement* and not parental alienation.

*PEP Formula (see **Primitive emotional power**):

This is the full range of ten primitive emotional powers that bullies use for dominating others, including the powers of *the bully's story, emotional repetition, negative advocates, polarization,* and so forth, as described in this book. Most bullies discover this formula by accident and are surprised at how powerful it is.

Personality disorder:

This is an adult mental health diagnosis contained in the *Diagnostic and Statistical Manual of Mental Disorders*, currently the fifth edition with text revisions (commonly known as the *DSM-5-TR*). A person with a personality disorder has an enduring pattern of dysfunctional interpersonal behavior that is unlikely to change over their lifetime, except for a small percentage of cases. There are ten personality disorders identified in the *DSM-5-TR* with different types of dysfunctional behavior, three of which are in Cluster B and are briefly discussed in this book: *borderline, narcissistic,* and *antisocial.* The *DSM-5-TR* indicates that approximately 10 percent of adults worldwide have a personality disorder. Based on the author's experience, many bullies have one of these disorders, but some do not.

Polarization:

A division into two strongly opposed groups with no middle ground. As used in this book, polarization is driven by the primitive emotional power of bullies and defined as when opposite opinions become highly emotional and personal, such that one group wants to eliminate the people in the other group, not just their ideas. With such polarization, one group's language may include disparaging remarks about the other group being stupid, immoral, incompetent, evil, inhuman, and so forth. This can occur within families, work groups, communities, and nations.

Predisposed:

As used in this book, predisposed refers to people who enter adulthood with a personality preference for or against others with domineering personalities, other characteristics, or points of view. They are unaware of these predispositions and are unlikely to change them because they are personality based.

Primed:

As used in this book, primed refers to recent experiences and exposure to ideas that create a like or dislike for certain people, actions, or points of view. For example, after a year of listening to Hate Radio, many people in Rwanda were *primed* to kill others with machetes.

**Primitive emotional power (PEP):*

This is the ability of bullies to unconsciously activate three primitive emotional responses in others: fear, anger, and love/loyalty. This is usually communicated through *images of strength, sounds of strength,* and *words of strength (hyperbole),* which tend to emotionally hook the right hemisphere of the brain, especially the right amygdala, without the person's awareness.

**Target of blame:*

Bullies cannot see their part in problems, so they see themselves as blameless. Therefore, they intensely blame all their problems on individuals or groups who are often completely unrelated to their problems. Because of their emotional intensity, they are often able to convince other people (who become their *negative advocates*) that their target of blame is an evil person who has done terrible things, so they join in attacking that person or group, verbally, violently, or otherwise.

APPENDIX 3:

List of Examples by Categories

All these examples help in spotting the common patterns of adult bullying behavior. Some show bullying that was not stopped, but most show how it was stopped.

NOTES

CHAPTER 2

1. Brad Boserup, Adele Elkbuli, and Mark McKenny, "Alarming Trends in US Domestic Violence During the COVID-19 pandemic," *American Journal of Emergency Medicine* 38 (2020): 2753–55.

2. Gary Namie, "2021 WBI U.S. Workplace Bullying Survey, the Fifth Representative WBI National Study, Zogby Analytics, Pollster, Results Summary," Workplace Bullying Institute, accessed November 18, 2023, https://workplacebullying.org/2021-wbi-survey/.

3. Namie, "Bullying Survey."

4. Peter Beinart, "America's Foes Are Joining Forces," *New York Times*, July 3, 2023, https://www.nytimes.com/2023/07/03/opinion/iran-cuba-usa-partnerships.html?searchResultPosition=1.

CHAPTER 3

1. American Psychological Association, "Bullying," July 2022, https://www.apa.org/topics/bullying.

2. "Ex-Surgeon Confesses He Took His Wife's 'Body out of the Airplane over the Ocean," Good Morning America, October 22, 2021, https://www.goodmorningamerica.com/news/video/surgeon-confesses-wifes-body-airplane-ocean-80724005.

3. "Ex-Surgeon Confesses."

4. "Ex-Surgeon Confesses."

5. American Psychiatric Association (APA), *Diagnostic and Statistical Manual of Mental Disorders*, 5th ed., Text Revision (Washington, DC:

American Psychiatric Association, 2022), 734. (Hereafter DSM-5-TR.)

6. Sylia Wilson, Catherine B. Stroud, and C. Emily Durbin, "Interpersonal Dysfunction in Personality Disorders: A Meta-Analytic Review," *Psychology Bulletin* 143, no. 7 (July 2017): 677–734, 691, doi: 10.1037/bul0000101.

7. *DSM-5-TR*, 748, 753, and 760.

8. Katherine L. Collison and Donald R. Lynam, "Personality Disorders as Predictors of Intimate Partner Violence: A Meta-Analysis," *Clinical Psychology Review* 88 (2021): 1–2.

9. Wilson, "Interpersonal Dysfunction," 720.

10. Aaron Beck, A. Freeman, D. D. Davis, et al., *Cognitive Therapy of Personality Disorders*, 2nd ed. (New York: Guilford Press, 2004), 19.

11. Press conference with Lance Armstrong, YouTube, February 12, 2009, https://www.youtube.com/watch?v=nZgns7CXeUI.

12. Book interview with Floyd Landis, YouTube, July 19, 2017, https://www.youtube.com/watch?v=aPjneqtRufY.

13. *Associated Press*, "Lance Armstrong Loses $10 Million in Arbitration Ruling," New York Times, February 16, 2015.

14. Excerpt from *5 Types of People Who Can Ruin Your Life: Identifying and Dealing with Narcissists, Sociopaths, and Other High-Conflict Personalities* (New York: TarcherPerigee, 2018), 187–88. Used with permission.

15. Report of Investigation into Allegations of Sexual Harassment by Governor Andrew M. Cuomo, State of New York Office of the Attorney General Letitia James, August 3, 2021, https://ag.ny.gov/sites/default/files/2021.08.03_nyag_-_investigative_report.pdf.

16. Bill Eddy and L. Georgi DiStefano, "A Respectful Meeting Policy," *High Conflict Institute Newsletter*, April 8, 2017, https://highconflictinstitute.com/workplace-conflict/a-respectful-meeting-policy/.

17. California School Boards Association, "Governance in a Time of Chaos: Managing Board Meetings in Turbulent Times,"

Governance Best Practices Guide, accessed January 27, 2024, https:/
/www.csba.org/-/media/CSBA/Files/GovernanceResources/CSBA
-Difficult-Meetings-Roadshow-Guide-09-2021ashx?la=en&rev
=4c91c4292322412da8e4ce6bf2d8992a.

18. Deborah S. Brennan, "You Can Cuss, but Please Don't Clap: The Perils of
    Managing Public Discourse," *San Diego Union-Tribune*, May 22, 2022,
    https://www.sandiegouniontribune.com/news/politics/story/2022-
    05-22/civic-conduct.

19. *White v. City of Norwalk*, 900 F. 2d, 1421 (1990).

20. Brad Wilson, *Travis Kalanick: A Biography of the Uber Founder* (Scotts
    Valley, CA: CreateSpace Independent Publishing Platform, 2017),
    Track 9, Audiobook.

21. Wilson, *Kalanick*, Track 10.

22. Wilson, *Kalanick*, Track 9.

23. Suhauna Hussain, "Uber Agrees to Pay $9 Million California Settle-
    ment on Sexual Assault Reporting Failure," *Los Angeles Times*, De-
    cember 2, 2021.

24. Janet R. Johnston and Joan B. Kelly, "Rejoinder to Gardner's Commen-
    tary on Kelly and Johnston's 'The Alienated Child: A Reformulation of
    Parental Alienation Syndrome,'" *Family Court Review* 42, no. 4 (Oc-
    tober 2004): 622–28, 622.

25. Scott Carrier, "The One Mighty and Strong: To Put God's House in
    Order, Brian David Mitchell Needed to Kidnap a Virgin Bride," *Salt
    Lake City Weekly*, December 1, 2010, 1.

26. Carter Williams, "A Look Back at the Frantic Search for Elizabeth
    Smart 15 Years Ago," *KSL News Utah*, June 7, 2017, https://www.ksl.
    com/article/44554474/a-look-back-at-the-frantic-search-for-elizabeth
    -smart-15-years-ago.

27. Cathy Free, "Elizabeth Smart, Rescued Twenty Years Ago, Now Teaches
    Others to Fight Back," *Washington Post*, March 10, 2023, https:/

/www.washingtonpost.com/lifestyle/2023/03/10/elizabeth-smart
-kidnap-rescue-anniversary/.

28. Free, "Elizabeth Smart."

CHAPTER 4

1. Jaak Panksepp and Lucy Biven, *The Archaeology of Mind: Neuroevolu-
tionary Origins of Human Emotions* (New York: W. W. Norton and Company, 2012), loc. 42–43 of 1075, iBooks.

2. Panksepp and Biven, *Archaeology of Mind*, loc. 549.

3. Jen Percy, "What People Misunderstand About Rape," *New York Times*,
August 22, 2023, https://www.nytimes.com/2023/08/22/magazine
/immobility-rape-trauma-freeze.html.

4. Percy, "What People Misunderstand."

5. Allan Schore, *Right Brain Psychotherapy* (New York: W. W. Norton and
Company, 2019), 220.

6. Antonio Damasio, *The Feeling of What Happens: Body and Emotion in
the Making of Consciousness* (Orlando, FL: Harcourt Brace & Company,
1999), 187.

7. Hope Gillett, "What Is Mobbing at Work and How Do You Stop
It?" PsychCentral, July 21, 2022, https://psychcentral.com/health/
mobbing-at-work-group-bullying#what-is-mobbing.

8. Yuval Noah Harari, Sapiens: A Brief History of Humankind (New York:
Harper Perennial, 2015), loc. viii of 444, iBooks.

9. Catherine Mattice, e-mail correspondence with the author, December
21, 2023. Mattice is author of *Back Off! Your Kick-Ass Guide to Ending
Bullying at Work* (Conshohocken, PA: Infinity Publishing, 2012).

10. Jane Wright, "Bullying Claim Results in Significant Damages," *Work-
dynamic Australia*, accessed January 28, 2024, https://workdynamic
.com.au/bullying-claim-results-in-significant-damages/.

11. Wright, "Bullying Claim."

12. Ronan Farrow, "Abuses of Power," *New Yorker*, October 23, 2017, 44–45.

13. Farrow, "Abuses of Power," 44.

14. Lauren Herstik, "Harvey Weinstein Sentenced to 16 Years for Los Angeles Sex Crimes," *New York Times*, February 23, 2023, https://www.nytimes.com/2023/02/23/us/harvey-weinstein-sentence-los-angeles.html?searchResultPosition=1.

15. California Family Code Section 6320 (implemented starting in 2021).

16. Wright, "Bullying Claim."

17. Jaron Lanier, *Ten Arguments for Deleting Your Social Media Accounts Right Now* (New York: Picador Henry Holt and Company, 2018), loc. 20 of 157, iBooks.

18. Pam Kragen, "Anti-Bullying Activist Promotes Self-Love," *San Diego Union-Tribune*, August 8, 2022, B1.

19. Kragen, "Anti-Bullying Activist," B4.

CHAPTER 5

1. Megan Meier Foundation, "Megan's Story," accessed January 28, 2024, https://www.meganmeierfoundation.org/megans-story#utm_source=google&utm_medium=cpc&utm_campaign=MMF percent20- percent20KLC&utm_content=Megan. This is an abridged version of a story by Steve Pokin in the *St. Charles (MO) Journal*, November 13, 2007.

2. Panksepp and Biven, *Archaeology of Mind*, loc. 47.

3. Editorial Board, "Jeffrey Epstein Is Dead. His Victims Still Deserve Justice," *New York Times*, July 8, 2019, https://www.nytimes.com/2019/08/10/opinion/jeffrey-epstein-suicide.html?searchResultPosition=5.

4. Editorial Board, "Jeffrey Epstien." New York Times, July 8, 2019, https://www.nytimes.com/2019/08/10/opinion/jeffrey-epstein-suicide.html?searchResultPosition=5.

5. Sarah Berman, *Don't Call It a Cult: The Shocking Story of Keith Raniere and the Women of NXIVM* (Lebanon, NH: Steerforth Press, 2021), loc. 415 of 861, iBooks.

6. Berman, *Don't Call It a Cult*, loc. 60.

7. Megyn Kelly, *Settle for More* (New York: HarperCollins, 2016), loc. 307 of 341, iBooks.

CHAPTER 6

1. Jonathan Haidt, *The Righteous Mind: Why Good People Are Divided by Politics and Religion* (New York: Vintage Books, 2013), 276.

2. Katie Benner and Melena Ryzik, "FKA twigs Sues Shia LaBeouf, Citing 'Relentless' Abusive Relationship," *New York Times*, January 22, 2021.

3. Benner and Ryzik, "FKA twigs."

4. Benner and Ryzik, "FKA twigs."

5. Benner and Ryzik, "FKA twigs."

6. Benner and Ryzik, "FKA twigs."

7. Richard Warshak, *Divorce Poison: How to Protect Your Family from Bad-Mouthing and Brainwashing* (New York: Harper, 2010), loc. 78 of 520, iBooks.

8. Panksepp and Biven, *Archaeology of Mind*, loc. 47.

9. Johnston and Kelly, "Rejoinder to Gardner's Commentary," 622.

10. Barbara Jo Fidler, Nicholas Bala, and Michael A. Saini, *Children Who Resist Postseparation Parental Contact* (New York: Oxford University Press, 2013), 8.

11. Janet R. Johnston and Linda E. G. Campbell, *Impasses of Divorce: The Dynamics and Resolution of Family Conflict* (New York: Free Press, 1988), xi.

12. Tom McTague, "Inside the Controlled Chaos of Downing Street," *The Atlantic*, July–August 2021, 38–51, 48.

13. Tom McTague, "Is Boris Johnson a Liar? And If He Is, Why Don't His Supporters Seem to Care?" *The Atlantic*, October 4, 2021.

14. McTague, "Is Boris Johnson a Liar?"

15. Matthew Smith, "Most Britons Say Brexit Has Been 'More of a Failure,'" YouGov.co.uk, May 22, 2023, https://yougov.co.uk/politics/articles/45733-most-britons-say-brexit-has-been-more-failure.

16. McTague, "Is Boris Johnson a Liar?"

17. McTague, "Is Boris Johnson a Liar?"

18. Julia Jacobs, "Court Rejects Jussie Smollett's Appeal of Hoax Case Conviction," *New York Times*, December 1, 2023, https://www.nytimes.com/2023/12/01/arts/jussie-smollett-appeal.html.

CHAPTER 7

1. Aumyo Hassan and Sarah J. Barber, "The Effects of Repetition Frequency on the Illusory Truth Effect," *Cognitive Research: Principles and Implications* 6, no. 38 (2021): 1, https://doi.org/10.1186/s41235-021-00301-5.

2. Hassan and Barber, "Effects of Repetition Frequency," 2.

3. Hassan and Barber, "Effects of Repetition Frequency," 3.

4. Tom Stafford, "How Liars Create the 'Illusion of Truth,'" *BBC*, October 26, 2016, https://www.bbc.com/future/article/20161026-how-liars-create-the-illusion-of-truth.

5. FBI, "History: Patty Hearst," accessed January 28, 2024, https://www.fbi.gov/history/famous-cases/patty-hearst.

6. FBI, "History."

7. FBI, "History."

8. Jeff Guinn, *The Road to Jonestown* (New York: Simon & Schuster, 2017), loc. 561 of 862, iBooks.

9. Guinn, *The Road to Jonestown*, loc. 704.

10. Guinn, *The Road to Jonestown*, loc. 716.

11. Warshak, *Divorce Poison*, loc. 71–72.

12. Elizabeth Williamson, "Sandy Hook Families Say Alex Jones Cannot Hide behind Bankruptcy," *New York Times*, August 15, 2023.

13. Elizabeth Williamson, "Judge Won't Let Alex Jones Use Bankruptcy to Avoid Sandy Hook Damages," *New York Times*, October 11, 2023.

14. Williamson, "Sandy Hook Families," August 15, 2023.

CHAPTER 8

1. Beibei Kuang and Shenli Peng, "Universality vs. Cultural Specificity in the Relations Among Emotional Contagion, Emotion Regulation, and Mood State: An Emotion Process Perspective," *Frontiers in Psychology* 10 (February 12, 2019): 186.

2. Daniel Goleman, *Social Intelligence: The New Science of Human Relationships* (New York: Bantam Book, 2006), 39.

3. Kuang and Peng, "Universality."

4. Guin, *Road to Jonestown*, loc. 488.

5. John Carreyrou, *Bad Blood: Secrets and Lies in a Silicon Valley Startup* (New York:Vintage Books, 2018), loc. 298 of 325, iBooks.

6. Carreyrou, *Bad Blood*, loc. 196.

7. Carreyrou, *Bad Blood*, loc. 196.

8. Carreyrou, *Bad Blood*, loc. 197.

9. Carreyrou, *Bad Blood*, loc. 198.

10. Max Rollwage, Alisa Loosen, Tobias U. Hauser, Rani Moran, Raymond J. Dolan, and Stephen M. Fleming, "Confidence Drives a Neural Confirmation Bias," *Nature Communications* 11 (2020): 2634, https://doi.org/10.1038/s41467-020-16278-6.

11. Carreyrou, *Bad Blood*, loc. 299.

12. Megan Twohey and Jacob Bernstein, "The 'Lady of the House' Who Was Long Entangled with Jeffrey Epstein," *New York Times*, July 15, 2019, https://www.nytimes.com/2019/07/15/us/ghislaine-maxwell-epstein.html.

13. Rebecca Davis O'Brien and Benjamin Weiser, "Partners or Partners in Crime? Maxwell-Epstein Bond Is Key to Her Trial," *New York Times*, December 7, 2021, https://www.nytimes.com/2021/12/06/nyregion/jeffrey-esptein-ghislaine-maxwell-trial-strategy.html.

14. Twohey and Bernstein, "'Lady of the House.'"

CHAPTER 9

1. Nicholas Bogel-Burroughs and Mike Baker, "Authorities Say DNA Links Las Vegas Official to Killing of Reporter," *New York Times*, September 8, 2022, https://www.nytimes.com/2022/09/08/us/las-vegas-reporter -german-telles-dna.html.

2. Bogel-Burroughs and Baker, "Authorities Say DNA Links."

3. Katelyn Newberg, "Robert Telles Says He Was Under Surveillance in Bribery Investigation," *Las Vegas Review-Journal*, July 7, 2023, https:/ /www.reviewjournal.com/crime/courts/robert-telles-says-he-was -under-surveillance-in-bribery-investigation-2804969/.

4. Heather Murphy, "El Paso Shooting Suspect Indicted on Capital Murder Charge," *New York Times*, September 12, 2019, https://www.nytimes .com/2019/09/12/us/el-paso-suspect-capital-murder.html.

5. Nellie Bowles, "'Replacement Theory', a Racist, Sexist Doctrine, Spreads in Far-Right Circles," *New York Times*, March 18, 2019, https://www .nytimes.com/2019/03/18/technology/replacement-theory.html.

6. U-T News Service, "Hate Crimes Increased 20.2% in California Last Year," *San Diego Union-Tribune*, June 27, 2023, A-1.

7. U-T News Service, "Hate Crimes."

8. Jonathan Haidt, "How Social Media Dissolved the Mortar of Society and Made America Stupid," *The Atlantic*, May 2022, 54–66, 59.

9. Teri Figueroa, "Man Gets Prison in 'Evil' Scam Targeting Seniors," *San Diego Union-Tribune*, August 19, 2022, B-1, 8.

10. Figueroa, "Man Gets Prison," 8.

11. Courtney E. Martin, "Stopping Culture Wars in Their Tracks," *Christian Science Monitor Weekly*, June 12, 2023, 18–24, 21.

12. Martin, "Stopping Culture Wars," 22.

13. Martin, "Stopping Culture Wars," 23.

14. Martin, "Stopping Culture Wars," 24.

CHAPTER 10

1. Timothy Bella, "He Refused to Give Up His Coveted Twitter Handle. Then He Was 'Swatted' and Died of a Heart Attack," *Washington Post*, July 24, 2021.

2. Bella, "He Refused."

3. Avi Selk and Eli Rosenberg, "A Twitter User Claims to Have Made the 'Swatting' Call That Led Police to Kill a Man," *Washington Post*, December 30, 2017.

4. Selk and Rosenberg, "A Twitter User Claims."

5. Bella, "He Refused."

6. Bill Eddy and Megan Hunter, *Dating Radar: Why Your Brain Says Yes to "The One" Who Will Make Your Life Hell* (Scottsdale, AZ: Unhooked Books, 2017), 22.

7. Ruby Mellen, "The Shocking Speed of the Taliban's Advance: A Visual Timeline," *Washington Post*, August 16, 2021.

8. Helene Cooper and David Sanger, "U.S. Warns of Grim Toll If Putin Pursues Full Invasion of Ukraine," *New York Times*, February 5, 2022, https://www.nytimes.com/2022/02/05/us/politics/russia-ukraine -invasion.html?searchResultPosition=4.

9. David Remnick, "In the Cities of Killing," *New Yorker*, November 6, 2023, 29–41, 36.

10. Remnick, "In the Cities of Killing," 36.

11. Observer, "Ukraine Invasion: How Vladimir Putin Built His Career on Waging War," *The Guardian*, February 26, 2022.

12. Observer, "Ukraine Invasion."

13. For information about the EAR Statement method, see Bill Eddy, *Calming Upset People with EAR: How Statements Showing Empathy, Attention, and Respect Can Defuse a Conflict* (Scottsdale, AZ: Unhooked Books, 2021).

14. *Weigert v. Georgetown University* (2000), 120 F. Supp. 2d 1.

15. *Weigert v. Georgetown University*.

16. David Wexler, "Conversations on Domestic Violence in Family Law with 16 Experts" (video), *High Conflict Institute*, October 2022.

17. *The Late Show*, "Interview with New Zealand prime minister Jacinda Ardern," hosted by Stephen Colbert and produced by CBS Television, May 24, 2022.

CHAPTER 11

1. Jason Cowley, "From a Young Age Boris Johnson Longed to Be World King—But the Gods Are Mocking Him," *New Statesman*, November 4, 2020, https://www.newstatesman.com/politics/uk-politics/2020/11/young-age-boris-johnson-longed-be-world-king-gods-are-mocking-him.

2. Yuval Noah Harari, *Sapiens: A Brief History of Humankind* (New York: Harper Perennial, 2015), loc. viii of 444, iBooks.

3. Harari, *Sapiens*, 27.

4. Harari, *Sapiens*, 103.

5. Harari, *Sapiens*, 27.

6. Erich Fromm, *The Heart of Man: Its Genius for Good and Evil* (Riverdale, NY: American Mental Health Foundation, 2010), loc. 824 of 2243, Kindle Books. Originally published in New York by Harper & Row, 1964.

7. UK Parliament, "Magna Carta," accessed August 22, 2023, www.parliament.uk.

8. Bertelsman Transformation Index, "Democracy Report 2022," accessed January 28, 2024, https://bti-project.org/en/reports/global/democracy-report#Efficiency percent20versus percent20democracy.

9. Masha Geffen, *The Future Is History: How Totalitarianism Reclaimed Russia* (New York: Riverhead Books, 2017), loc. 220 of 515, iBooks.

10. Tatiana Stanovaya, "Putin's Age of Chaos: The Dangers of Russian Disorder," *Foreign Affairs*, August 8, 2023, https://www.foreignaffairs.com/russian-federation/vladimir-putin-age-chaos?utm_medium=promo_email&utm_source=special_send&utm_campaign=Putin_Age_of

_Chaos_Actives&utm_content=20230808&utm_term=all-actives.

11. David Nather and Margaret Talev, "Axios/Ipsos Two Americas Index," *Axios*, September 12, 2022, https://www.axios.com/2022/09/12/two -americas-index-democracy.

12. Sasha Abramsky, "High Noon in Clallam County," *The Nation*, February 21–28, 2022, 23–30.

13. Jill Cowan and Shawn Hubler, "L.A. City Council Member Resigns amid Uproar over Remarks," *San Diego Union-Tribune*, October 13, 2022, A-1, 8.

14. *Collins v. Quinn, Collins, Gipson and Arquitt, D.D.S., P.C.*, 2011 U.S. Dist. LEXIS 164494.

15. *Collins v. Quinn et al.*

16. Kristina Davis, "Lawsuit: UCSD Coach Was Reason Student Killed Self," *San Diego Union-Tribune*, October 1, 2021.

CHAPTER 12

1. Karyl McBride, *Will the Drama Ever End?* (New York: Atria Books, 2023), 66.

2. McBride, *Will the Drama Ever End?*, 207.

3. Marsha Linehan, *Cognitive-Behavioral Treatment of Borderline Person-ality Disorder* (New York: Guilford Press, 1993), 431.

4. Cass Sunstein and Reid Hastie, *Wiser: Getting Beyond Groupthink to Make Groups Smarter* (Boston: Harvard Business Review Press, 2015), 84–85, 87.

5. Sunstein and Hastie, *Wiser*, 86.

6. Sunstein and Hastie, *Wiser*, 82.

7. Marlise Simons and Alison Smale, "Slobodan Milosevic, 64, Former Yugoslav Leader Accused of War Crimes, Dies," *New York Times*, March 12, 2006, https://www.nytimes.com/2006/03/12/world/europe /slobodan-milosevic-64-former-yugoslav-leader-accused-of-war.html ?searchResultPosition=8.

8. Ezra Klein, *Why We're Polarized* (New York: Avid Reader Press, 2020), loc. 148–49 of 312, iBooks.

9. Emily Badger and Kevin Quealy, "These 526 Voters Represent All of America. And They Spent a Weekend Together," *New York Times*, October 2, 2019, https://www.nytimes.com/interactive/2019/10/02/upshot/these-526-voters-represent-america.html.

10. Emily Krauser, "Who Is Alec Baldwin and Kim Basinger's Daughter? All about Ireland Baldwin," *People*, October 25, 2023, https://people.com/parents/all-about-alec-baldwin-kim-basinger-daughter-ireland/#:~:text=All percent20About percent20Ireland percent20Baldwin,-Alec percent20Baldwin percent20and&text=Alec percent20Baldwin percent20and percent20Kim percent20Basinger's percent20marriage percent20may percent20have percent20ended,through percent20their percent20daughter percent20Ireland percent20Baldwin.

11. Simons and Smale, "Slobodan Milosevic."

12. John Colapinto, *This Is the Voice* (New York: Simon & Schuster, 2021), 228.

CHAPTER 13

1. Glenn Thrush and Matt Richtel, "A Disturbing New Pattern in Mass Shootings: Young Assailants," *New York Times*, June 2, 2022, https://www.nytimes.com/2022/06/02/us/politics/mass-shootings-young-men-guns.html.

2. Thrush and Richtel, "Disturbing New Pattern."

3. Thrush and Richtel, "Disturbing New Pattern."

4. E. Alison Holman, Dana Rose Garfin, Pauline Lubens, and Roxane Cohen Silver, "Media Exposure to Collective Trauma, Mental Health and Functioning: Does It Matter What You See?" *Clinical Psychological Science* 8, no. 1 (2020): 111–24.

5. Holman et al., "Media Exposure to Collective Trauma," 112.

6. Holman et al., "Media Exposure to Collective Trauma," 119.

7. Daniel Goleman, *Social Intelligence: The New Science of Human Relationships* (New York: Bantam Book, 2006), 39.

8. Steven Pinker, *Enlightenment Now: The Case for Reason, Science, Humanism and Progress* (New York:Viking, 2018), 51.

9. Dominick Mastrangelo, "Fox News Top Rated Cable Channel for Eighth Straight Year," *The Hill*, December 14, 2023, https://thehill.com /homenews/media/4360708-fox-news-top-rated-cable-news-channel /#:~:text=Overall percent20cable percent20news percent20ratings percent20have,and percent20568 percent2C000 percent20who percent20watched percent20CNN.

10. Gabriel Sherman, *The Loudest Voice in the Room: How the Brilliant, Bombastic Roger Ailes Built Fox News—and Divided a Country* (New York: Random House, 2014) loc. 16 of 1086, iBooks.

11. Bertelsman Transformation Index, "Democracy Report 2022."

12. Bertelsman Transformation Index, "Democracy Report 2022."

13. Andrew Nagorski, *Hitlerland: American Eyewitness to the Nazi Rise to Power* (New York: Simon and Schuster Paperbacks, 2012), 101.

14. Steven Levitsky and Daniel Ziblatt, *How Democracies Die* (New York: Crown Publishing Group, 2018), 102–3.

15. Matt Stefon, "Fairness Doctrine: United States Policy (1949–1987)," *Britannica*, December 8, 2023, https://www.britannica.com/topic/Fairness -Doctrine.

16. Sherman, *Loudest Voice in the Room*, loc. 16 and 333.

17. Wikipedia, "Social Media History," accessed December 30, 2023, https://en.wikipedia.org/wiki/Social_media#History.

18. Global Social Media Statistics, accessed December 30, 2023, https:/ /datareportal.com/social-media-users.

19. Allan Schore, *Right Brain Psychotherapy* (New York: W. W. Norton & Company, 2019), 222.

20. Klein, *Why We're Polarized*, loc. 149.

21. Klein, *Why We're Polarized*, loc. 149.

22. United Nations International Residual Mechanism for Criminal Tribunals, "Three Media Leaders Convicted for Genocide," press release, December 3, 2003, https://unictr.irmct.org/en/news/three-media-leaders-convicted-genocide.

23. United Nations International Residual Mechanism for Criminal Tribunals, "Three Media Leaders."

24. Simons and Smale, "Slobodan Milosevic."

25. *Schenck v. United States*, 249 U.S. 47 (1919).

26. Stefon, "Fairness Doctrine."

CHAPTER 14

1. Interview with David Wexler, as part of a six one-hour video series, *Conversations about Domestic Violence in Family Law Cases with 16 Experts*, High Conflict Institute, 2021. See https://www.highconflicttraining.com/conversations-about-domestic-violence-in-family-law-with-16-experts.

2. Sheila M. Eyberg et al., "Parent-Child Interaction Therapy with Behavior Problem Children: One- and Two-Year Maintenance of Treatment Effects in the Family," *Child & Family Behavior Therapy* 23, no. 4 (2001), 1-20.

3. Elizabeth J. Latourneau and Charles M. Borduin, "The Effective Treatment of Juveniles Who Sexually Offend: An Ethical Imperative," *Ethics and Behavior* 18, no. 2–3 (2008): 286–306, doi:10.1080/10508420802066940.

4. For information about the New Ways for Families method for separation or divorce, see www.HighConflictInstitute.com/new-ways-for-families.

5. Michael Housman and Dylan Minor, "Toxic Workers," Harvard Business School Working Paper 16-057, October 2015 (revised November 2015).

6. Bill Eddy and L. Georgi DiStefano, "New Ways for Work: A New Coaching Method," *High Conflict Institute Newsletter*, November 11, 2015, https://highconflictinstitute.com/workplace-conflict/new-ways-for-work-a-new-coaching-method/.

7. Bill Eddy, "How to Write a BIFF Response," *High Conflict Institute Newsletter*, June 22, 2007, https://highconflictinstitute.com/communication/how-to-write-a-biff-response/. For additional information about the BIFF Communication method, see any of four short books at https://www.unhookedmedia.com/high-conflict-institute.

8. Lauren Landry, "Why Emotional Intelligence Is Important in Leadership," Harvard Business School Online, April 3, 2019.

9. Landry, "Why Emotional Intelligence."

10. Academy of Professional Family Mediators, www.APFMnet.org.

11. Association for Conflict Resolution, www.ACRnet.org.

12. For information about the EAR Statement method, see Eddy, *Calming Upset People with EAR.*

13. Steven Pinker, *The Better Angels of Our Nature: Why Violence Has Declined.* (New York: Viking, 2011), 208.

ACKNOWLEDGMENTS

THIS BOOK IS THE RESULT OF MANY DISCUSSIONS over the past three years with many people. I particularly appreciate my wife, Alice, for her patience with my writing, her willingness to endlessly discuss many of the ideas in this book, and her feedback at all stages of this book—at times saving me from myself. She is the love of my life, and her positive spirit keeps me going in this often-difficult line of work.

I have a big thanks for my literary agent, Scott Edelstein, who has guided me through many books over the past twenty years. He helped me with the structure for this book, its final title, and many editing suggestions for the book proposal. His knowledge of the rapidly changing publishing world has been extremely valuable, as well as his steadfast belief that what I teach is important.

I want to thank my editor at Health Communications, Darcie Abbene. Her highly detailed feedback has made this book much better overall and taught me how to be a better writer. Her commitment to this book has energized me beyond my expectations. I want to thank Lindsey Triebel Mach of Health Communications for all her work on the marketing and promotion of this book. Kelli Daniels also gets a big thank-you for her promotional work on this book, her third with me.

Thanks go to Megan Hunter, my colleague and business partner with High Conflict Institute, who encouraged me to write this book over the past three years. She has been a wonderful collaborator in all our endeavors over the past fifteen years to educate professionals worldwide about managing high-conflict situations. As CEO of High Conflict Institute, she has done a skillful job of managing our staff and speakers, growing the institute, and allowing me time to focus on teaching and writing. I also appreciate our whole team, especially Meggen Romine, Susie Rayner, Rehana Jamal, Jessiah Stokes, Katerina Ricci, Michael Lomax, Georgi DiStefano, Cherolyn Knapp, John Edwards, and Ginger Gentile, and our alumni of former staff and speakers.

Lastly, I want to thank the many people who read early versions of this book and gave me valuable suggestions over the past year, especially Cathy Eddy, Rehana Jamal, Denny Doyle, and Jess Abramson.

ABOUT THE AUTHOR

BILL EDDY is a lawyer, therapist, mediator, and the cofounder and chief innovation officer of the High Conflict Institute. He has trained professionals in forty states of the United States, eight provinces in Canada, and twelve other countries. He is the author of over twenty books and manuals regarding high-conflict disputes and personalities. Eddy is on the part-time faculty of the Straus Institute for Dispute Resolution at the Pepperdine University School of Law and is a Conjoint Associate Professor at the Newcastle Law School in Newcastle, Australia. He has taught at the National Judicial College in the United States and for the National Judicial Institute of Canada. He is the developer of the New Ways for Families skills training program for parents going through high-conflict separation and divorce, and the developer of the New Ways for Mediation method for potentially high-conflict mediation cases. He is the codeveloper of the New Ways for Work coaching method and the creator of the BIFF Response and EAR Statement methods for calming potentially high-conflict communications. His popular blog on Psychology-Today.com has received over six million views. His website is www. HighConflictInstitute.com.